I0867446

Containing chapters from some of the leading specialists in the Revolutionary and Napoleonic Wars, this volume covers a diverse range of topics. Philip Ball looks at the unfortunate General Mack, Terry Crowdy covers military intelligence in Napoleon's Italian Campaign and Alexander Mikaberidze examines Kutuzov's role before Austerlitz. There is a chapter by Alistair Nichols on the French émigré units in British pay and one by Mark Edward Hay on the rebuilding of the Dutch army before Waterloo. The Peninsular War is also covered with chapters by Kenton White on French strategy and tactics, John Marsden on the sieges of Astorga, and Robert Griffith covering the long-overlooked role of the battalions of light companies in Wellington's Army.

Robert Griffith is the author of *Riflemen: The History of the 5th Battalion, 60th (Royal American) Regiment – 1797–1818*, and *At the Point of the Bayonet: The Peninsular War Battles of Arroyomolinos and Almaraz 1811–1812*. He works as a freelance editor specialising in military history.

Armies and Enemies of Napoleon 1789–1815

Proceedings of the 2021 Helion and Company 'From Reason to Revolution' Conference

Edited by Robert Griffith

Helion & Company

Helion & Company Limited
Unit 8 Amherst Business Centre
Budbrooke Road
Warwick
CV34 5WE
England
Tel. 01926 499619
Email: info@helion.co.uk
Website: www.helion.co.uk
Twitter: @helionbooks
Visit our blog at http://blog.helion.co.uk/

Published by Helion & Company 2022
Designed and typeset by Mach 3 Solutions Ltd (www.mach3solutions.co.uk)
Cover designed by Paul Hewitt, Battlefield Design (www.battlefield-design.co.uk)

Cover: The French surrendering at Bailén, by Maurice Henri Orange (Anne S.K. Brown Collection).

ISBN 978-1-915070-41-8

British Library Cataloguing-in-Publication Data.
A catalogue record for this book is available from the British Library.

Helion and Company gratefully acknowledges the assistance of the Waterloo Association (https://www.waterlooassociation.org.uk/ and the British Commission for Military History (http://www.bcmh.org.uk/) in supporting the conference from which these papers are drawn.

Contents

Contributor Biographies		viii
Foreword		x
Introduction: Armies and Enemies of Napoleon, 1789-1815		xii
1	Miseria en la Maragatería The French and Spanish Sieges of Astorga During the Peninsular War. John Marsden	15
2	The Unfortunate General Mack Phillip Ball	49
3	Military Intelligence in Napoleon's Italian Campaigns (1796–1800) Terry Crowdy	70
4	General Mikhail Kutuzov and the Allied Headquarters on the Eve of the Battle of Austerlitz Alexander Mikaberidze	91
5	The Raising of the White Cockade Regiments, 1794–1802 Alistair Nichols	111
6	The House of Orange and the Re-establishment of the Dutch Army, 1810–1814 Mark Edward Hay	135
7	The French Method of Warfare in the Peninsula Kenton White	158
8	Light Bobs and Jäger Battalions of Light Companies in the Peninsular War Robert Griffith	175
Index		208

Contributor Biographies

Philip Ball has a long-standing interest in military history and worked for a number of years in museums, archaeology and the heritage sector. He is the author of *Neither Up Nor Down: The British Army and the Flanders Campaign 1793–1795*, published by Helion, and *A Waste of Blood and Treasure: The 1799 Anglo-Russian Invasion of the Netherlands*. Holding degrees from St David's, Leicester, and Birmingham Universities, he is currently researching British amphibious operations in the Revolutionary and Napoleonic Wars.

Terry Crowdy is a well-established, military history author specialising in the Napoleonic Wars. Author of *Incomparable: Napoleon's 9th Light Infantry Regiment*, *Napoleon's Infantry Handbook* and *French Light Infantry 1784–1815,* which was recently published by Helion. He has studied in detail the role of French chasseurs and voltigeurs through the wars of the French Revolution and First Empire, and the minutiae of French soldiers' daily lives. With a broad interest in irregular warfare throughout the ages, Crowdy has also written on military espionage and deception subjects. His account of the Battle of Marengo is definitive, revealing the true identity of the famous Marengo spy.

Robert Griffith read Economics and International Relations at the University of Warwick and then had a long career in the graphic arts industries, during which he wrote several novels set during the Napoleonic Wars. His first work of military history was *Riflemen: The History of the 5th Battalion, 60th (Royal American) Regiment – 1797–1818*, and he has subsequently written *At the Point of the Bayonet: The Peninsular War Battles of Arroyomolinos and Almaraz 1811–1812*, both published by Helion. He now works as a freelance editor, working mainly on the From Reason to Revolution series for Helion, and is currently writing a history of the campaign that culminated in the Battle of Vimeiro.

Dr Mark Edward Hay is an assistant professor of history at the Erasmus University, Rotterdam. He read history in Amsterdam, Paris, and Oxford, before taking up an AHRC-funded doctorate in history at King's College London. His doctoral thesis explored Dutch financial diplomacy in the Revolutionary and Napoleonic era. His current research explores international relations, war and diplomacy, financial and economic history, and women's history in the Atlantic World, 1750–1850.

John Marsden After graduating from the University of Sheffield, John Marsden spent some years teaching Computer Science to sixth form students at Mexborough

School, before returning to university to take a postgraduate degree in Control Systems. He then pursued a successful career in the IT industry. Marriage to his Spanish wife has stimulated an interest in Spanish culture, literature, and history: mainly, though not exclusively, relating to the Peninsular War. His knowledge of Spanish has allowed him to bring to light a number of documents relating to that conflict currently lying in the Spanish military archives. He is the author of *Napoleon's Stolen Army: How the Royal Navy Rescued a Spanish Army in the Baltic.*

Alexander Mikaberidze is Professor of European History at Louisiana State University at Shreveport, where he also holds Ruth Herring Noel Endowed Chair for the Curatorship of the James Smith Noel Collection. He is the author of several books, including *The Napoleonic Wars: A Global History, The Burning of Moscow: Napoleon's Trial by Fire, Napoleon's Great Escape: The Battle of Berezina*, and most recently *Kutuzov, A Life in War and Peace.*

Alistair Nichols is a former police officer with a social science degree from Portsmouth University. Over the last 20 or so years he has researched and written about the foreign units in the British Army during the French Revolutionary and Napoleonic Wars. His work includes books on the history of the Chasseurs Britanniques, the Watteville Regiment and the Independent Companies of Foreigners. For Helion he has co-authored *For God and King: A History of the Damas Legion 1793–1798: A Case Study of the Military Emigration during the French Revolution* and written *The Soldiers are Dressed in Red: The Quiberon Expedition of 1795 and the Counter-Revolution in Brittany.*

Kenton White is a lecturer in Strategic Studies and International Relations at the University of Reading. He also is an active organiser for the Ways of War Centre at Reading. His main areas of research are British defence policy over the last 200 years, the Peninsular War, and the study of strategy through history, and is also keen wargamer. He is the author of *The Key to Lisbon: The Third French Invasion of Portugal, 1810–11* and *Never Ready: NATO's Flexible Response Strategy, 1968–1989*, both available from Helion.

Foreword

The third From Reason to Revolution conference, from which these papers are taken, broke new ground for a number of reasons and these published proceedings do the same.

The event should have taken place in April 2020, but for obvious reasons this did not prove possible. As the world struggled to adapt to the realities of the COVID pandemic, we initially hoped to postpone the live event to 2021 only to be forced by the ongoing situation to accept that the continued uncertainty and risk mandated a switch to an online format. One of the few positives to come out of the last two years has been the proliferation of online events and the platforms to host them, and when the event finally took place online, just under a year after its intended date, everything went off without a hitch. The only drawback of this switch online was that one of the speakers lacked the technology to be able to participate in this format; nevertheless, their paper has been included in this work so that the published proceedings reflect the conference as it would have taken place in a non-COVID environment.

The other new development is reflected in the editorship of this volume. As the series has grown, so too has the team working on our titles. Now that our output of new titles is exceeding 20 books in a year it is no longer possible for a single editor to oversee the whole production process in detail and in 2021 I was pleased to welcome Rob Griffith as a freelance editor working with me to share the load. As series editor I had felt a certain amount of guilt that the first two sets of conference proceedings went out with my name on the cover but with only an introductory essay to mark my own contribution. Far better that the credit should go to someone who has contributed a chapter to the work in question, and who was a great help in organising and running the conference itself. It therefore seemed fitting, as we dusted ourselves off after the online event, that Rob should take the lead on preparing the proceedings for publication.

Lastly, the conference broke new ground in that it was the first to focus on a specific sub-section of the series' 1721–1815 timeframe. The first two conferences were thematic – in 2018 looking at command and leadership and in 2019 following the experience of soldiering from enlistment through to combat – but this one took as its theme the period which, if judged by the numbers of titles that we release, remains the most popular part of the From Reason to Revolution era. Its popularity is not to be wondered at, featuring as it does such a memorable cast of characters beginning with the man who give his name to the era. The Emperor makes an appearance in this work of course, although primarily, in Terry Crowdy's chapter on intelligence during the Italian campaigns of 1796–1800, as general and consul in that portion of his career when Bonaparte had not yet become Napoleon. Other big names are here too, with Mack and Kutusov getting their moment in the spotlight thanks to Philip Ball and Alexander Mikaberidze respectively. At the same time, it seemed important when putting together the conference panels to include armies and theatres of the war that might otherwise be overlooked; hence the inclusion of the Dutch experience courtesy of Mark Edward Hay, the émigré story thanks to Alistair Nichols, and the Spanish side of the Peninsular conflict as related by John Marsden. This last paper, along with Kenton White and Rob Griffith looking at aspects of the French and British experience respectively, rounds out a coverage of the 'Spanish Ulcer' that manages to open up the context beyond the Wellington-focused perspective that still dominates much of the literature on this theatre.

In concluding this foreword, I would like to take the opportunity to thank again all of the contributors and also to recognise the behind-the-scenes work by Helion's social media manager Leonni Ward and our managing director Duncan Rogers – who rolled up his sleeves to act as tech support on the day – for making the inaugural online conference a success. It is pleasing to report that at the time of writing we have been able to run our first live in-person conference since the outbreak of the pandemic, with plans well underway for a second. However, the success of the online format, not least in facilitating the participation of speakers and audience members from around the globe, means that we have every expectation of running further events in this format in the future too.

Andrew Bamford
Series and Commissioning Editor,
From Reason to Revolution 1721–1815
February 2022

Introduction
Armies and Enemies of Napoleon, 1789-1815

Walk into any good high street bookshop, find the military history section, scan along the many shelves of First and Second World War books and you will eventually find a small selection of books on the French Revolutionary and Napoleonic Wars, often tucked away on a lower shelf. Crouch down, look at the spines and every title will probably include either 'Waterloo', 'Napoleon', 'Wellington', or perhaps 'Nelson'. As far as mass market publishing goes the history of the period is still very much following the 'great man' or 'great battle' model.

However, we are lucky enough to be experiencing what could be termed a golden age of military history publishing. If you leave the high street chain-store bookshop and find either a specialist retailer or go online, you will find that there are countless authors who have carved out niches that cover obscure but fascinating topics – little known campaigns, long neglected regiments, and commanders who died never dreaming that people would be writing and reading about them 200 years later. The internet, online archive catalogues, digitisation and many other innovations mean that it is far easier now to write such books than it was 20 years ago. The rise of specialist publishers, like Helion, also means that it is now easier to get a book published on a topic other than the headline battles or the famous protagonists.

For example, in the last year Helion's From Reason to Revolution series has published a broad range of titles that cover the French Revolutionary and Napoleonic Wars. There were biographies of Admiral Sir Pulteney Malcolm (*The Sea is My Element*), who had a long career and knew Nelson, Wellington and Napoleon, as well as surgeon James McGrigor (*Sir James McGrigor*) who did a lot to advance medical services in the British Army. There were also titles such as Mark Thompson's *Wellington and the Lines of Torres Vedras*, probably the most complete study of the defences around Lisbon yet; R.N.W. Thomas' *No Want of Courage*, a seminal study of the Duke of York's army in Flanders in 1793–1795; and Wayne Stack's examination of the British Army in Ireland during the period, *Rebellion, Invasion and Occupation*. Two books also covered the conflicts in India where Wellington and others cut their teeth: Andy Copestake's *Their Infantry and Guns will Astonish You* and Josh Provan's *Bullocks, Grain and Good Madeira*.

Significant recent titles from other publishers include Alexander Mikaberidze's *The Napoleonic Wars: A Global History*, which looks at the wars from a wider perspective and illustrates how they influenced developments across the world, and also Moisés Gaudêncio's and Robert Burnham's and *In the Words of Wellington's Fighting Cocks*, which covers the much neglected Portuguese contribution to the

Peninsular War. Matilda Greig has also made a very valuable contribution with her *Dead Men Telling Tales*, which tells the story of how and why so many men who fought in the wars published their memoirs.

The collection of chapters in this book highlights the work of some of those authors seeking out such over-looked subjects, or at least looking for a different take from the popular histography. The theme of the armies and the enemies of Napoleon, both as emperor and as a general, has allowed the inclusion of a broad range of topics. As far as Napoleon's own armies are concerned, Kenton White examines one of the French army's longest campaigns of the two decades or so of warfare that ebbed and flowed across Europe, and indeed many other parts of the world, but one in which Napoleon himself on played a fleeting role. In the Iberian Peninsula the French fought a very different war to the one in central and northern Europe. The geography was different, and the enemies were different, but the French still tried to fight the same kind of war they had elsewhere and did not adapt. White outlines the French strategic, operational and tactical failings that allowed the Spanish Ulcer to fester.

One of the main reasons that the French failed in the Peninsula was the resistance of the Spanish and Portuguese peoples, but their part has long been downplayed by British historians from William Napier onwards. The works of Charles Esdaile started the trend to correct this and John Marsden's chapter on the sieges of Astorga is another valuable contribution. The small city in northwest Spain was briefly but brutally occupied by the French in early stages of the Peninsular War and then the Spanish forces holding it were besieged by the French in 1810. The siege lasted little more than a month before the Spanish surrendered just before the city was stormed, but Astorga's resistance still influenced the timing of French invasion of Portugal. In 1812 it was the Spanish army's turn to besiege the French garrison holding the city. The Spanish were under-resourced, and the siege lasted longer but the result was the same; the defenders surrendered when it became clear that their situation was hopeless. The details of the two sieges provide interesting counterpoints to the better-known sieges such as Ciudad Rodrigo and Badajoz.

Even within the British histography of the Peninsular War there are distortions that have masked the true contributions of different elements of Wellington's Anglo-Portuguese army. There are more books about the Light Division than any other part of the army, whether memoirs or books about the division and its regiments. You could be forgiven for thinking that the men of the Light Division were the only light infantry that Wellington had, but the current editor's own chapter highlights an ad hoc collection of units that were by far the most important light infantry elements of the army in battle. The battalions of light companies formed in each brigade composed the majority of the skirmish screen that faced off with the French voltigeurs. Formed from the light companies of the line regiments and companies of German light infantry and riflemen, and often supported by Portuguese Caçadores, they are seldom mentioned in any detail in the histories of the campaigns. The chapter outlines their training, selection, and evolution from the initial landings in Portugal to the march over the Pyrenees and into France.

Whilst the Peninsular Campaign may have been one of the longest and least successful for the French, and Britain was probably Napoleon's most implacable enemy, it was not the hills of Iberia or the waters off Cape Trafalgar that were the most decisive battlefields. The armies of Austria and Russia did more to defeat the French than did the small British Army. Two of the opponents that the French faced elsewhere in Europe are the subjects of Philip Ball's and Alexander Mikaberidze's chapters.

From the early campaigns of the 1790s through to the disastrous defeat at Ulm in 1805 the story of Austrian staff officer and general Johann Christoph Carl Mack illustrates how the Austrian army struggled to adapt to the new realities of warfare that followed the French revolution. Philip Ball outlines how Mack may have had new ideas and attempted to innovate, but the Austrian army proved to be too cumbersome a beast to turn quickly and evolve to counter such a brilliant field commander as Napoleon.

Ulm set the stage for Austerlitz a few weeks later and Alexander Mikaberidze's chapter reveals the tensions of coalition warfare and factional infighting in the allied headquarters before the Battle of Three Emperors. Whereas Mack's career could be characterised as illustrative of over-promoted mediocrity, Mikhail Kutuzov's shows the struggle of talent and ability to be recognized and utilised. The unwillingness of Czar Alexander to accept Kutuzov's cautious and prudent approach to the campaign led to a more aggressive and ultimately disastrous Austrian plan being adopted, making Austerlitz another example of how Napoleon's victories were often the result of his enemy's mistakes more than his own successes.

In the build-up to Austerlitz Napoleon deceived the allies into thinking that his position was weaker than it was, all the while striving to gather his own intelligence on his enemy's intentions. Terry Crowdy's chapter on military intelligence during Napoleon's earlier Italian campaigns outlines how the use of accurate and timely intelligence led to the successes that are often attributed to Napoleon's genius. The tale of spy and counter-spy are worthy of any Cold War thriller and Crowdy manages to throw some long overdue light onto a very shadowy subject.

Another thing that Napoleon excelled at was turning friends into enemies, and many of the armies of Europe served both for and against the emperor over the years. Mark Edward Hay's chapter on the Dutch army covers how it became completely integrated into the French army in 1810, suffered greatly in the 1812 invasion of Russia, but then was rebuilt as the noose tightened around France in 1813 and eventually fought against its former master to help in the liberation of its homeland.

The political and ideological divides of the revolution and the wars that followed also created conflict between countrymen. The Royalists who fled from France in the 1790s were a pool of manpower that Britain was quick to see the potential of. With a small standing army, Britain had always relied on foreign soldiers to help rapidly expand its forces following a declaration of war. Alistair Nichol's chapter on the émigré white cockade regiments details the slightly chaotic way the units were raised and how they failed to live up their promise or make an impact on the battlefield.

While history may be written by the victors, it should never just be written about the victors. The chapters in this book that cover the mediocre, the failures, and the defeats are as much a part of the story as the grand victories and great men. The richness and diversity of military history today is what makes it a fascinating subject of study.

1

Miseria en la Maragatería
The French and Spanish Sieges of Astorga During the Peninsular War.

John Marsden

Introduction

The small, cathedral city of Astorga is the capital of a region in northwest Spain known as la Maragatería; an area roughly bounded by Astorga itself to the east, the village of Manzanal to the north, Peñalba de Santiago in the west and Castrocontrigo in the south. Its inhabitants, known as los Maragatos, have struggled for centuries to eke a living from a land of poor, high and sparse pastures lying scattered across the lower slopes of the craggy peaks that overlook them. It is a land which, even in the best of years past, has struggled to produce harvests bountiful enough to guarantee the survival of its people throughout the frequently severe winters that scour the high steppe of northern Spain.

Such conditions of climate and geography led to the evolution of a way of life, perhaps unique across the Iberian Peninsula, in which the men, as muleteers or arrieros, would trudge along mountain trails and open plains, trading whatever goods they could acquire by transporting them from their place of origin to those where their relative scarcity provided for a small profit from local wholesalers. Whilst the men were absent from their families, the women of the Maragatería would take on the roles of farmer, mother and family figure–head; and woe betide any muleteer who failed to bring home a reasonable bounty on the rare occasions he returned to his village in the course of a year. Almost inevitably, such a way of life encouraged many a familia Maragata to set up as retailers in the larger towns and cities of northern Spain, thus allowing them to add the profits from sales to those of transportation. Today, their presence in places such as Madrid, León and Valladolid, is still borne witness to by the number of traders whose stalls and businesses continue to bear those surnames common amongst los Maragatos, such as Botas, Luengo, Crespo and Fuertes. For the interested reader, the life and culture of the Maragatería is beautifully described by Concha Espina in her novel, *La Esfinge Maragata* (*The Maragatan Sphynx*) a book she wrote whilst living in Astorga, which was published in 1914.

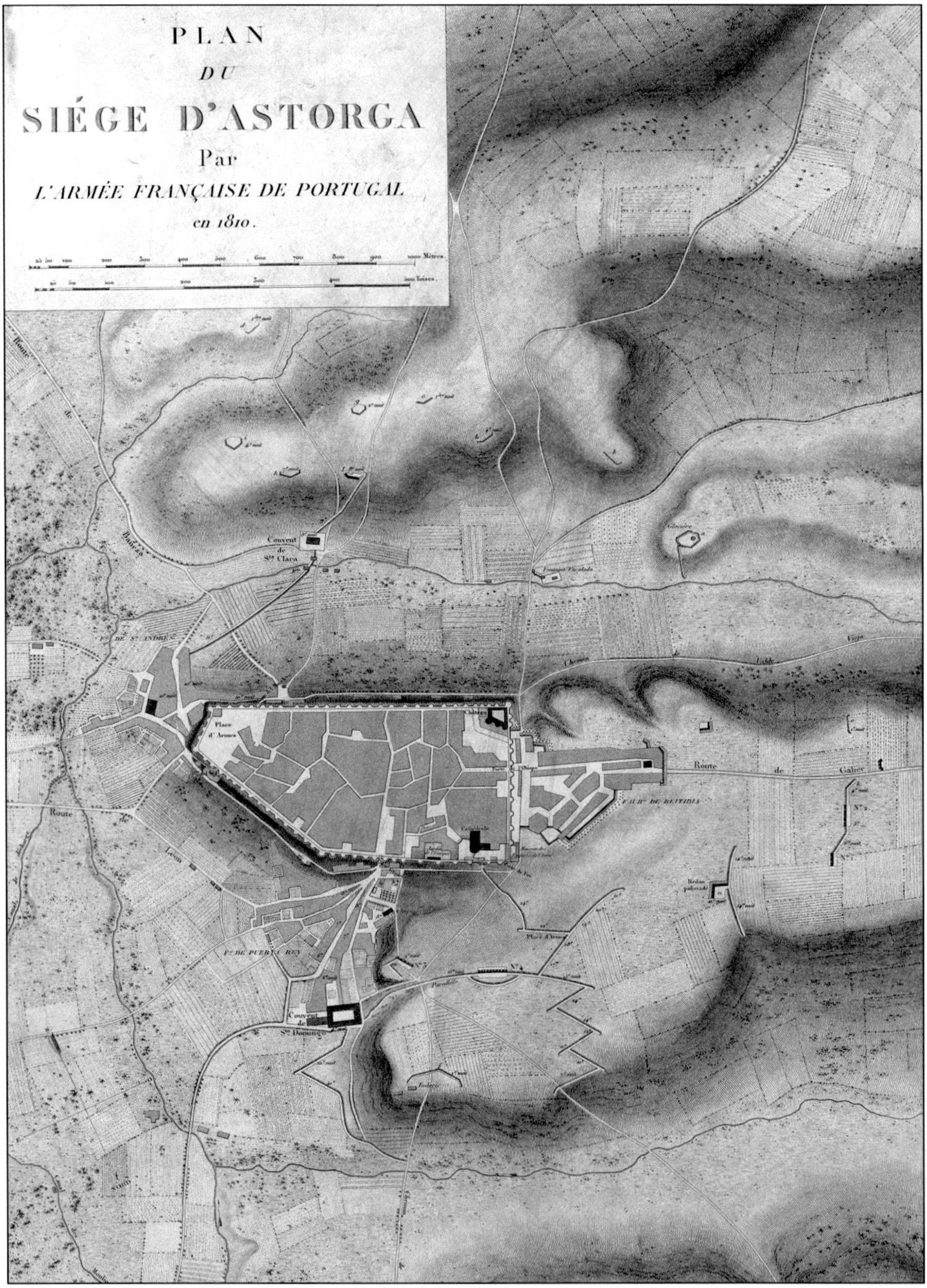

Plate 1. French plan detailing their siege works at Astorga, 1810. (Biblioteca Virtual del Ministerio de Defensa. Astorga SG. Ar.E-T.7-C.1-309)

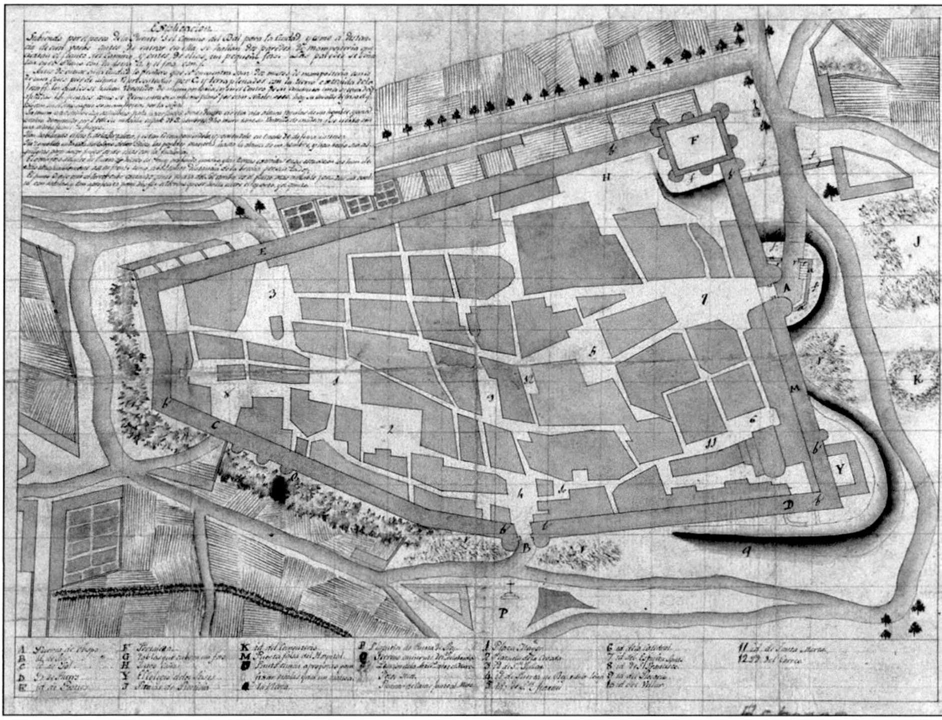

Plate 2. An early plan of Astorga showing its walls and gates. (Biblioteca Virtual del Ministerio de Defensa. Plano de la Plaza de Astorga, Ar. E-T.7-C.1-315)

The walls of Astorga are clearly shown on Plate 2. The old castle, labelled 'F' in the top right-hand corner of the periphery, is joined by a long, straight, uninterrupted section of wall which ends at what we might call the top left-hand corner of the periphery. Drawing a line from that corner towards the point labelled 'D', just short of the bottom right–hand corner of the walls, will roughly define true north. In other words, the city wall on the right of the plan with gate 'A' at its centre (la Puerta del Obispo) we shall refer to as the north wall, with the other walls named relative to it with respect to the cardinal points of the compass. This convention applies to all plates herein which show the city of Astorga in plan.

Astorga lies directly upon the old Madrid-La Coruña royal highway, and its proximity to León means that it is also just a few miles from one of the main routes which lead from south-central Spain to the province of Asturias. Thc city first figured in the history of the Peninsular War when it briefly became a major hub and supply depot for Lieutenant General Sir John Moore's army during its ill-fated campaign of 1808–1809. In addition to Moore's force, which landed in Portugal in late August 1808, a second corps command by Lieutenant General Sir David Baird landed at La Coruña in September, and by the end of the year Baird was in full control of the section of royal highway which ran between that place and Astorga.

On travelling the highway from south to north, one finds Astorga lying at the commencement of the foothills which climb towards the difficult mountain country dominating the province of Galicia. In fact, the little city stands at what is known as the gateway to Galicia, and as such it is of importance in military terms for any army intending to control movement between that province and its neighbouring provinces of León and Asturias.

Both the British Army under Moore and the Spanish Ejército de la Izquierda (Army of the Left) under the Marqués de La Romana, were to come together at Astorga in late December 1808 as they retreated northwards in the face of strong French advances from the south and east. The student of the Peninsular War knows well what happened next: by the middle of January 1809 the British army was at La Coruña, where it fought a desperate rear-guard battle against the French in which Moore was killed. After the action the Royal Navy arrived to lift the army from the Spanish shore and return it to England, leaving La Romana and the remnants of his army to fend for themselves.

With the British gone their erstwhile pursuers, *Maréchaux* Ney and Soult, found themselves in possession of the remote province of Galicia in the midst of winter's grip, and as they strengthened their hold on the region, La Romana was forced to move his army south towards the frontier with northern Portugal. When the spring of 1809 arrived, the Marqués was still unable to present a realistic threat to the enemy, thus allowing Soult to mount a virtually unopposed invasion of Portugal in February that year. By March he was in possession of the city of Oporto on the river Douro, planning his next move whilst Ney, who remained in Galicia, was beginning to grapple with an increasing level of civil unrest, which was supported whenever possible by the kernel of the old Ejército de la Izquierda, by then referred to as the Ejército de Galicia.

In April 1809 Lieutenant General Sir Arthur Wellesley returned Portugal and took command of the British forces there. Once familiarised with the situation he commenced a march upon Soult in the north, and due to a lack of intelligence or concern on the part of his opponent, he was unopposed during his advance to the Douro until he came upon the French outposts at Albergaria Nova on 9 May and Grijon on the 11th. Pushing on to Oporto, he managed to ferry his troops across the river at a point out of sight from the French, who had inexplicably kept their forces tightly concentrated around the city centre. Once a sizeable corps had been established on the north bank, the British were able to block Soult's avenue of retreat into Spain, and as more troops arrived the French were decisively beaten and forced to flee across the mountains of the Sierra de Santa Catalina into Galicia, abandoning their artillery and baggage as they went. After a fatiguing five-day march, Soult and his troops emerged from Portugal in the vicinity of the Spanish town of Orense.

Neither Soult nor Ney would remain in Galicia much longer. Once the former's corps had recovered from the ordeal of its retreat from Oporto, the *maréchaux* met at a somewhat fractious conference held at Lugo on 30 May. Frustrated with his colleague's illusions of grandeur, Ney demanded that Soult help him to deal once and for all with the Galician insurgents, along with the small corps of regular troops comprising the División del Minho, led by the Conde de Noroña and La Romana's force. The two eventually agreed upon a combined pincer movement against their enemy, which was set in motion on 1 June 1809, but it failed in its aim to entrap the Spaniards, Ney's column being stopped by Noroña at Sampayo whilst Soult was apparently 'resting' his column near Orense. In truth the latter's heart was never in the battle for Galicia, and after some acrimonious letters had been exchanged between the two, Soult decided to take his army where he felt it was most needed; that is onto the plains of León where it could find sufficient supplies of grain. Without his comrade in arms, Ney realised that he too had to bring his army out of Spain's Celtic province, and after concentrating at Lugo on 22 June, he marched out of Galicia leaving it free from French occupation, arriving at Astorga on the final day of the month.[1]

Spanish Forces Take Possession of Astorga

By the time Ney arrived at Astorga his men had become well-practised in the art of plunder, their commander having allowed them an undue measure of license as they passed through the villages of El Bierzo, leaving a trail of destruction and worse in their wake. According to the testimony of *Coronel* Santocildes, the Spanish officer given command of the city on 22 September 1809 after Soult had left, it would seem

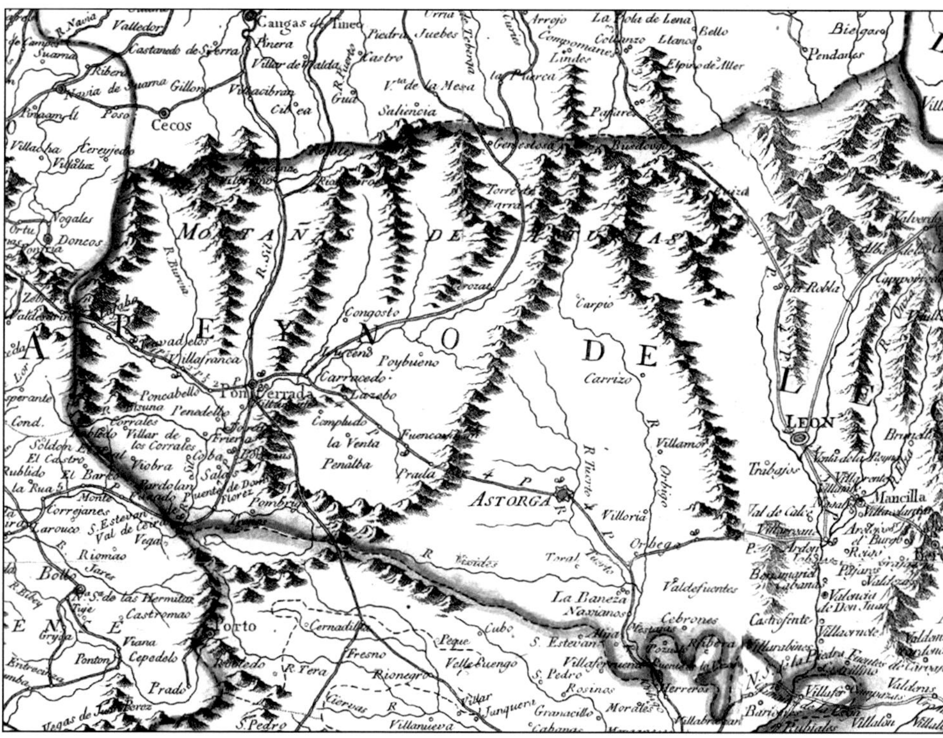

Plate 3. Northwest Spain. Detail from a map once used by the Marqués de la Romana showing, from left to right as one traces the line of the royal highway snaking down through Astorga: Villafranca del Bierzo, Ponferrada, Astorga and La Bañeza, with León to the northeast. *(Mapa de España y Portugal al Ex. S. Marques de la Romana, Mapes d'Espanya (s.XV-XX)* Institut Cartogràfic i Geològic de Catalunya)

1 Sir Charles Oman, *A History of the Peninsular War* (London: Greenhill Books, 1995), vol.2, pp.389–405.

that such behaviour was also given free rein during their stay in the little capital of the Maragatería.[2]

At Astorga, the force at Santocildes' disposal was meagre: some 1,100 soldiers, two 8-pounder guns which had to be repaired after the French had spiked them before withdrawing from the city, three 4-pounders and three 3-pounders, all served by just 30 artillery men so inexperienced they had not yet begun their training.

The French Siege of 1810

Once it became clear to the French that newly ennobled Viscount Wellington intended to spend the winter of 1809–1810 within the borders of Portugal, they began to probe beyond their front line on the Órbigo towards Astorga. On 9 October 1809 *Général de division* Kellerman sent a force of some 3,000 infantry and cavalry under *Général de brigade* Jean Augustin Carrié to occupy the place, taking with them just two pieces of artillery in ignorance of the presence of Santocildes and his garrison. Once he realised that a straightforward occupation of the city was out of the question, Carrié took possession of the extramural suburbs of San Andrés, Puerta del Rey and Reitivia and, after positioning his two guns amongst the dwellings of the latter, he began to pound the Puerta del Obispo (Bishop's gate) in an effort to force his way into the walled city.

After four hours of bombardment and several attempts to storm the north wall, Carrié called off his attack and headed back towards the Órbigo, thus allowing the Spaniards to bring in some of their own artillery from El Bierzo via the passes of Manzanal and Foncebadón. The temporary absence of the enemy also allowed some improvements to be made to Astorga's defences, especially those of the north wall and the suburb of Reitivia, whose buildings sat on an area of high ground, thus allowing a view into the fortress city from their rooves and upper floors. Sallies were made from the city towards the Órbigo with the intention of displacing the enemy and collecting food supplies, but the land and its villages had been so thoroughly picked over by the French that little was ever brought back to the city. This was the way things continued into the new year, which would see events such as the French siege of Ciudad Rodrigo, the Battle of Buçaco and *Maréchal* Masséna's invasion of Portugal.[3]

In 1810, Napoleon's overriding priority for the war in the Peninsula was the expulsion of the British. Once rid of them, he felt that the Spanish and Portuguese resistance would soon be reduced to the point where they would be forced to sue for peace. Masséna, Duc de Rivoli, was Napoleon's choice to lead what would become the third and final French invasion of Portugal during the course of the war. Once his route of approach had been defined there would be a number of supporting

2 *General* Josef María De Santocildes of Catalunya, *Resumen Historico de los Ataques, Sitios y Rendición de Astorga, de su Reconquista y Segundo Sitio puesto a la Ciudad, Siendo Gobernador en la Primer Ëpoca, y Comandante General del Sexto Ejército en la Segunda …* (Madrid: Imprenta Real, 1815), pp.13–14.

3 Santocildes, *Resumen Historico de los Ataques, Sitios y Rendición de Astorga*, pp.17–22.

operations to complete before launching his army into Portugal, where he would seek out Wellington and push him into the sea. Ciudad Rodrigo, on the Spanish side of the frontier, and Almeida in Portugal, were to be taken, and although on the extreme periphery of the zone of operations relating to Masséna's campaign, it was felt that his northern flank would be more secure with Astorga under French control. On this basis resources were designated to what the French felt would prove to be but a short distraction from the focal point of their efforts in 1810.

On 11 February *Général de division* Louis-Henri Loison arrived before Astorga with some 8,000 men and a field artillery consisting of six guns. Once he had arranged his forces to form a blockade of the place, he decided to chance his luck by sending a courier to the gates of the city with a letter for Santocildes; it contained an invitation to the Spaniard to state his terms for surrender or agree to a face-to-face meeting with the French commander. The governor refused to parley and Loison, having had time to assess the probable durability of Astorga's walls against the capabilities of his field artillery, decided that he would require some siege guns to make any rapid impression upon them. At that, he simply marched the bulk of his forces some 15 miles down the road to the small crossroads town of La Bañeza, where he would await the arrival of a siege train from Burgos or beyond, leaving just a small and ineffective blockading force behind.[4] The real reason for Loison's keenness to billet his men at La Bañeza may well have been the atrocious weather. Situated on the high plains of northern Spain, surrounded by mountains and regularly lashed by freezing rain or snow during the winter months, the prospect of digging, maintaining and manning the trench works required for a regular siege must have been daunting. In fact, during the French pursuit of Moore's army in December 1808, *Général de division* Pierre Bellon Lapisse described how, on arriving at Astorga after a day on the road, the only means he could find of staving off hypothermia was to strip himself naked from his sodden clothing and have his servants tie him between two wool-stuffed mattresses, before laying him in front of a blazing fire.

Santocildes took full advantage of Loison's absence to remove a large number of civilians from within the walls of Astorga, shepherding them through the leaky French blockade towards the passes leading to El Bierzo, and at the same time managing to bring more field guns and ammunition into the city, as well as a small but significant quantity of rations.[5]

Unimpressed by Loison's torpidity, the French high command ordered him take his force towards Salamanca in order to provide closer support for Masséna's coming operations. Once he had vacated La Bañeza, the apparently more energetic *Général de division* Bertrand Clausel arrived with his force of 3,000 men and orders to take control of the situation at Astorga. On 26 February he marched his men the short distance up the road to the little city and sent a letter from his commander in chief, *Général de division* Jean-Andoche Junot, to Santocildes, demanding its surrender. In response the governor sent the courier away without reading the document, telling Clausel that he would not accept letters relating to the surrender of Astorga, as he had already given his answer on that subject to Loison some 10 days earlier. At

4 Santocildes, *Resumen Historico de los Ataques, Sitios y Rendición de Astorga*, pp.22–26.
5 Oman, *A History of the Peninsular War*, vol.3, p.223.

that, Clausel came the same conclusion as Loison, and marched his men back to La Bañeza to await the arrival of the siege guns requested by the latter. It would be some weeks yet before a regular siege of Astorga could be commenced.

Junot, commander in chief of the French VIII Corps and unhappy with his subordinate's lack of activity, ordered Clausel to return to Astorga, place himself before its walls and begin work on the trenches, not forgetting to prepare the artillery batteries to receive the siege guns when they finally arrived. In the meantime, Junot requisitioned 16 field guns from various sources which he then ordered to the front, and although these proved to be ineffective, by 21 March 1810 he could nevertheless claim that a start had been made on laying a formal siege to the city.

Santocildes kept a diary of the 1810 siege, and in his entries for the dates between 22 March and 1 April, he described how the French continued their work of digging approach trenches whilst at the same time constructing batteries at various points around the city, and how his own men, still in occupation of the now heavily fortified extramural suburbs, carried out a number of sallies in an attempt disrupt the work of the enemy and engage in combat with them. In the course of one of those days, 26 March, the French attempted to dislodge the significant Spanish force in possession of the city's water mills, all of which were situated along the banks of a brook which ran to the east of the suburb of Puerta del Rey and were within cannon shot of the defenders on its walls. The French were repulsed, but then resorted to the expedient of redirecting the water course upstream of the mills, thus forcing the Spaniards to the necessity of grinding their corn and wheat by hand. Despite the gallant efforts of Santocildes and his men, Clausel was slowly tightening the noose around the city; steadily dislodging the Spaniards from their positions in its suburbs and forcing them ever closer to its walls.[6]

On 3 April, three soldiers, who in disguise had earlier been sent out in various directions to discover both the strength of French forces committed to the siege and to make contact with elements of the Ejército de Galicia then in occupation of El Bierzo, returned to Astorga. The news they brought was hardly encouraging. The French were found to be in possession of La Bañeza, Benavente, León and the passes of Foncebadón and Manzanal; and they put the strength of Junot's army at about 16,000 men. Santocildes was also informed that *Teniente-General* Nicolás de Mahy was at Villafranca in command of a force of no more than 4,000 Spaniards, with which he intended to throw supplies into Astorga; a forlorn hope it would seem.

On 7 April the French gained possession of the convent of Santa Clara, situated on the edge of the extramural suburb of San Andrés. The nunnery, made famous by Hippolyte Lecomte's portrait of Napoleon at its doors during the French pursuit of Moore's army in December 1808, was set alight during the fighting as the Spaniards were forced into an ever-shrinking pocket around the walls of Astorga.[7]

By 13 April there was growing concern amongst the city's defenders about the depletion of their stockpiles of food and ammunition, and even though Santocildes was well aware of the impossibility of any help coming from Mahy's Galicians in El Bierzo, a signal was made via Astorga's telegraph mast in the hope that it would be

6 Santocildes, *Resumen Historico de los Ataques, Sitios y Rendición de Astorga*, pp.31–32.
7 Santocildes, *Resumen Historico de los Ataques, Sitios y Rendición de Astorga*, pp.37–41.

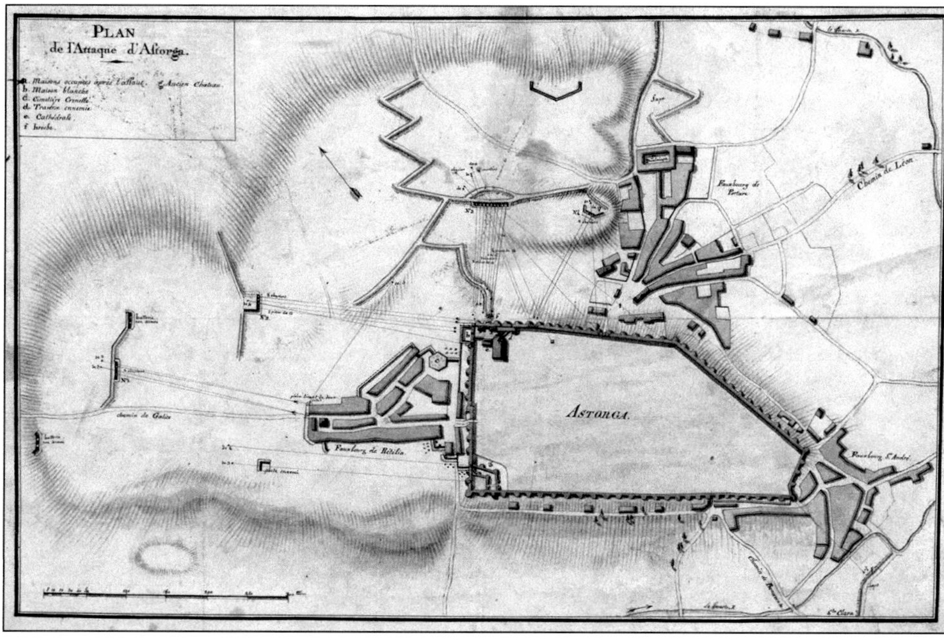

Plate 4. French map showing their siege works of 1810 and the lines of fire of their artillery. Note that the breaching battery is located beneath the crescent shaped trench (top, centre) and is concentrating its fire upon the Puerto de Hierro in the NE corner of the walls, close to the cathedral. (Biblioteca Virtual del Ministerio de Defensa. Plan de L'Attaque d'Astorga Ar.E-T.7-C.1-311)

seen by Mahy's outposts. In response, an agent sent by the commander of Mahy's vanguard, *Brigadier* Josef Meneses, on the 14th, entered Astorga carrying a note from his chief which read: '*Sr. Gobernador*, Later, later you will receive strong support. Commander General of the Vanguard of [the Army of] Galicia, JM'.[8] It was hardly an encouraging message, and it gave cause for some confusion in the mind of Santocildes as he attempted to interpret its meaning.

From Plate 4 it may be seen that at the commencement of the siege of Astorga, the Spaniards were still in possession of the northern, extramural suburb of Reitivia, as the French battery on the far left is directing its fire against the Spanish trenches on its northern fringes. The cathedral is the building at the north-east corner of the city.

Until this point in time, mid-April, 16 small-calibre field guns were all that Clausel had in terms of artillery, and these were found incapable of making sufficient impression on the walls of Astorga. However, Masséna had been promised a huge train of siege artillery for his planned invasion of Portugal. These large-calibre guns were destined to be used against the fortresses blocking the route into Portugal, such as Ciudad Rodrigo, Almeida and even Badajoz if necessary. But between 15 and 19 April, Santocildes noted in his diary the appearance of a significant artillery

8 Santocildes, *Resumen Historico de los Ataques, Sitios y Rendición de Astorga*, p.45.

train being drawn along the Madrid-La Coruña highway, clearly visible from the walls of Astorga, with some of the guns peeling off into the smaller roads leading to the villages in the surrounding area. He also noted the frenetic activity of the French besiegers as they dug more and more approach trenches and extended their artillery batteries, improving them as they did so. It would seem that some of Masséna's artillery had been diverted to Astorga, and on 20 April Santocildes wrote in his diary:

> At daybreak the besiegers opened fire from the breaching battery with four 24-pounder cannon, one 16-pounder, two 12-pounders and two howitzers; and with six howitzers and four 12-pounder cannon from other batteries situated around the walls [see Plate 4 above]. So continuous was the fire between five in the morning and midday, that it was impossible to know how many rounds were fired. From that point on and throughout the night it continued, but at a slower rate. As soon as the enemy batteries opened fire the artillery of the city began to play upon them but at a slow rate due to a lack of shot, which was remedied only by collecting any spent enemy shot of a calibre equal to our own and firing it back at him ... Observing the rapid progress being made in forming the main breach, I determined to construct three barricades using just large sacks and barrels instead of sand bags, fascines and more appropriate materials, which could not be found. Two of these were laid on the terreplein of the wall along the flanks of the [main] breach, with the third beneath them at another point accessible from the breach, close to the cathedral, where the enemy could enter the city. As most of this work was carried out at the place where the enemy was concentrating his fire, it was impossible to avoid casualties. [However] because the terreplein of the wall was just six feet wide at that point and constructed of stone, it was impossible to dig a ditch [along its top]. Instead, all that could be done was to raise a wall some 12 feet long and four and a half feet high [behind it].
>
> The smaller breach was [also] situated close to the cathedral, but [in the north wall, facing towards Reitivia, and as the top of the wall at that point was at street level] it was possible to dig a ditch [behind it] having a parapet and firing step along its bank. The breaches could only be defended by musket fire as there was not enough room to employ artillery effectively.[9]

On 21 April Santocildes wrote: '... At eleven in the morning, a lance corporal belonging to the *Voluntarios de Ribera*, who had been taken prisoner four days earlier at Foncebadón, left the [French] trenches close to Reitivia carrying a white flag ...'[10]

9 Santocildes, *Resumen Historico de los Ataques, Sitios y Rendición de Astorga*, pp.49–51. The reader should note that the 'walls' of Astorga are really a 'render' of stone (albeit some 10 feet thick) against the face of a naturally occurring 'cliff', hence the description of the 'top of the wall' being at 'street level' in some places.

10 Santocildes, *Resumen Historico de los Ataques, Sitios y Rendición de Astorga*, pp.51–52.

The prisoner had been sent to convince Santocildes of the hopelessness of his situation, and that with a viable breach already made in the walls of the city, any further resistance on his part would result in an assault during which everybody found within the place would be put to the sword. But Santocildes was not ready to surrender, writing his reasons as to why in a short note which the Spanish corporal refused to carry back to the French trenches. At that, he had a French prisoner of war brought before him who was asked to do the job. He too refused, and the task was left to one of Santocildes' officers who, after crossing the lines, was brought before Junot to deliver his commander in chief's refusal to capitulate. In the meantime, orders were given to repair and improve Astorga's defences in preparation for the inevitable attack.

At 2:30 p.m. two strong columns, each of about 1,000 men, attacked the suburb of Reitivia from the north and east. Santocildes claimed that the resultant fighting was severe, with ground being gained and lost again by both sides, the Spanish defenders making use of two 3-pounder guns located in their trenches which were supported by two more 3-pounders mounted on the walls of the city. Then, at 3:00 p.m., about 1,000 grenadiers and skirmishers climbed out of the trenches opposite the main breach, many of them carrying scaling ladders, picks and shovels, and advanced upon it before scaling it under a lively supporting fire from their lines. Santocildes' diary entry for the day continued:

> With many of the first wave being killed more waves came forward from the trenches but, caught in the open with no cover whatsoever, only a few of them reached the breach, many being killed or wounded by our terrible shrapnel fire and musketry. Those who entered through the breach were bayoneted to death at the barricades or the house situated close to the cathedral.[11]

The diversionary attack made by the French upon Reitivia went on for two hours before they withdrew to their starting positions, whilst at the main breach the fighting went on for some half an hour after sunset, when the survivors of the storming party retired to take cover amongst the rubble of the wall. During the moonlit night which was to follow, the French sappers dug a trench which ran from their main battery all the way up to the foot of the main breach, and with the Spanish having spent almost all of their ammunition and seen several of their artillery pieces dismounted or vented, they knew that there would be no stopping the next assault. A council of war was thus convened at 1:00 a.m., during which concerns were raised about the impossibility of Mahy being able to lift the siege; the certainty of what would become of the civilian population still within the walls should the French be forced to fight their way in; the enormous disparity in strength between besieged and besiegers, and the vanishingly small chance of success should the Spaniards attempt a general sally in the hope of breaking through the French cordon. When the conference came to an

11 Santocildes, *Resumen Historico de los Ataques, Sitios y Rendición de Astorga*, pp.13–15.

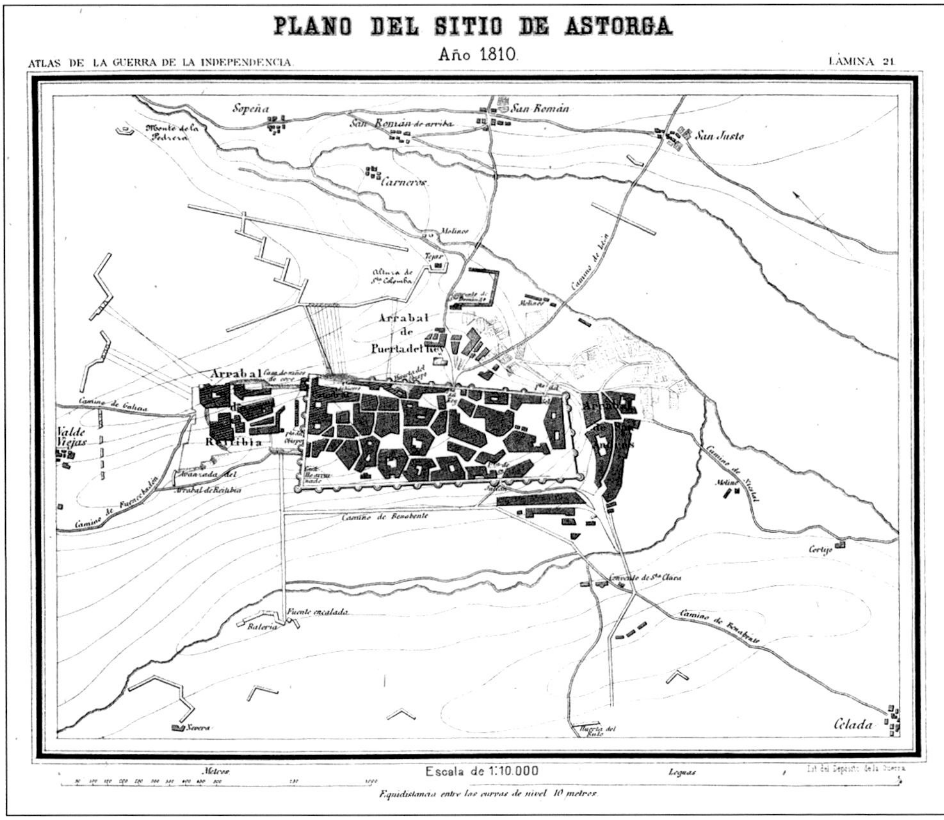

Plate 5. Map showing the French siege works of 1810 and the location of the main breach. (Biblioteca Virtual del Ministerio de Defensa. Plano del sitio de Astorga: Año 1810 Ar.E-T.7-C.1-312(2))

end, there was a unanimous decision to raise a flag of truce at daybreak and send out *Teniente-Coronel* Don Pedro Guerrero to offer terms for an honourable surrender.

As dawn broke on 22 April with the French storming party poised behind the wall of sandbags they had erected at the foot of the main breach, Guerrero walked out through the minor breach into the streets of Reitivia. Two hours later he returned with the terms of surrender offered by the French, and by 11:00 a.m. the acts of surrender began when the commander of the French artillery, *Général de division* Boyer, entered the city in company with a member of his commissary to exchange letters. In the meantime, Santocildes made his way to French headquarters to confer with Junot. At 2:00 p.m., after sustaining the siege for some 32 days, the Spanish defenders of Astorga marched out of the city through the Puerta del Obispo towards the road leading south to La Bañeza. Their flags were flying, their arms shouldered and their drums beating. At the cited road junction they were met by Junot and his *État Major*, who observed them lay down their arms and march off into captivity.[12]

12 Santocildes, *Resumen Historico de los Ataques, Sitios y Rendición de Astorga*, pp.15–17.

Miles Byrne was a soldier serving with the 2e bataillon du Légion Irlandaise, the unit chosen to scale the main breach, and he has left us an interesting account of his service with the French army during the Peninsular War, it includes the following description of the capture of Astorga:

> On the night of the 18 April 1810 the general in chief, Duc d'Abrantes, arrived, and as the Spanish garrison would not surrender, he ordered the breach to be made ... A battalion of chosen troops was organised to mount the breach, and Captain Allen's company of voltigeurs, consisting of 150 men of the 2nd Battalion of the 1st Irish Regiment, would march at its head. ... At 5 o'clock pm, when the signal was given, he had to pass more than 200 yards, uncovered, before he got to the bottom of the breach under the fire of about 2,000 men; he, however, mounted it with such bravery and decision, that when he arrived at the top, he turned around and saluted the general ... he took possession of a house near the rampart ... in order to keep up communication between the breach and the trenches; and this he defended the whole night. ... The rest of Commandant Fitzhenry's battalion remained all night near the breach, ready to mount first [thing] in the morning, and suffered much ...
>
> After the town surrendered, Captain Allen was ordered to return [to the trenches] via the breach, as an honour, with the remains of the battalion, which was reduced to about 150 men out of 900, the rest being killed or wounded ...[13]

The Butcher's Bill

On the day of the Spanish surrender, *Général de division* Junot finalised his report on events at Astorga and sent it to *Maréchal* Berthier, then acting as Napoleon's chief of staff, in it he gave the total losses amongst his units taking part the actual siege of Astorga as 111 killed and 330 wounded. Amongst supporting units in the surrounding area 49 were killed and 70 wounded.[14]

Interestingly, the casualties amongst the voltigeurs of the regiment referred to by Byrne as the '2nd battalion of the Irish Regiment,'[15] the unit which led the 'forlorn hope' through the breach, are stated at 11 killed and 16 wounded during the action; whilst the 'Régiment Irlandaise' is said to have lost 21 killed and 51 wounded during the entire period of the siege. Whether the former set of figures is included in the latter or not is unclear, but whatever the case, it would seem that the figures quoted above by Byrne are a wild exaggeration.

---

13 Mrs M Byrne (ed.), *Memoirs of Miles Byrne* (London: A. H. Bullen, 1907), vol.II, pp.73–75.

14 J. Belmas, *Journaux des Sieges Faits ou Soutenus par les Francais dans la Peninsule de 1807 a 1814* (Paris: Firmin-Didot, 1837), vol.3, pp.61–70.

15 Probably the 2e bataillon du Légion Irlandaise or, as Belmas refers to it, the Régiment Irlandaise.

Plate 6. The southern profile of the main breach in the east wall at Astorga. (Author's collection)

The French historian, Belmas, provides Santocildes' figures for the number of Spanish casualties, putting them at about 50 killed and 100 wounded. However, in his report to Berthier, Junot puts the Spanish losses at 1,500 killed and 5,000 taken prisoner![16] One need only take a brief look at Santocildes' return for the garrison troops he commanded at Astorga, a document which he handed to Junot on his surrender, to see that Junot's figures are grossly exaggerated. Santocildes stated that his total strength at Astorga on the day the siege began was just 2,759.[17]

16 Belmas, *Journaux des Sieges*, pp.61–70. 'Nous avons tué quince cents hommes, et fait environ cinq mil prisoniers.'

17 Belmas, *Journaux des Sieges*, pp.61–70.

Plate 7. The southern edge of the main breach as seen by the approaching French troops. The rear of the cathedral is clearly visible beyond the opening in the wall. (Author's collection)

Plate 8. The western profile of the breach made in the north wall of Astorga. This was roughly the location of the lesser breach made by the French in 1810, at which the damage was not as great as it appears today. In 1812 the whole of the north-east corner of the walls was demolished by the Spanish to discourage any further occupation of the city by the French. (Author's collection)

Plate 9. The breach in the north wall in profile, looking westwards along the line of the north wall roughly from the point where it used to meet the east wall, thus forming the north-east or 'cathedral corner' of the fortifications. (Author's collection)

Plate 10. The east wall of Astorga looking towards Gaudi's Episcopal Palace, beyond which the cathedral can be seen, occupying the north-east corner of the walled city. (Author's collection)

Plate 11. El Fuente Encalada, situated about half a mile from la Puerta del Obispo, the gate in the north wall of Astorga through which (recently promoted) *Brigadier* Santocildes led his men when surrendering to Junot in April 1810. It was here where the Spanish soldiers lay down their arms before marching into captivity. (Author's collection)

Effects of the Spanish Resistance at Astorga on the Allied Campaign of 1810

As stated earlier, the hopes harboured by the French for their 1810 offensive amounted to nothing less than the total defeat of the British and their Portuguese allies. Careful planning on their part mapped out a step-by-step campaign designed to clear the way for Masséna's advance to the Portuguese frontier, whence he would launch his thrust upon Lisbon, corralling the British within the city where they would be destroyed or forced to evacuate.

Besides the supporting operations on the northern and southern flanks of Masséna's planned route to Portugal, the intentions of which were to quell any allied attempts to put pressure on his communications, there were two fortresses lying directly in his path which would have to be reduced: Ciudad Rodrigo and Almeida. With regard to Masséna's northern flank, those historians supportive of Spanish claims that their contributions to the eventual defeat of the French on the Peninsula have been understated, might say that the well planned and bravely executed defence by Santocildes at Astorga was the cause of significant delay to the French invasion of Portugal in 1810. They back up such claims by observing that a sizable part of the French siege train assigned to the reduction of the two fortresses just mentioned, was diverted to the little city in order to guarantee its surrender, and that Junot's corps was subsequently late in taking up its supporting role for Masséna's advance because of Santocildes' efforts. Supporters of this theory claim that the resulting setback to the commencement of the siege of Ciudad Rodrigo had a knock-on effect at Almeida, and that every day of delay in the French timetable for Masséna's operation, gave another day to Wellington's engineers to improve the defences along the Lines of Torres Vedras. Students of the war who take a different view of things point to the content of Napoleon's correspondence relating to Masséna's invasion, and claim it shows that the Emperor was not in his usual rush for results from the 1810 offensive in Iberia. Instead, he was insisting upon a slow, steady and methodical campaign, which would be more likely to deliver the kind of success he sought. To back this up they make the supposition that if the British were to be driven into the sea, then the Emperor would rather they be forced to take to their boats during the stormy weather of October or November, than at the height of a more tranquil season. In other words, Napoleon may have considered that the defence of Astorga was actually helping rather than hindering the hoped-for outcome of his plans, making it more likely that Lisbon would fall late in the year. Perhaps there is some substance in both theories.

Wellington's thoughts about the situation at Astorga during the spring of 1810 come to the surface in a letter to Charles Stuart. As he pondered the approach of the French towards the Portuguese frontier, he told Stuart that:

> I have for some time turned over in my mind the expediency of making an attempt on the magazine at Salamanca at least, with a most anxious desire to carry it into execution. The fact is, however, that, according to the accounts we have of the enemy's strength, it is probable that I should not be able to accomplish anything, excepting probably the relief of Astorga, which I do not conceive of such importance as to induce me to incur the risk and inconvenience of moving my troops out of the strong country into the plains …
>
> I do not think the possession of Astorga, by the enemy, to be an object of any great importance in the existing situation of affairs. It is better they should not have it undoubtedly; but it is not an object of such importance as to induce me to incur the risks and to submit to the inconveniences of a forward move at present …[18]

Despite the thoughts expressed here, it is clear from his ensuing correspondence with various parties that Wellington's opinions underwent a subtle change when he realised that the French were not strong enough to mount simultaneous sieges at Astorga and Ciudad Rodrigo. Just 10 days after writing to Stuart, when he finally received the news from Brigadier General William Cox at Ciudad Rodrigo that Astorga had fallen, he mused: 'The fall of Astorga is of great consequence at the

18 J. Gurwood (ed.), *The Dispatches of Field Marshal the Duke of Wellington During his Various Campaigns in India, Denmark, Portugal, Spain, the Low Countries and France from 1799 to 1818* (London: John Murray, 1838), vol.VI, p.51. Wellington to Stuart, 21 April 1810.

present moment, and it is obvious that it is the cause of all the late movements of the enemy ...'[19]

After its fall to Clausel, Astorga would remain in French hands for some two years.

The Spanish Siege of 1812

After surrendering Astorga to Junot on 22 April 1810 Santocildes, along with some 2,500 of his troops, was marched off to captivity in France. In his resumé of the French siege, the Spanish general described how he eventually ended up in the town of Macon, some 35 miles north of Lyon. It was there where he began to resent both his status and treatment as a simple prisoner of war, expecting the French to have requested his word of honour that he would not escape, in exchange for the usual lax regime of incarceration which went with compliance. Had that been the case, he would have been able to move about freely in his local environment. Such privileges having been denied him he decided to make a break for freedom. The only insight he provided us with into how he made his way back to Spain is simply that, on the night of 22 October 1810, he made a 'risky but fortunate' dash for freedom, which led to his eventual arrival at Cádiz during February of the following year, where he was informed that he had unknowingly held the rank of *brigadier* since 9 October 1809.[20] The news of his promotion had not reached him before his capture by the French, due to the lack of communication which existed between Castilla and Andalucía at the time.

Upon hearing of his reappearance in Spain, *Teniente-General* Francisco Javier Castaños nominated him temporary general commander of the Spanish 6° Ejército (also known as the Ejército de Galicia) which meant an immediate return to his old stomping ground of Galicia and north-west León. After making an initial assessment of the situation in the north he decided that, due to the overwhelming superiority of the French cavalry in the region, he would be unable to conduct operations on the plains of Castilla. Instead, he determined upon taking up a defensive stance behind the passes of Foncebadón and Manzanal, threatening and sometimes executing incursions onto the plains towards the cities of Astorga and León whenever an opportunity arose.[21]

After gaining possession of Astorga the French, having had sufficient time to analyse the strengths and weaknesses of the place during their siege, decided to improve its fortifications by constructing a large hornwork in front of its north wall. The reason for identifying this area as the main weakness in the defences, was that some of the buildings comprising the extramural suburb of Reitivia overlooked it, thus providing any besieging force with a platform from which to observe the defenders of the city and to direct a plunging musketry fire into it, as we saw earlier. The project would mean the eventual demolition of the little settlement lying there,

19 Gurwood (ed.), *The Dispatches of Field Marshal the Duke of Wellington*, vol.VI, p.74. Wellington to Cox, Celorico, 1 May 1810.

20 Santocildes, *Resumen Historico de los Ataques, Sitios y Rendición de Astorga*, p.68.

21 Santocildes, *Resumen Historico de los Ataques, Sitios y Rendición de Astorga*, p.69–70.

but before things could get underway on the hornwork, the more immediate task of repairing the two breaches from the recent siege had to be undertaken. Astorga was going to become an important forward base for the French forces under *Général de division* Jean Mathieu Serás, which were occupying the region lying between the rivers Órbigo and Esla.

Santocildes' Minor Offensive of June 1811

After taking possession of Badajoz in Extremadura during May 1811, Wellington continued with his offensive, defeating the French at Fuentes de Oñoro and at Albuera. The reaction from Paris was swift; Masséna, having failed in Portugal, was replaced as commander in chief of the Armée du Portugal by Marmont; and to head off an anticipated crisis in the south of Spain, French forces from the north were sent to reinforce him. None of this went unnoticed by Santocildes, who decided to take advantage of the situation by mounting an offensive against Serás in June, sending his 3ª División under La Carrera towards La Bañeza, and his 2ª División under Taboada towards Astorga. To counter these movements Bessières and Bonnet made a combined movement upon the city of León, arriving there on 17 June before pushing on to Astorga where, on 20 June, its governor, Jeanin, was given orders to retire with his garrison once he had demolished parts of the city's defences by exploding 14 mines at different points along its walls. Two days later, with the French out of sight, Santocildes re-entered the city just 14 months after marching out through its Puerta del Obispo into French captivity.[22]

During the following weeks of the summer there would be much to-ing and fro-ing of the contending French and Spanish forces between the banks of the Esla and the passes of Foncebadón and Manzanal. During one of the French advances their cavalry actually entered a deserted Astorga on 18 July, before leaving to report on the results of their reconnaissance.

In early August 1811, Castaños relieved Santocildes of his command of the 6° Ejército, replacing him with *Mariscal de Campo* Francisco Javier Abadía; it was an act which would lead to unhappy consequences. Soon after, on 25 August, *Général de division* Jean-Marie-Pierre-François Dorsenne crossed the Esla to attack him, and by the following day he was in Astorga whence he sent orders for Bonnet to pursue the Spaniards into El Bierzo. However, by 30 August, having found no means of subsistence within that devasted region, Bonnet was back at Astorga, where he received instructions to place the city in a state of defence and to use his division to hold the line of the Esla, leaving Dorsenne to lead the bulk of his Armée du Nord south towards Ciudad Rodrigo, then under threat of attack from Wellington.[23]

On 26 August Castaños wrote to Santocildes, informing him that he would soon be confirmed in the rank of *mariscal de campo*. No doubt his superior felt he had been harshly treated, and that his promotion would be the first step towards his

22 Arsenio García Fuertes, *No Sin Nosotros* (Madrid-Astorga: Editorial CSED, 2016), pp.144–146.

23 Fuertes, *No Sin Nosotros*, pp.156–163.

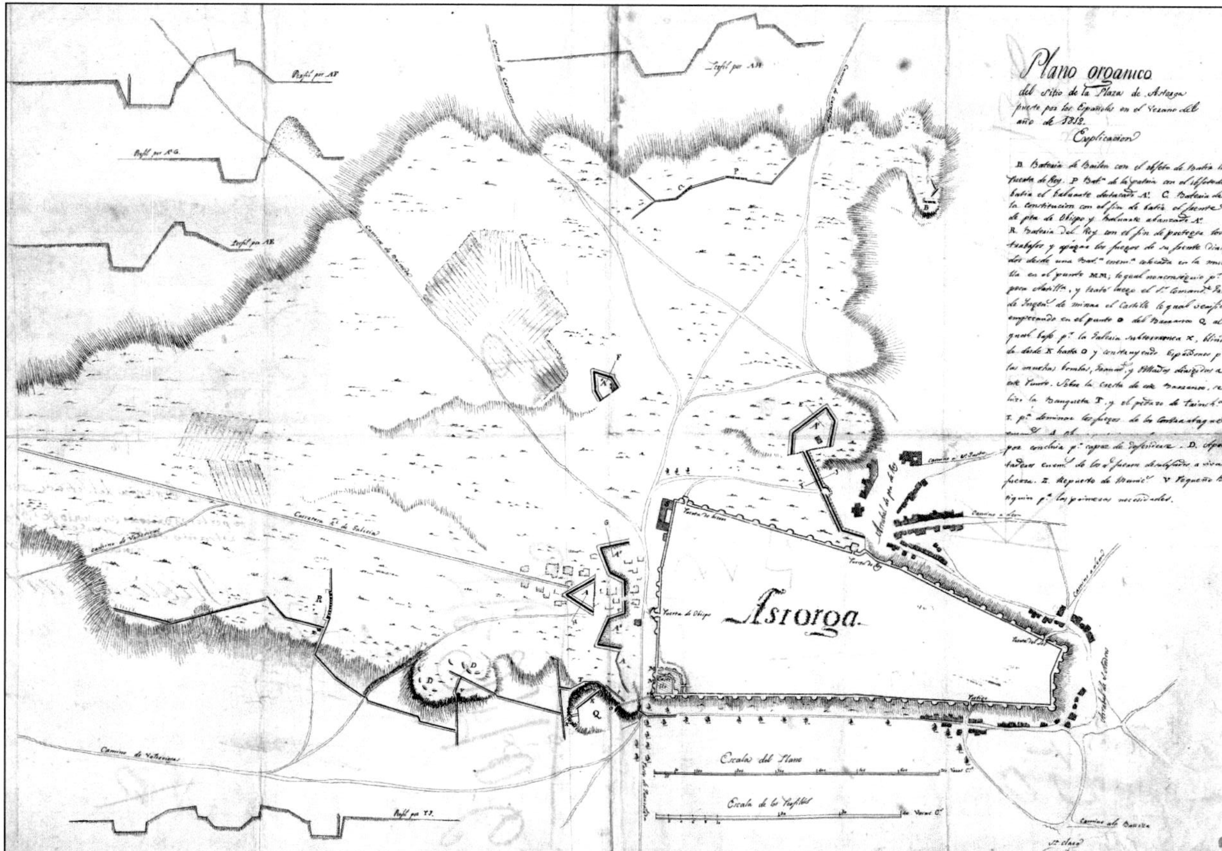

Plate 12. A Spanish plan showing the new hornwork constructed by the French at Astorga in 1811. Also shown are the approach works dug by the Spanish (lower L-H quadrant) during their (later) siege of 1812. (Biblioteca Virtual del Ministerio de Defensa. Plano orgánico del sitio de la Plaza de Astorga puesto para los españoles en el verano de 1812 [LE-1/7])

eventual rehabilitation. Meanwhile, at Astorga Bonnet soon set his engineers to work on the new defences in front of the Puerta del Obispo, and as a result the dwellings of Reitivia were systematically destroyed, the stone and other materials from them being put to use in the construction of the new fortifications, which would become a significant obstacle to both the infantry and, more importantly, the artillery of a besieging force.

The French would continue their work at Astorga throughout the winter of 1811 and into 1812, the year of Ciudad Rodrigo, Badajoz, Salamanca and Burgos; a period during which the internal politics of Abadía's 6° Ejército became more and more fractious.

Preparations for the Spanish Siege of 1812

After months of continual squabbling with the Junta de Galicia, and showing a lamentable lack of respect for his subordinates, things in north-west Spain came to a head in January 1812 when Abadía's chief of staff, Juan Moscoso, sent an eviscerating report on the situation to the Spanish government in Cádiz. As a result, Abadía was removed from command of the 6° Ejército and replaced by a reluctant Santocildes, the man who had been forced to hand over to Abadía just a few months earlier. Whilst Santocildes vacillated over re-assuming command, the Marqués de Portago was placed in charge of the army, finally handing over to the former on 6 June 1812.[24]

Wellington's 1812 offensive in the valley of the Duero had been long in the planning and it was to be a combined operation in the broadest sense of the word, in that he was insisting upon the cooperation of all Spanish forces in the northern half of the Peninsula. These were asked to prepare local plans for tying down the various French armies which, if left unmolested, could soon come to the aid of Marmont's Armée du Portugal and thwart British plans for a broader offensive towards Madrid and Burgos, should Marmont be destroyed early enough in the campaign. Wellington saw the role of Santocildes' army as being that of offering a credible threat to Marmont's right flank and rear-guard, and he seemed to be expecting them to advance towards Zamora and Tordesillas on the Duero, as well as laying siege to Astorga. But his ambitions for the Galicians seemed to take no account of the weakness of the 6° Ejército, which consisted of a force of about 12,000 infantry, just 400 cavalry and virtually no artillery to speak of. With men the likes of Castaños and Santocildes in command, Wellington's unjustified hopes would be treated with a healthy scepticism; these men were realists and fully aware of the limited capacity of the 6° Ejército to operate as a genuine field army. In their minds it would do well to tie down significant French forces at Astorga for any appreciable period of time, and to offer a threat towards La Bañeza and Benavente. To venture forth onto the wide-open plains of northern Spain with little cavalry support, would be to invite disaster.

24 Fuertes, *No Sin Nosotros*, p.257.

On 12 June, Portago led his small force of cavalry towards Astorga, and after two days of skirmishing with French outposts, he managed to establish an initial blockade of the place.[25] As the Spaniards subsequently probed towards the west bank of the Órbigo, the French withdrew their forces from La Bañeza, Benavente and the city of León, and soon the whole province of León would be free from French occupation – apart from the garrison at Astorga. By 14 June troops belonging to the 2ª División of the 6° Ejército were moving into positions surrounding the little city. Three days later Cabrera's 3ª División arrived before the walls of the place, making the possibility of an escape by Rémond's garrison of some 1,200 less likely than it had been. Finally, on the 19th, Santocildes arrived on the scene and established his headquarters in the village of Santa Catalina de Somoza, after having reconnoitred the defences he had last inspected some two years earlier and finding them much improved by the French in the meantime. But with Astorga now blockaded, the Spanish general found himself in the same position as Loison was at the end of 1809: he had no heavy siege artillery and his field artillery was inferior to that possessed by the French defenders of the city.[26] What was worse, was the fact that he had nowhere near enough cavalry to shield the besiegers, and by 23 June only a small detachment of sappers had arrived, comprising 24 officers and NCOs together with 108 rank and file. But there was no time to lose; fascines were prepared, and on the night of the 26th work began on a number of batteries and trenches to the north of the city. However, still on its way from La Coruña, the heavy artillery had gotten only as far as Lugo, and a number of medium-heavy guns were still three days march away.[27]

Come the beginning of July 1812, Wellington was asking questions about the 6° Ejército, suggesting that it should by then have been making its presence felt towards Zamora on the banks of the Duero. He was hoping to prevent Marmont crossing to its south bank, or at least to catch him in the act of doing so, and a Spanish presence on his right flank would confine the Frenchman to the area along its course between Zamora and Tordesillas. On 30 June Wellington wrote to Lord Liverpool saying, 'I have not yet heard that *General* Santocildes has commenced his attack upon Astorga …,'[28] and on 7 July he wrote to Bathurst saying that, after his arrival at Pollos near Tordesillas on the 3rd:

> We have since been employed in endeavours to discover the fords of the Duero … and are waiting till they become practicable for infantry.
>
> By that time, I hope that the Army of Galicia [6° Ejército] under General Santocildes, will have been able to advance, the siege of Astorga having been brought to a conclusion. The fire against that place opened on the 2nd instant, but I have not heard with what effect; and I have recommended to

25 Fuertes, *No Sin Nosotros*, pp.552–553.
26 Fuertes, *No Sin Nosotros*, pp.557–560.
27 José Maria Sánchez de Toca, *Los Desastres de la Guerra* (Astorga: Editorial Akrón, 2009), p.411.
28 Gurwood (ed.), *The Dispatches of Field Marshal the Duke of Wellington*, vol. IX, pp.261–264, Wellington to Liverpool 30 June 1812.

> General Santocildes to leave a small body of troops to continue the siege, and to move forward with the remainder.[29]

At the time Wellington was composing his letter to Bathurst, the early signs of hunger amongst Santocildes' men were beginning to appear. The area around Astorga was exhausted, and detachments were already having to explore the country some two days march away in order to procure the half-ton of meat which was the army's daily requirement. However, the siege artillery comprising a number of 16-pounders had finally arrived on 2 July, allowing Santocildes to try his luck at effecting a surrender of the French garrison. But Rémond was having none of it, and the Spanish commenced fire on the morning if the 3rd when, according to Santocildes:

> The battery finally opened fire on 3 July with all the accuracy and effect one could desire, and in such a manner that I am sure that if it could have been maintained at the necessary rate, the true point of [our] attack would have been swept clear of the enemy … but as we had only 2,000 shot to share between the four guns, and some of these being of too small a calibre, it was necessary to maintain a slow rate of fire despite the recovery of enemy shot … thus allowing the enemy to remain under cover.[30]

On 6 July, *Mariscal de Campo* Bárcena arrived with the 1ª División to join the siege. But as Santocildes increased the number of troops at Astorga, Wellington was still unconvinced of his intention to take it by storm. On 9 July he wrote to Bathurst from Rueda: 'I hear that a breach was open at Astorga on the 7th, but I fear that the Spaniards will not storm it. If they do not, the Governor will not surrender.'[31] It was during this period that Wellington had his army deployed along the south bank of the Duero, hoping to block Marmont's anticipated attempt to cross it from the north. The reason he was pressing Santocildes to come forward towards Zamora, or make a move towards the Esla, was that his army would then threaten the right flank of the French, either drawing enemy forces towards him or forcing the French commander to limit his room for manoeuvre in that direction.

On 13 July Santocildes finally sent a detachment of some 1,100 men towards Benavente in pursuance of Cabrera's small cavalry brigade, sent there two days earlier. It would seem to have been little more than a gesture to Wellington; the Spaniards were no match for the kind of forces available to Marmont and were determined not to fall victim to the French cavalry once more, having suffered greatly at their hands on previous occasions. But Wellington's frustrations with the 6° Ejército surfaced once again when he wrote to Bathurst from Rueda on the 14th:

29 Gurwood (ed.), *The Dispatches of Field Marshal the Duke of Wellington*, vol. IX, pp.274–276, Wellington to Bathurst, 7 July 1812.

30 Santocildes, *Resumen Historico de los Ataques, Sitios y Rendición de Astorga*, p.75–76.

31 Gurwood (ed.), *The Dispatches of Field Marshal the Duke of Wellington*, vol. IX, pp.279–280, Wellington to Bathurst, 9 July 1812.

> I have no authentic account of the siege of Astorga of a later date than the 5th instant, at which period General Santocildes, who was conducting that operation, entertained no hopes of bringing it to an early termination, and he expected to be in want of ammunition. It is reported that there are two breaches in the place; but I am apprehensive that there is no foundation for these reports …

Later in the same letter he said:

> I have again written to suggest the expediency that the siege of Astorga should be carried on by those troops only which are necessary for the operation, and that the remainder of the Army of Galicia should be brought forward to the Esla …[32]

At Astorga on 14 July, *Mariscal de Campo* Losada responded to a sally made by the French on the previous night by strengthening the artillery bombardment of their strongpoints. At the same time, the Spanish sappers began work on the approach trenches leading from the artillery battery, Rey, towards the ruins of the castle situated at the north-west corner of the city walls. The intention, once they had dug their way to the piece of sunken ground close to the castle, was to begin work on a mine designed to take them beneath its foundations (see F, D, E, Plate 13). In response, Rémond mounted five artillery pieces atop the walls between the castle and the Puerta del Obispo in order to provide counter-battery fire against the Rey battery, and encouraged the French troops manning the outposts (see B, B, B, Plate 13) to keep up a relentless fire on the Spanish sappers. This had such a demoralising effect on the engineers that Felix Carrera led a desperate attack on the outposts, forcing their occupants to seek safety closer to the walls of the city.[33]

On 16 July Marmont began his operation to cross the Duero, and it was on that day that Wellington wrote to Santocildes from Nava del Rey, asking him to march to the Esla via Carbajales and Villalcampo with the aim of crossing the Duero and uniting with the British left, but advising him to retire towards Galicia if attacked, thus drawing some of Marmont's forces away from the river.[34] On the same day an intense artillery duel was fought at Astorga between the Spanish guns in the Rey battery and those placed atop the city walls by Rémond, which resulted in significant damage on both sides. Energetic though they were whenever they had the necessary ammunition, the Spanish gunners had not yet created a viable breach in the defences of the city, and when the commander of engineers, *Teniente-General* Felipe la Paz, arrived on 18 July, it did not take him long to realise that the Spanish had too few guns of sufficient calibre to have any significant effect upon the walls. In a conference with Santocildes and Losada later that day, he advised them that their

32 Gurwood (ed.), *The Dispatches of Field Marshal the Duke of Wellington*, vol.IX, pp.284–287, Wellington to Bathurst, 14 July 1812.

33 Arsenio Garcia Fuertes, *El Sitio de Astorga de 1812* (Astorga: Centro de Estudios Astorganos, 2012), pp.194–197.

34 Fuertes, *El Sitio de Astorga de 1812*, p.201.

Plate 13. Astorga in three-dimensional aspect, showing clearly the hornwork constructed by Bonnet's engineers. The French outposts and hornwork are denoted A and B, the Spanish siege batteries and approach trenches constructed during the 1812 siege are denoted C, D, E, F, G, H and I. (Museo del Ejército, Toledo, Exp. Santocildes, Legajo 29/11, doc 376)

best chance of effecting a break-in was to push forward with the mining efforts near the castle, and use their disposable artillery to protect the sappers.[35]

By this time the pressure was beginning to mount upon Santocildes to bring the greater part of his forces into the theatre of allied operations on the Duero. On the 19th his commander in chief, Castaños, wrote to him from Lugo expressing his satisfaction that Cabrera and Castañón had been dispatched to Benavente, but urged him to bring the siege at Astorga to a swift conclusion.[36] With that, Santocildes finally decided to bow to pressure, and after placing Losada in overall command of the leaguer, he set off with a force of some 8,000 men towards Benavente on 20 July. Once there he wrote to Wellington, informing him of his intention to make a feint towards Marmont's rear-guard at Valladolid using only a small portion of his force, whilst directing the bulk of it upon Zamora.[37] For Santocildes' men, the march down the course of the Esla to its confluence with the Duero was to be a severe test of their fortitude; the summer temperatures were at their peak, they had no pack animals to transport their rations, and there was very little cavalry to protect the infantry.

35 Fuertes, *El Sitio de Astorga de 1812*, p.206.
36 Museo del Ejército, Toledo (MET): Exp. Santocildes, Legajo 29/11, doc. 376. Castaños to Santocildes, 19 July 1812.
37 MET: Exp. Santocildes, Legajo 29/11, doc. 376. Santocildes to Wellington, 21 July 1812.

At Astorga the absence of some 8,000 men had a debilitating effect on the siege; work on the approaches to the location where the mine was to be sunk continued, but the chronic lack of ammunition for the artillery meant that any covering fire for the sappers could not be continuous, the result being a series of short bombardments until supplies were exhausted, at which point the French would set to work and repair the damage before the next bombardment could begin. Then, on the morning of the Battle of Salamanca, Wellington wrote to Santocildes warning him to expect an attack at any moment from Marmont's newly reinforced host.[38] One may then imagine his relief when, at midnight on the 24 July, he received another letter from Wellington informing him of his victory over the French, expressing his hopes for a swift unification with the Galicians and asking Santocildes to make known his requirements for uniforms to Castaños.[39] The Spaniard sent his congratulations before the midnight hour was out.[40]

Oblivious to the news from Salamanca, the mining operation at Astorga proceeded at a snail's pace, but with *Teniente-General* la Paz on hand more method had been brought to the works, and the Spanish infantry was energetic in its nocturnal attacks upon the advanced posts of the French, pushing the occupiers away from the sappers. Sadly, this did not eliminate the risks to the men in the trenches who, having to work within sight of the walls of Astorga, were subjected to artillery and musket fire which caused them many casualties.

Soon, Santocildes was being urged by *Mariscal de Campo* Miguel Ricardo de Alava, a member of Wellington's headquarters staff, to ford the Duero at Castronuño and make contact with the Allied army, promising him that he would be released to go to the aid of Astorga should the French send forces to lift the siege. But it was at about this time, late July or early August, that deserters from the French garrison at Astorga began to tell the Spanish besiegers of the lack of munitions within its walls, estimating that there was only about one week's worth of ball and powder available to the infantry and no more than a thousand rounds for the artillery.[41]

With Marmont in flight, Wellington was trying to decide between turning south towards Soult in Andalucía, advancing upon Madrid, or making a dash for Burgos to threaten French communications; and the demands being made upon Santocildes were ever increasing. On his arrival at Zamora on 27 July, he wrote to Wellington asking for the extra resources he would require if he was to besiege the garrisons of Zamora and Toro.[42] Cavalry and artillery were his main requirements, but he made no mention of the fact that his men were in urgent need of rations. By Wellington's reply of the 29th it was clear that he was losing patience with Santocildes, urging him to re-cross the Duero and make for Nava del Rey where, he said, he would be within easy reach of his army which was then at Olmedo. His demands were sweetened by an offer to give the Spaniard five pieces of French artillery captured at Salamanca; all he had to do was to send an officer with some draught animals to transport them

38 MET: Exp. Santocildes, Legajo 29/12, doc. 349. Wellington to Santocildes, 22 July 1812.
39 MET: Exp. Santocildes, Legajo 249/5, doc. 350. Wellington to Santocildes, 23 July 1812.
40 MET: Exp. Santocildes, Legajo 29/12, doc. 354. Santocildes to Wellington, 25 July 1812.
41 Fuertes, *El Sitio de Astorga de 1812*, pp.218–227.
42 MET: Exp. Santocildes, Legajo 249/5, doc 356. Santocildes to Wellington, 28 July 1812.

from the city.[43] When Santocildes replied on the following day, saying that he had neither the necessary animals or artillerymen to make use of the offer, signs of the British commander in chief's exasperation were apparent in his subsequent letter, when he wrote: 'I should hope that your excellency would experience no difficulty in procuring mules to draw the artillery which I have placed at your disposition, by requisition on the large towns of León, the Asturias and Castilla.'[44] Wellington made his entry into Valladolid on the following day, the French having withdrawn to Burgos.

At Astorga on 27 July, it occurred to Losada that he should send a flag of truce to Rémond to inform him of Marmont's total defeat at Salamanca, it was a clear intimation that his position was now hopeless and that he should surrender. In his reply, the Frenchman stated:

> *Sr. General,*
> Even if the news you send me is true, I cannot debase my honour and my duty by accepting the terms of surrender which you propose, as the means of defence available to me are yet far from being exhausted.
> I have the honour to address you with the highest consideration.
> *Brigadier Général, Gouverneur d'Astorga*, Rémond.[45]

Having complied with Wellington's request that he should occupy Nava del Rey, Santocildes arrived there on 1 August and it was not long before Wellington was in communication with him, this time urging him to take possession of Tordesillas which, he claimed, was occupied by a token force of just 200 French soldiers.[46] *Mariscal de Campo* Castañón was duly dispatched to the place with a force of about four battalions, but found the French in some strongly fortified positions awaiting his arrival. His task would not prove as easy as it may have seemed according to Wellington's dispatch, but Castañón persevered with his mission, finally forcing the French, who by then were confined within the fortified walls of the church of San Antolín, to surrender on 4 August (we shall hear of this group of prisoners later in the story). This was the day upon which Santocildes finally came face to face with Wellington at his headquarters in Cuellar. By this time Wellington had decided to take his army south to Madrid, leaving Clinton's 6th Division in the region of Valladolid in company with the 6° Ejército, both corps having been given their own set of instructions to follow should Clausel drop down from Burgos and attack them. That being the case, Santocildes was to retreat westwards and take up a defensive position on the Esla. However, Wellington was still urging him to have the affair at Astorga brought to a successful conclusion, emphasising that once the city was under

43 MET: Exp. Santocildes, Legajo 29/13, doc 302. Wellington to Santocildes, 29 July 1812.
44 Gurwood (ed.), *The Dispatches of Field Marshal the Duke of Wellington*, vol.IX, p.320, Wellington to Santocildes, 1 August 1812.
45 Sánchez de Toca, *Los Disastres de la Guerra*, p.431.
46 Gurwood (ed.), *The Dispatches of Field Marshal the Duke of Wellington*, vol.IX, p.320, Wellington to Santocildes, 1 August 1812, Wellington to Santocildes, 1 August 1812.

Allied control it would completely change the situation in the north-west of León.[47]

Finally, on 5 August, the sappers at Astorga pushed the approach trench to the location at which the intended mining gallery could be opened, but at some cost in casualties despite la Paz's energetic attempts to keep the engineers and infantry safe from the plunging fire directed upon them from the walls.[48] Perchance, on the following day, the Conde de Belvedere left Astorga for Valladolid to take up the role of second in command to Santocildes; it was to be a fortuitous decision.

After some 50 days of maintaining the siege at Astorga, signs of malnutrition were becoming noticeable amongst the besiegers due to a lack of fresh food. In response a hospital was established in the nearby village of Castrillo de los Polvazares to help treat the increasing number of soldiers with scurvy, and Losada passed a regulation forbidding the sale of unripe fruit.

Elsewhere, Clausel, now commander in chief of the French Armée du Portugal, decided to make an advance towards Valladolid, knowing that Wellington had taken the bulk of his army south to Madrid. The only forces standing in his way were Clinton's division, much weakened after its hard fighting at Salamanca, and Santocildes' 6° Ejército; both of whom resorted to the instructions left them by Wellington should such a situation arise, Clinton falling back towards his commander in chief, whilst Santocildes withdrew westwards towards the Esla.

Santocildes' movement was fraught with danger; he was about to embark upon a retreat of more than 100 kilometres across the wide-open plains of Castilla with his corps of some 8,000 men, the vast majority of them infantry, many of whom were unshod and all of them weakened after a long campaign on short rations. He had not a single piece of field artillery, and his cavalry strength amounted to no more than 400 horsemen. If discovered by the French they would be cut to pieces by their numerous and well-practiced cavalry, a fate which had already overtaken the Spanish on more than one occasion in the course of the war. Had the Spanish general been aware that *Général de division* Maximilien Sébastien Foy had been given specific orders to re-supply the French garrison of Astorga, his anxiety would no doubt have increased, as there would now be no prospect of a halt on the banks of the Esla in the face of a French pursuit.[49] In his memoirs of the period Santocildes wrote:

> Consequent to [the orders given to me by Wellington] I moved upon Valladolid, occupying the city and its surroundings together with an English division of some 10,000 men. In the meantime, the Duke of Ciudad Rodrigo [Wellington] took possession of Madrid with the rest of his forces. However, as Maréchaux Soult and Suchet, ... came to the aid of the defeated armies, including that of Marmont, which had been reformed and reinforced with troops from Biscay and Navarra, the French were far superior to

47 Gurwood (ed.), *The Dispatches of Field Marshal the Duke of Wellington*, vol.IX, p.341, Wellington to Santocildes (via Douglas or Álava) 5 August 1812.
48 Fuertes, *El Sitio de Astorga de 1812*, pp.232–245.
49 Fuertes, *El Sitio de Astorga de 1812*, p.257.

> the force under my command, together with the English, which now stood in their way. As a result, when they threatened to attack us the [British] retired upon Madrid whilst we, engaging with the enemy vanguard every day … retreated towards Astorga.[50]

On 13 August, the 200 French prisoners taken by Castañón at Tordesillas were being marched along the Madrid-La Coruña road at the point where it passes within a few yards of the west-facing wall of Astorga. On seeing the column approaching Losada sent for the senior officer amongst them, one *Capitaine* Antoine Bernard, who agreed to enter Astorga under a flag of truce to inform Rémond of the defeat recently inflicted upon the French at Salamanca. The news spread quickly throughout the garrison, demoralising many amongst its ranks to the point where they decided to surrender to the Spanish.[51]

By the 15th, out on the plains, Santocildes was coming under increasing pressure from the French, and as he began his retreat in fear of the consequences of an attack by the French cavalry, Lieutenant Colonel Sir Howard Douglas, a British military attaché to the 6° Ejército, was demanding to know the details of his intentions, which he intended to communicate to Wellington. This produced an inevitable spat between the two men and increased the pressure on the Spaniard whose health, already poor, took a turn for the worse, resulting in what may have been a nervous breakdown. It was at this moment that the newly-arrived Conde de Belvedere took command.

By this time, news of the French counter-offensive had reached Losada at Astorga, who immediately gave orders for the withdrawal of his artillery towards the safety of El Bierzo. It now seemed that everything rested upon the success of the mining operation, and la Paz took personal command of the works in situ. But then, on 16 August, with morale within the walls at its lowest point since the siege began, Rémond finally gave signs that he was willing to enter into talks, calling for a truce during which initial negotiations could take place under the condition that, should the garrison surrender, it would be allowed to return to France. Before giving his answer to Rémond, Losada read a strict order to all of his troops, demanding that absolutely nothing be said to the French about the continuing retreat of the 6° Ejército towards Astorga and its pursuance by a relieving force, nor anything about the fact that the besiegers were already making preparations to move away from the city. He then sent a reply to Rémond, informing him that he was not authorised to accept his basis for surrender, adding that if he failed to receive a reply indicating that he was willing to capitulate, he would suspend the truce and recommence the siege. Rémond refused.

Elsewhere, at dawn on the 17 August Belvedere received intelligence indicating that Foy had left Valladolid in search of his corps, at which he immediately ordered his men to begin a forced march across the arid, burning plains of the Tierra de Campos towards Benavente. It was to be known as the día terrible, a 40 kilometre dash across the baking earth, under a merciless sun. By nightfall they were safe, and

50 Santocildes, *Resumen Historico de los Ataques, Sitios y Rendición de Astorga*, pp.80–81.
51 Fuertes, *El Sitio de Astorga de 1812*, pp.259–264.

the exhausted soldiers claimed that, on that day, just as the Spanish soldiers who 'miraculously' overcame their Dutch enemies at Empel, Flanders in December 1585 had claimed, 'Díos fue español' (God was Spanish).[52] But their race was not yet run; Foy was at Toro and about to march on Astorga.

By the end of that día terrible for their comrades in the field, the sappers at Astorga had pushed their gallery to within 20 metres of the castle foundations, but they would require another three days before they reached the spot where the explosives were to be placed. All the time the French were keeping up a tremendous assault upon the trenches leading to the gallery entrance and, pushing forward all the time, were themselves within 20 metres of the Spanish trenches. The end game finally began when Castaños arrived to help direct operations at the siege. When a clear picture of the situation was put to him, Castaños came to the conclusion that Foy would probably arrive on the scene before the mine could be blown, but rather than conclude the siege he decided to appeal to Rémond's vanity. He knew that the French commander would find it easier to surrender to a *teniente-general* than to a lower ranking officer, especially the *teniente-general* famous for his victory at Bailén. Calling his secretary to his side, he dictated a flattering and mildly threatening letter to Rémond, offering him honourable terms of surrender and adding a footnote stating that there was no hope of his being relieved, as Marmont's army had been destroyed.[53]

Meanwhile, on the burning meseta, as Belvedere arrived at the east bank of the Esla on the afternoon of 18 August, he decided to rest his troops before fording the river, but in the evening he received news that no time could be lost as the French, in two columns, were attempting simultaneously to cut his line of retreat and to engage his rear-guard. At 8:00 p.m. he began to cross the river, but there were a further 60 kilometres of sparse, open territory to cross before reaching Benavente.

Back at Astorga, on the 17th Castaños' able and mentally agile negotiator, *Coronel* Enrile, was allowed through the gates bearing his superior's message. Earlier that day Rémond had conversed with his staff; he was in favour of surrendering on the best terms available, but others proposed a dash for freedom through the Spanish lines. However, when Castaños's proposals were found to contain a clause which promised that, upon surrendering, the whole garrison would be conducted under escort to the French lines, the news was the cause of great relief to the French commander. Some of his staff remained sceptical of such a generous offer until it was claimed that the Spanish had arranged a like-for-like prisoner exchange with the French high command. This seemed to assuage the doubts still held by some, allowing Rémond to issue notice of his intention to surrender on the evening of the 18th and hand-over the city at 8:00 a.m. on the following morning after a resistance of 67 days.[54]

On the 19th, as the French prisoners were handing their weapons over to their Spanish escorts at Astorga, the Conde de Belvedere's corps, after another gruelling forced march of some 24 hours, met with one of Losada's cavalry outposts guarding the bridge which crosses the Órbigo at la Vizana. Just a few miles further on they

52 Fuertes, *El Sitio de Astorga de 1812*, p.265.
53 Fuertes, *El Sitio de Astorga de 1812*, pp.268–269.
54 Fuertes, *El Sitio de Astorga de 1812*, pp.265–275.

were finally allowed to rest at La Bañeza. By then the French prisoners were on their way to Burgos with their Spanish escort, and Losada's men were already dismantling as many of the critical parts of Astorga's defences as they could before Foy's arrival, knowing that it would be impossible for the Spanish to defend it and not wanting to leave it in a tenable condition for the French. As the work of destruction continued, Belvedere's two weary brigades trudged their way into the city; but there would be little respite for them. On the following day, after ascending the passes of Manzanal or Foncebadón, they entered the relatively safe territory of El Bierzo.

Foy rode into Astorga on the morning of the 21st, collected the sick and wounded left behind by Losada and marched away. The French would never return.

By the beginning of September 1812, Santocildes has recovered his health sufficiently to lead his men back to Astorga, the French were by then holding a line beyond the east bank of the Órbigo. Having been the scene of enormous suffering amongst its population for more than two years, a decision was taken to reduce its defences to the point where they would be considered useless, thus dissuading any future army from occupying it as a stronghold. Astorga's war was finally over.

Plate 14. The bridge at La Vizana where Belvedere met Losada's cavalry scouts. (Author's collection)

Plate 15. The causeway of the bridge at La Vizana. (Author's collection)

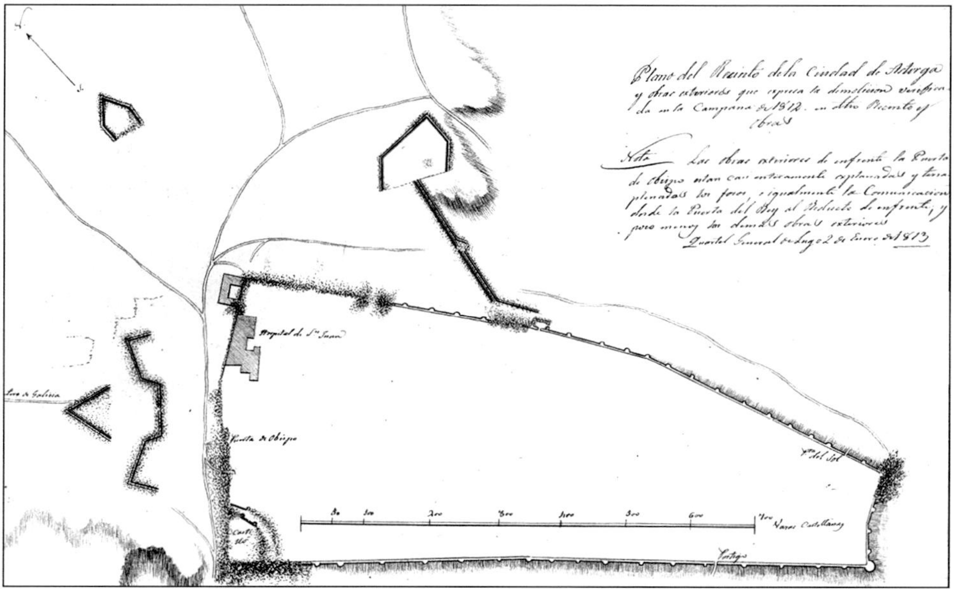

Plate 16. Plan showing the extent of the demolition of the walls and fortified outposts of Astorga (heavy shading) carried out by the Spanish in September 1812. (Biblioteca Virtual del Ministerio de Defensa, Plano del Recinto de la Ciudad de Astorga y obras exteriores que expresa la demolición verificada en la Campaña de 1812 … Ar.E-T.7-C.1-314(3))

Bibliography

Archival Sources

Biblioteca Virtual del Ministerio de Defensa:

Plano del Recinto de la Ciudad de Astorga y obras exteriores que expresa la demolición verificada en la Campaña de 1812 ... Ar.E-T.7-C.1-314(3)

Astorga SG. Ar.E-T.7-C.1-309

Plan de L'Attaque d'Astorga Ar.E-T.7-C.1-311

Plano de la Plaza de Astorga, Ar. E-T.7-C.1-315

Plano del sitio de Astorga: Año 1810 Ar.E-T.7-C.1-312(2)

Plano orgánico del sitio de la Plaza de Astorga puesto para los españoles en el verano de 1812 [LE-1/7]

Institut Cartogràfic i Geològic de Catalunya:

Mapa de España y Portugal al Ex. S. Marques de la Romana, Mapes d'Espanya (s.XV-XX)

French Army Archive, Vincennes:

Vue de la Place d'Astorga et des travaux de siege fait au mois d'avril 1810

Museo del Ejército, Toledo:

Exp. Santocildes, Legajo 29/11

Exp. Santocildes, Legajo 29/13

Exp. Santocildes, Legajo 249/5

Published Sources

Belmas, J., *Journaux des Sieges Faits ou Soutenus par les Francais dans la Peninsule de 1807 a 1814* (Paris: Firmin-Didot, 1837)

Byrne, Mrs M. (ed.), *Memoirs of Miles Byrne* (London: A. H. Bullen, 1907)

Dunne-Lynch, Nicholas, 'An Irish Draper at Astorga', Proceedings of the International Conference: *Juntas, Guerra y Constitución en Astorga y el Noroeste Peninsular*. Astorga 2014

Garcia Fuertes, Arsenio, *El Sitio de Astorga de 1812* (Astorga: Centro de Estudios Astorganos, 2012)

García Fuertes, Arsenio, *No Sin Nosotros* (Madrid-Astorga: Editorial CSED, 2016)

Gurwood, J. (ed.), *The Dispatches of Field Marshal the Duke of Wellington During his Various Campaigns in India, Denmark, Portugal, Spain, the Low Countries and France from 1799 to 1818* (London: John Murray, 1838)

Sánchez de Toca, José Maria, *Los Desastres de la Guerra* (Astorga: Editorial Akrón, 2009)

Santocildes, General Josef María de, *Resumen Historico de los Ataques, Sitios y Rendición de Astorga, de su Reconquista y Segundo Sitio puesto a la Ciudad, Siendo Gobernador en la Primer Ëpoca, y Comandante General del Sexto Ejército en la Segunda ...* (Madrid: Imprenta Real, 1815)

Oman, Sir Charles, *A History of the Peninsular War* (London: Greenhill Books, 1995)

2

The Unfortunate General Mack

Phillip Ball

The name of General Mack, according to a recent historian, 'Has become synonymous with military failure, for rigid adherence to outdated views and refusal to take note of new developments.'[1] Certainly, if Mack is remembered at all today it is for his surrender at Ulm in 1805 at the beginning of Napoleon's famous Austerlitz campaign. This particular humiliation provoked Lady Louisa Erskine to write of 'the black treachery of that odious wretch Mack' suggesting that he had been bribed and of her astonishment that 'the Emperor did not order him strangled instantly.'[2]

Is this a fair reflection on the career of a man who once enjoyed a high reputation as a military planner and reformer throughout Europe? A glance at Mack's career reveals little that would proclaim him as a genius or indeed change the minds of those who view him as a failure so how did his star rise so high and why has his reputation fallen so low today? Was he a hapless foil for the genius of Bonaparte? A general whose movements were so ponderous that Horatio Nelson was to claim that, 'he cannot move without five carriages'?[3] Was he simply 'unfortunate' as his epithet suggests? Or was there more to it than that?

Johann Christoph Carl Mack. (Public Domain)

1 E. Gramm, *Der unglückliche Mack Aufstieg und Fall des Karl Mack von Leiberich* (Doctoral Dissertation, University of Vienna, 2008), p.1.

2 Louisa Erskine to Arthur Paget, 24 November 1805, A. Paget, *The Paget Brothers* (London: J Murray, 1918), pp.50–51.

3 H. Nelson, quoted in *The Saturday Magazine. Published Under the Direction of the Committee of General Literature and Education Appointed by the Society for Promoting Christian Knowledge* (London: JW Parker, 1835), vol.5, p.91.

Johann Christoph Carl Mack was born on 25 August 1752 to humble parents in Nennslingen, Bavaria and baptised a Lutheran. Although his father rose in status from a clerk to a bailiff, this background was pretty unusual for generals in the Imperial Army who tended to be Princes of the Hapsburg dynasty or high ranking nobles and were almost invariably Roman Catholics. Mack therefore was an outsider from the start.[4]

In 1770, a maternal uncle, who was an officer in a cavalry regiment in the Austrian army, obtained a place for the young Mack as a *fourier* (quartermaster) in his regiment and Mack's career began.[5] He rose slowly, because of his background and his father's lack of influence, not becoming an officer until 1777. The British historian, Colonel Maude described Mack as being 'as devoid of powerful protection as a man could well be.'[6] However, he was fortunate to secure an appointment to the staff of Count Kinsky during the War of the Bavarian Succession and subsequently caught the eye of the commander-in-chief, *Feldmarschall* Count Lacy. These officers were particularly impressed with Mack's work and he rose quickly from then on, becoming a *lutnent* in 1777, *hauptmann zum Generalstab* (a captain on the General Staff) in 1783 and being ennobled as Mack von Leiberich in 1785. Another war with Turkey saw Mack becoming personal aide-de-camp to the Emperor and by 1789 he was a *oberstleutnant*.[7]

Part of the reason for Mack's rise to prominence was work he did on the Emperor's ideas for training cavalry remounts.[8] He also cemented his reputation in the eyes of Count Lacy winning the latter's esteem and praise for his 'ceaseless energy and devotion to duty.'[9] In most armies of the time, being noticed by a powerful patron was a useful pathway to further advancement and this would explain Mack's rise to prominence at this time. His service on the Emperor's staff allowed Mack to expand his military knowledge from just a familiarity with cavalry and he gained a good knowledge of Belgian geography when he accompanied the Emperor there in 1784. This was to stand Mack in good stead later in his career but his next important appointment came in 1787 when *General der Kavallerie* Graf Kinsky expressly requested Mack to serve as his chief of staff in Hungary, in a new war against the Turks. This campaign gave Mack useful experience in exercising high command; planning the deployment of the units under his jurisdiction and organising their logistical support. Mack also distinguished himself at the storming of Belgrade where he was not only involved in the planning of the operation but took it upon himself to lead the most crucial of the storming parties.[10] It was whilst leading this

4 Gramm, *Der unglückliche Mack,* p.20.

5 Gramm, *Der unglückliche Mack,* p.29.

6 F.N. Maude, *The Ulm Campaign: 1805* (Driffield: Leonaur, 2007), p.28.

7 H. Chisholm (ed.), 'Mack Von Leiberich, Carl', *Encyclopaedia Britannica*, 1911, < https://en.wikisource.org/wiki/1911_Encyclopædia_Britannica/Mack_von_Leiberich,_Karl>, (accessed 26 February 2021); D. Smith, 'Biographical Essay' <https://www.napoleon-series.org/research/biographies/Austria/AustrianGenerals/c_AustrianGeneralsM.html>, (accessed December 2021).

8 Gramm, *Der unglückliche Mack,* p.40.

9 Maude, *Ulm,* p.29.

10 Gramm, *Der unglückliche Mack,* p.59.

assault that Mack received a wound to the head that was to trouble him for the rest of his life.

It would seem that Mack's star was in the ascent but shortly after this crowning point of his early career, a change of commander led to the first of a series of clashes he was to have with high command. The retirement of *Feldmarschall* Hadik led to his replacement by *Feldmarschall* Loudon an officer whom, it seems, was heavily embroiled in court politics and professional jealousy. Loudon regarded Mack as a protégé of his rival Lacy and was resentful of the young staff officer's elevated position and popularity with the Emperor. He had objected to Mack's plan for Belgrade and after that relations between the two deteriorated to such an extent that Mack requested a court martial and removed himself from the front. He was compensated with the colonelcy of a cavalry regiment and the Order of Maria Theresa and was later reconciled with Loudon, but this incident set a pattern for his later relations with the upper echelons of the Imperial Army.[11] However, this was a period that had quickly established Mack as a first-rate planner and a military thinker. What it was that caused Lacy, and indeed the Emperor, to view Mack in these terms is a bit of mystery. Certainly, his rise from humble ranker, to staff officer, to someone trusted to plan major tactical moves is rapid and, despite the clash with Loudon, he continued to be viewed by the Austrian high command as a safe pair of hands. It would not be long before Mack's burgeoning talent for planning would be called on again.

At the outbreak of war with France in 1792 Mack was in command of the 3rd Chevaux Legers but the following year the man appointed to lead Austria's army in Flanders, Prince Josias von Coburg-Saalfeld, asked for Mack to act as his chief of staff. Mack apparently tried to refuse this honour as he was suffering ill-health, but he was soon prevailed upon to accept the post.[12]

Mack was given far ranging powers, way beyond those laid out in the imperial regulations for one of his rank and he was sent ahead of Coburg to liaise with allied forces and set the plan, to relieve Maastricht, in motion. He was (according to Von Prokesh Osten) 'the leading spirit of the Austrian headquarters.'[13] Contrary to traditional view of Austrian strategy during the ensuing campaign, rather than maintain a wide cordon across the frontiers of France and reduce important fortresses, Mack's first aim was to concentrate all allied forces to bring the French in Flanders to a decisive battle. To this end he sent instructions for the Dutch and Anglo-Hanoverians to move towards Antwerp to cover the main army's right flank and he went in person to visit the Duke of Brunswick who was commanding the Prussian forces on the left.

The Prussians under Brunswick's command were characterised by almost glacial movement and a slavish reliance on well-regulated supply magazines. It must be remembered that Brunswick's assault on France the previous year had ended at Valmy when a lack of supplies had persuaded him that the campaign was unwinnable. Therefore, it was a wise move of Mack to offer to supply the Prussians from

11 Chisholm (ed.), 'Mack Von Leiberich, Carl'.
12 Maude, *Ulm*, p.30.
13 A. Von Prokesch-Osten, *Kleine Schriften: Der Feldzug in den Niederlanden 1793, Dritter Band* (Stuttgart: Hallberger, 1842), p.108.

the imperial magazines at Liege and support them with *Generalmajor* Wenkheim's division.[14] Brunswick was impressed and immediately ordered his army to pack up and move with as much stealth as possible to Grave. The Prussian liaison officer Graf Von Tuentzien excitedly expressed the opinion that Mack would 'get things done.'[15]

At the headquarters of Mack's own army things were not to prove as easy. *Feldzeugmeister* Clerfait, a man who was to acquire a reputation for great caution, point blank refused to conform to Mack's plan. A veteran of the Seven Years War, Clerfait had been a general for some years and had exercised successful independent command during the Austro-Turkish war, gaining victories at Mehadia and Calafat, he was not about to be told what to do by an inexperienced staff officer. Clerfait had a plan of his own for a limited movement to Ruremond and would not advance without reinforcements.

Mack reported to Coburg that he was unable to win Clerfait over to his 'design' and that 'with inscrutable persistence he insists on his project on Ruremond.' Fortunately, Coburg approved of Mack's design, writing in reply that; 'The crossing over the Roer is now the most important object.'[16] With that, he ordered Clerfait to comply with Mack's plan and preparations were duly made for the river crossing.

The crossing was a complete success and accomplished with very little fighting or bloodshed on 1 March 1793. Mack duly won great praise for this operation, adding to his growing reputation as an organiser and a strategist. Coburg wrote to the Emperor on the day of the crossing: 'Today I opened the campaign, forced the enemy occupied Roer river, dislodged the enemy from its entrenched cantonments and struck it in its entrenched position at Hönichen... I owe this happy success to God, the Archduke Charles, Feldzugmeister Clerfait and Colonel Mack.'[17] The Archduke Charles was also fulsome in his praise, writing to the Emperor: 'It is to Colonel Mack that we all owe our thanks he has distinguished himself everywhere by his energy, ability and courage.' To Mack himself he wrote:

> ... the 1st March is your day. It is you we have to thank the line of the Roer was not abandoned. It was thanks to you that the decision was come to, to cross the river. You alone drew up and carried out the admirable dispositions for the operation which remain a model for all time. In fact but for you the opinion of others, who held the enemy's position as unassailable, would have prevailed, and we should have retired with nothing accomplished.[18]

Whether Mack let this praise go to his head or whether he was naturally arrogant we can only guess at but in August 1793 he penned this rather self-congratulatory note to Colloredo:

14 Prokesch-Osten, *Kleine Schriften*, p.108.
15 Gramm, *Der unglückliche Mack*, p.133.
16 Gramm, *Der unglückliche Mack*, p.134.
17 Gramm, *Der unglückliche Mack*, p.137.
18 Maude, *Ulm*, p.31.

> Whoever despises his enemy is a fool and whoever fears him is a villain. I did not see in this New Republican French like others, nothing but ancient Roman heroes, did not believe that their artillery men were nothing but Jupiters who hurled infallible thunderbolts, did not compare their numbers with the sand on the sea and because, after careful consideration, I found that we were villains if we were afraid of them, I advised Prince Coburg, implored him to attack them, defended my plan against others, and this was the first March that deserves to be recorded in the series of important days.[19]

Whilst this immodest tone can have done little to endear him to his contemporaries, Mack was right. His actions had broken the mould in terms of Austrian tactics, and he had broken a potential deadlock by advancing against a feared enemy. As the campaign progressed, some on the allied side would bemoan the departure from the defensive cordon system that Austria had traditionally adopted, but concentration and attack were to become the way of waging warfare in the coming century.[20] By seeking a decisive engagement with the most force that he could bring to bear against the enemy, Mack was predicting Napoleon Bonaparte and harking back to Frederick the Great of Prussia. It was a potentially dangerous and costly strategy but one that could bring results quickly. The decisive engagement that Mack sought was not long in coming but it occurred by accident rather than sophisticated design.

Although Brunswick had agreed to cover the Austrian left, he still was not in position by the time the whole Imperial army had crossed the Meuse and Mack had to divert forces to cover that flank. By 15 March, the army had taken up position behind the Lesser Greet River between Tirlemont (Tienen) and St Throne (Sint Truiden). French outposts had been encountered (and driven in) at Goetsenhoven and Halle (possibly Helecine) and the town of Tirlemont taken. The French fell back on Leuven but the whereabouts of their main force was unknown and the Austrians hoped to turn the French right and attack them at Hoegaarden.[21]

What then occurred was a series of messy encounters that evolved into the battle of Neerwinden. Like many battles of this period, what actually happened is a matter of dispute. The numbers involved are subject to some controversy with different sources claiming each side was outnumbered but it appears that the Austrians had the upper hand. Von Prokesh Osten (an Austrian staff officer in 1813 and the closest to a contemporary commentator) gives the Austrian strength as 42,568 and does not appear to include the six battalions of Dutch allies whom Digby Smith claims were present. Most sources agree that the French had 40–42,000 infantry and 4–5,000 cavalry so forces were probably fairly even.[22] Both sides claim to have had the better

19 Gramm, *Der unglückliche Mack,* p.138.

20 Anon., *Betrachten uber den Feldzug, welchen die Alliirten Armeen in Jahre 1794 in den Niederlanden führen warden* (Prague: Royal Library, 1796) pp.6–9.

21 Von Prokesch-Osten, *Kleine Schriften,* p.110.

22 D. Smith, *The Greenhill Napoleonic Wars Data Book* (London: Greenhill Books, 1998), pp.44–45; R.W. Phipps, *The Armies of the First French Republic: Volume I The Armée du Nord* (USA: Pickle Partners Publishing, 2011 [1926]), p.155; Von Prokesch-Osten, *Kleine Schriften,* p.109; Gramm, *Der unglückliche Mack,* p.141.

of the other and both claim that the other was surprised.[23] It does seem that whatever the odds and whoever was surprised, it was the French who recovered most quickly, apart from the brigade of *Generalmajor* Miaczinsky, which was lost in the woods around Leuven for two days.[24]

The Austrians had considerably more cavalry than their enemy and it was of much greater quality so they should have been able to out scout their enemies. However, Mack, not for the last time in his career, had underestimated his enemy and assumed they were in total retreat. This was an impression reinforced by the quick fall of the town of Tirlemont to Archduke Charles' *Avant Garde* but was actually entirely erroneous. Without checking the whereabouts of the French, Mack drew up a typically complex plan to turn what he thought was their right flank and to attack them at Hoegaarden with the main force of the army whilst Clerfait made a diversion around Velpen.

Far from retreating the French were actually already moving to attack the Austrians at St Throne and their commander Dumouriez quickly rallied his troops after they were thrown out of Tirlemont and retook the town. The Austrians had also failed to occupy the strategically important village of Goetsenhoven which dominated the area and, in spite of their attempts to drive the French from it, lost control of this area, which threatened the flank of their now overextended position. The Imperial Army therefore withdrew and reoccupied their positions of the day before; remaining on the defensive and surrendering initiative to Dumouriez.[25]

The battle itself was a typically confused affair with the French attacking in eight columns and quickly seizing a series of vital objectives on the Austrian left which completely wrong-footed Coburg who had expected their attack to come on his right. However, the French failed to occupy many key points on the battlefield and advanced too far, becoming over extended and allowing the Austrians to counterattack again and again. A series of mistakes and muddles further inhibited Dumouriez' chances of success and the failure of the Venezuelan revolutionary Miranda to make any headway on the Austrian right meant the French could not prevail.

What Mack's role was during the battle is uncertain, but we are told that he collapsed in the evening. He was already suffering from an unspecified illness and was apparently exhausted by his efforts on the day of battle so presumably he played a part in orchestrating the Austrian counterattacks. Having recovered slightly, Mack was making dispositions for the following day when Coburg came to him with the news that the fight was 'still undecided' on the left and Mack drew up orders for the necessary reinforcements to be sent. A little later Coburg returned, asking Mack to draw up plans for a retreat as he believed that the battle had reached a stalemate and that he could not win.[26] This defeatism apparently roused Mack from his sick bed and fortified with medication he, with some help from Archduke Charles, persuaded Coburg to hang on and rode out to inspect the position.

23 C. Dumouriez, *La Vie et Les Memoires du Général Dumouriez* (Paris: Bauduin Freres, 1823), vol.4, p.266; Gramm, *Der unglückliche Mack,* p.144.

24 Dumouriez, *La Vie,* p.78.

25 Von Prokesch-Osten, *Kleine Schriften,* p.109.

26 Von Prokesch-Osten, *Kleine Schriften,* p.143.

When he arrived at the threatened left wing, Mack could see that the French were in fact retreating and that the Austrians had gained a significant victory. It cannot really be called a great victory for it began with a series of blunders and seems to have been conducted in something of a panic with the Austrians merely holding their ground in the face of French ineptitude, but it was of great importance. The French advance had been checked and Dumouriez began to consider his position (both personal and strategic) with some concern.[27]

For his tireless staff work and for stopping his hesitant superior from throwing in the towel, Mack was credited with the victory. Another brick was laid in the foundation of his growing reputation. The Archduke Charles recommended that Mack be promoted and wrote to the Emperor that: 'all this good work must be attributed to Mack who, suffering most pitifully from ill health, gave himself with all his remaining energy to the cause, working literally day and night. In short the whole army loves and honours him and looks up to him as the originator of all its victories.'[28]

The pursuit of the French however was not pressed, and the advantage gained at Neerwinden was lost.[29] Mack can perhaps be excused from this omission on the grounds of his continuing ill health, but the inactivity set a precedent that would be repeated many times in the coming campaigns of the allied forces resting on their laurels. Not long afterwards however, Mack became involved in an intrigue that may have ended the war or seriously tarnished the reputation that he had laboured so hard to create.

Not long after Neerwinden, Dumouriez's adjutant general and confidante *Colonel* Montjoye arrived in the Austrian camp to discuss prisoner exchanges.[30] It is believed that the discussion expanded to encompass the terms of a possible truce and when Mack met Dumouriez to discuss this further the French general revealed his desire to stage a coup which would end the Republic and reinstate some form of the monarchy in France. Mack agreed in principle to hold back the Austrian army if Dumouriez withdrew from the Austrian Netherlands. The coup failed and Dumouriez fled to the Austrian camp where he was well received by Coburg and spent the rest of the war in exile (mostly in Britain).

Although the withdrawal from Belgium of the French forces was of advantage to the allies; Coburg was severely criticised for not following up on his success at Neerwinden. The allies also objected to any form of support being given to a proclamation issued by Dumouriez in favour of restoring the monarchy. Such tacit and obvious interference in Frances internal affairs was seen as contrary to coalition strategy and a statement to that effect was issued by (future chancellor) Metternich. The truce was nullified and a humiliated Coburg almost certainly blamed Mack.[31] There was worse to follow for Thugut had been appointed Austrian Chancellor and through his influence the Emperor made his displeasure known to all those

27 Von Prokesch-Osten, *Kleine Schriften,* pp.143–144.
28 Maude, *Ulm,* p.33
29 Gramm, *Der unglückliche Mack,* p.144.
30 Dumouriez, *La Vie,* p.109; Gramm, *Der unglückliche Mack,* p.145.
31 Gramm, *Der unglückliche Mack,* p.150; Maude, *Ulm,* p.32.

involved. According to the Austrian historian Gramm, Coburg continued to agitate for Mack's promotion to general rank, but some antipathy must have grown up between them at this point given Mack's later refusal to serve with him again.[32]

Mack continued to work, organising the responses to the newly invigorated French army which had returned to the offensive but on 1 May he once again collapsed and asked to be relieved. Some have suggested that Mack's resignation was down to dejection over the failure of the Emperor to promote him or the stigma from the Dumouriez affair but his health problems seem to have been genuine.

By this point the coalition had been joined by the British contingent bringing the allied force to a strength of around 80,000 men. In his final act before returning to Vienna, Mack planned an attack on the French base of operations at Famars, where he hoped to eradicate the 25,000 French troops under Lamarche in their fortified camp.[33] The plan bore many of Mack's later trademarks, such as wide flanking marches by separated columns and the inexperienced Duke of York declared it 'a master piece of military skill.'[34] As with many of Mack's plans it worked well in theory but took little account of topography, the distance the troops would have to march, or the difficulties in co-ordinating such widely dispersed units. The Duke's column could not cross the river in front of the camp and had to go downstream.[35]

One of the Austrian columns got across alright but could not get beyond the village of Atres which was heavily fortified.[36] Elsewhere there were friendly fire incidents between two Prussian columns and numerous delays and misunderstandings which could all have been prevented by a more thorough reconnaissance. The inflexibility of the plan was revealed when Mack himself, accompanying the Duke of York's column, was wounded early in the battle and no-one seemed to know how to proceed in his absence.[37]

The allies fought well and thoroughly drubbed the French defenders whenever they were able but errors in the planning led to delays with every column and it was almost nightfall when they reached the final French entrenchments. Mack having been wounded, the decision to halt for the night was taken by his more timid successor Hohenlohe.[38] It was the crowning mistake of the day for after the allies settled down for the night, their quarry slipped the net and escaped. Had it worked, Mack's plan would have sealed the fate of a goodly proportion of the French army but despite a tactical victory on the approaches to Famars, it was a failure. The shortcomings of this operation however, did not tarnish Mack's reputation and the wound he received in the battle gave him a good excuse to remove himself from the army honourably.

Mack now took a break from the army and went home to recover from his wound. In his absence things had ground to a halt. The eighteenth century predilection for

32 Gramm, *Der unglückliche Mack,* p.152.
33 J. Fortescue, *History of the British Army* (London: Macmillan 1899), vol.4, p.109.
34 A. Aspinall, *Later Correspondence of George III* (London: Cambridge University Press, 1963), vol.2, p.881.
35 York to the King, 24 May 1793 in Aspinall, *Correspondence*, vol.2, p.881.
36 Von Prokecsh Osten, *Schriften,* p.242.
37 A. Burne, *The Grand Old Duke of York* (London: Staples Press, 1949), p.52.
38 Burne, *York,* p.53.

laying siege to fortresses and supply depots quickly came to the fore. After Mack's departure the allies captured Valenciennes and then divided their forces with the British engaging in an unsuccessful siege of Dunkirk and the Austrians capturing Le Quesnoy. A series of battles followed which mostly went the allies' way but achieved little decisive and French victory at Wattignies undid most of the good work that had been done.

1794 did not begin well for the allies; the counter revolutionary uprisings in France were on the verge of defeat and the French had recaptured Toulon. The allies had been reinforced but there was a distinct lack of energy in their movements whereas the French seemed reinvigorated. In Britain fingers were pointed at the Duke of York and the coalition commander, Coburg.[39] It seemed to many that a change was required at the Austrian headquarters and, certainly in Britain, it was felt that Mack should return.[40]

On 4 January 1794 the Duke of York wrote to his father King George III expressing the view that:

> ... as long as Prince Hohenlo remains in his present situation of Quarter Master General and has the direction of all operations, nothing of any consequence can be expected ... It would therefore be very much wished that by some means or other the Emperor could be persuaded to let Colonel Mack return to the army. His presence alone would restore confidence in the troops, and instill a degree of spirit into the plans and execution which has been miserably wanting, since he has been removed.[41]

This view was not restricted to the Duke of York. The same day, the Archduke Charles wrote to his brother the Emperor:

> Since Mack has left us all has gone wrong ... Even the Hungarian Grenadiers say that things have gone from bad to worse since they no longer see 'the man with the white mantle' riding about amongst them. If Mack were fit to serve... he is above all the man for the Q.M. Generalship of this command. The whole army agrees in this, and longs for his return.[42]

Although Mack had not exactly been a runaway success as director of the army's operations, he was considered to be vastly superior to his successor Hohenlohe and all felt that he was the best hope for at least a resumption of offensive operations if not success.

Mack was duly promoted to the rank of *generalmajor* and his stipulation that he would only serve under the direct command of his Emperor was met as the latter assumed titular control of the coalition forces. Although Pitt expressed his concerns

39 Buckingham to Grenville, 6 January 1794, W. Fitzpatrick, *Report on the Manuscripts of J.B. Fortescue Esq., Preserved at Dropmore* (London: HMSO, 1894), vol.2, p.491.
40 The National Archives (TNA): WO 1/162: Murray to Pitt, 4 July 1793.
41 Aspinall, *Correspondence*, vol.2, p.143.
42 Maude, *Ulm*, p.34.

that the army was now being led by a committee, the British were overjoyed with this turn of events and immediately dispatched a frigate to bring Mack to London to discuss his plans with them.[43]

Mack remained in ill-health but having been hailed as the army's saviour in London and on his arrival at headquarters in Brussels, he threw himself into the business of planning the forthcoming campaign. York's brother, Prince Adolphus, met Mack on his arrival in Brussels and wrote to the King that: 'he looks exceedingly ill and complains; he can never write but in bed or in a carryage, which is so made that he lays down in it. He speaks with a prodigious fire; and seems to be just the man everybody takes him for ... His coming has caused great joy.'[44]

A further English description of Mack was left to us by the cavalry commander Gaspard Le Marchant who met him in April 1794:

> Mack is a man of forty ... he has a complaint in the head that keeps him in constant pain. In consequence he wears a black caul over his skull, sewed round the bottom with thick black hair, which gives him a very grotesque appearance. He lies all day on his bed, writing with a pencil his instructions for the movements of the army: when an action takes place, he is lifted from his bed to his horse.[45]

Initially Mack remained on the defensive and concentrated the forces available to him. This was the very thing that should have been done the year before but now it backfired on the allies for the French swarmed into those areas where they were weakest and popped up whenever the allies moved. The allies continued to get the better of their enemies whenever they met on the field of battle and although they seemed to be making little impact on the growing legions of the republic an offensive movement was certainly underway.

A string of minor victories enabled the coalition to re-enter West Flanders and the credit for this success must surely go to Mack for although things were not going entirely to plan the campaign was progressing. It had been hoped that the Prussians were going to add their weight to the offensive and perhaps end the war at last, but it was not to be and Mack wrote in person to the British foreign minister, Lord Grenville, expressing his great distress at their decision to withdraw.[46] It was therefore up to the allies already in the field to bring the campaign to a successful conclusion. A defeat of the French attacks across the Sambre convinced the Emperor that the opportunity had arisen to deal the French a major blow in Flanders. A sizeable portion of the French army was occupying a position roughly quadrilateral in shape and around 15 miles square from Tourcoing to Messines. This position was isolated and was protruded into the allied lines. Mack saw an opportunity to surround and

43 Grenville to Dundas, 29 January 1794; Pitt to Grenville, 2 February 1794; Elgin to Grenville, 2 February 1794, *Dropmore*, vol.2, pp.501–502.

44 Aspinall, *Correspondence*, vol.2, p.176.

45 D. Le Marchant, *Memoirs of the late Major-General Le Marchant* (Uckfield: Naval & Military Press, 2006), p.35.

46 Mack to Grenville, 21 March 1794; *Dropmore*, vol.2, p.534.

destroy them. His plan was dubbed the 'Plan of Destruction' and had it worked it would have been the crowning moment in his career but it was not to be.

Although it appeared that the Austrians were united in purpose with their allies and keen to make a decisive move in the war, things were not as straightforward as it seemed. A revolt in Poland had moved the focus of Austrian foreign policy east once more. The Austrian Chancellor, Thugut, had long harboured a desire to be rid of the troublesome and indefensible Austrian Netherlands. Although the Belgian revolt against Hapsburg rule had ended in 1790 resentment against the Emperor had continued and Thugut preferred to exchange this province for land in Bavaria and Poland. Therefore, it was not in the slippery chancellor's interests to save Belgium at all and he had little interest in fighting the French who had nothing that he wanted.

In addition to this conflict of interest it seems that a certain amount of antipathy had grown up between Mack and the other commanders of the Austrian army. Perhaps they supported the supplanted Hohenlohe or maybe they just considered Mack to be an upstart, certainly they seemed to dislike their British allies and in particular the Duke of York who was known to be loudly critical of all his allies and whose dealings with them were less than diplomatic. Whatever the motives of the generals in question, it seems that (possibly in concert with Thugut), they conspired to undermine the plan of destruction. The Hessian chronicler Von Ditfurth wrote: 'Regarding the other generals, the opinion of contemporaries was that hate against the Duke of York and friction with Colonel Mack, as a military upstart, had led them to forget their duties completely.'[47]

Even without any intrigue it seems that Mack's plan was unworkable. Once again, Mack had drawn up a plan which required several parts of the army to converge upon a single point and to a specific timetable which did not take into account the distance each had to travel or the obstacles they would face on their journey. Nor, as usual, had Mack made any allowance for the difficulties that the various columns of the army would have in communicating with each other; or indeed with him. The flaws in the plan were apparent to many of those involved in implementing it including some in the British headquarters where some of its elements are believed to have originated. Colonel Sir James Craig, York's adjutant general, wrote afterwards that he had been concerned from the start:

> I had my fears as to the termination of the operation which depended upon the link up of six different parts. It is impossible to even bring the Austrians to act otherwise than in small corps and I cannot, I own but lament, tho I didn't invent the great probability of our being some day destined to become victims of their folly and ignorance...'[48]

47 M. Von Ditfurth, *Die Hessen in den Feldzügen von 1793, 1794 und 1795 in Flandern, Brabant, Holland und Westphalen, ein Beitrag zur hessischen Kriegsgeschichte. Geschichte des Feldzugs von 1793 in Flandern* (Kassel: Bohné, 1839), vol.2, p.144. See also: Fortescue, *British Army*, vol.V, p.269–270 & Gramm, *Mack*, p.172.

48 TNA: WO 1/169: p.97, Craig to (probably) Evan Nepean (under-secretary of state for war), 19 May 1794.

The problems on the first day of the operation (17 May) however were more to do with poor planning than any reluctance on the part of the Austrians. It seems that Clerfait, whose column was supposed to have linked with York's, received his orders late and so was delayed setting off. Clerfait was further delayed when he found the river crossings to be heavily fortified and his bridging train had to work its way up from the back of the lengthy column to span the Lys. Everywhere similar problems were encountered. The plan had not made any allowance for the crossing to be defended or the French to put up any kind of resistance.

Similarly little allowance was made for the distance the various divisions had to travel or the state of the roads they would be forced to traverse. The Archduke Charles, whose arrival on the right of the French camp at Sainghin was key to operations in the southern sector, had to march his column 15–16 miles to act in conjunction with Kinsky, who only had to march five miles. Kinsky, whose loyalties would turn out to be questionable, would not march until he was sure of Charles' support and then was also delayed by strongly defended river crossings. At the end of the first day only York and Otto had reached their objectives. Both were dangerously exposed, and the French knew exactly where they were and what Mack's plan was. Far from remaining inactive as Mack seems to have hoped, the French quickly planned a counterattack against the two exposed columns, now in the centre of the French salient.

What happened the next day is shrouded in mystery and controversy for whether by previous consent or on the spot reluctance, the Austrian commanders literally stood and watched while Mack's plan unravelled. Rather than stay put while the allies got their troops into the right positions to destroy them as a fighting force the French attacked at dawn over unguarded bridges and inflicted a heavy defeat on the isolated columns in the centre of their position. It was an easily foreseeable reaction to the allies bumbling on the first day of the battle but what was less predictable was that the columns of Archduke Charles and Kinsky did not make the slightest move to assist their beleaguered allies.

Archduke Charles suffered from epilepsy and had apparently been taken ill in the evening of the first day. What is extraordinary however is that the next day his staff refused to wake him or take any action in his stead whilst the British contingent was cut to pieces just a few miles away. Even more extraordinary was the inaction of Kinsky whose troops had already made dispositions to march at dawn and who could see the smoke and hear the cannon fire at Tourcoing six miles from where they stood. A Hessian officer named Ochs did not receive his marching orders as expected on the morning of 18 May, so he went to visit Kinsky himself. Reporting to the Count's headquarters Ochs was received coldly and says that Kinsky 'pretended illness, and indeed relinquished command.'[49] Kinsky's response to the further, increasingly desperate entreaties by messengers from the Emperor and the Duke of York to move against Sainghin was; 'Kinsky knows what he has to do.'[50]

49 A. Von Ochs, *Biographie des Generals von Ochs, Eine politische-militarisher beitrag zur geschichte des nordamerikanischen und des franzosischen revolutionskrieges, so wie der feldzuge in Spanien, Russland und Deutschland* (Kassel: J.B.Hampe, 1827), p.103.

50 Phipps, *Armies,* p.301.

The suggestion was made at the time, and has been repeated since, that this was a deliberate plot to undermine Mack and his plan. The finger of suspicion is pointed at the Austrian Chancellor, Thugut, who may have seen this as an opportunity, both to move the war in a direction that fitted more with his strategy and of discrediting Mack.[51] The latter was probably seen by some in the Austrian camp as having undue influence over the Emperor and exceeding his authority on numerous occasions. Following his departure York's adjutant general, Colonel Craig, remarked that Mack had kept the Austrian staff officers in line and so perhaps this caused resentment, or maybe he was just disliked for his humble origins.[52] Whatever the reason, Mack's plan was in ruins, the coalition was falling apart and the Emperor was planning to return to Vienna.

Despite consolidating the allied position after the disaster at Tourcoing and winning the battle of Tournai, Mack's confidence was clearly shaken. Perhaps an element of paranoia set in; certainly he became desperate and after a further setback at La Tombe on 26 May 1794 he suggested opening the sluices to flood Flanders.[53] This would deny the region to the enemy but it would mean that no-one could live there, and it would mean that the Emperor could derive no benefit from ruling it. The plan was rejected and Mack resigned, returning to Austria even before the planned departure of his ruler.

Mack was not present to witness the collapse of the first coalition and the defeat of what remained of its forces as the French overran Flanders and the Netherlands, but his career was not over. In fact, despite the numerous mishaps and defeats forces under his direction suffered, his reputation remained intact. So highly considered were his strategic skills that when the War of the Second Coalition began and the King of Naples asked Austria for assistance, he was content to be sent Mack to command his army and direct its strategy.

On 2 March 1797, having been promoted *feldmarschalleutnant,* Mack was duly dispatched to Naples to take command of what was widely reported to be one of the finest looking armies in Europe. Splendidly turned out and well drilled, the Neapolitan army was unfortunately something of a paper tiger. Its ranks were filled by mercenaries and convicts, and the army had shown itself to be rather unreliable at Toulon. Sir Gilbert Elliot wrote from Toulon, 12 December 1793: 'The misfortune is that a great proportion of our troops cannot be depended on. We have 7,000 Neapolitans, who are well-looking and well-appointed, but they do not like danger. Yesterday four of them were killed by bombs at an outpost, and the rest of the party sent to the commanding officer of the post to beg to be relieved as they were all sick. If a serious attack is made, such troops as these will beg to be excused.'[54] The commander of the British Fleet, Admiral Samuel Hood, described them as 'dastardly trash.'[55]

---

51 Elgin to Grenville, 1 July 1794, *Dropmore Papers,* vol.2, p.594.

52 Craig to Nepean, June 1794, quoted in Fortescue, *British Army,* vol.IV, p.278–279.

53 Anon., *An Accurate and Impartial Narrative of the War, by an Officer of the Guards* (London: Cadell & Davies, 1796), vol.2, p.68.

54 Lady Minto, *Life and Letters of Sir Gilbert Elliot First Lord of Minto from 1751 to 1806* (London: Longmans, 1874), vol.2, p.198.

55 C. Calwell, *Military Operations and Maritime Preponderance: Their Relations and Interdependence* (London: William Blackwood & Sons, 1905), p.16.

It was in Naples that Mack encountered Rear Admiral Sir Horatio Nelson who it seems developed a rather low opinion of the 'most scientific soldier' in Europe.[56] Nelson, in keeping with his usual opinion of military affairs, believed the Neapolitans should attack immediately and was distressed that; 'General Mack cannot move without five carriages. I have formed my opinion; I heartily pray, I may be mistaken.'[57] Apparently a later blunder during some kind of manoeuvres which Neslon had witnessed caused him to doubt Mack's competence further but on meeting the man face to face he seems to have revised his opinion: 'He is active and has an intelligent eye, and will do well, I have no doubt.'[58] Of course, Mack did not do well at all...

The nineteenth century historian Sir Archibald Alison wrote of Mack that he was: '[A]n officer who stood high at Vienna in the estimation of military men, but who, though skilled in sketching out plans of a campaign on paper and possessed of considerable talent in strategic design, was totally destitute of the penetration and decision required for success in the field.'[59]

Not an entirely fair estimation but it was certainly increasingly the case that Mack made war on maps without taking into account the strengths of his enemy, the nature of the terrain or the weakness of his own forces.[60] Certainly this was the case in Naples for though the French were widely dispersed, Mack split his own force into six columns and advanced on a broad front rather than concentrate on one or other of the French corps.[61]

Part of the Neapolitan host converged on Rome and, meeting no resistance, they took the city allowing their king to make a triumphal entry into the ancient city on 29 November. However, so undisciplined were the Neapolitan troops that they had fallen out en route and become disordered just from the march. While Mack was reordering his troops in Rome three of his outlying columns were defeated: one surrounded at Terni and forced to surrender en masse; another forced back upon the main body and the third forced to flee back to Naples. The French encouraged by this success closed in on Mack and defeated another two of his detached forces.

Realising that he was isolated Mack, uncharacteristically, changed his plan and fell back across the Tiber hoping to catch *Général de division* Louis Lemoine unsupported. However, the Neapolitans moved so slowly that Lemoine became aware of the movement and *Général de brigade* Karol Kniazwitz, coming to his aid with the Polish Legion, hit the would be attackers in the flank causing such panic that 4,000

56 G. Rothenberg, *Napoleon's Great Adversary, Archduke Charles & the Austrian Army 1792-1814* (Staplehurst: Spellmount, 1985), p.47.

57 Nelson to Earl Spencer, 9 October 1798, in N. Nicholas, *Dispatches and Letters of Vice Admiral Lord Viscount Nelson* (London: Henry Colburn, 1845), vol.3, p.140.

58 Nelson to St Vincent, 13 October 1798, in Nicholas, *Nelson,* p.148.

59 A. Alison, *History of Europe from the Commencement of the French Revolution to the Restoration of the Bourbons in MDCCCXV* (London: Blackwood & Sons, 1854), vol.4, p.139.

60 Baron Thiebault, later a *général de division* under Napoleon, wrote in detail of the tactical failings of Mack's subordinates who were a mixture of Germans and French émigrés: Thiebault, *The Memoirs of Baron Thiebault* (Felling: Worley Publications, 1994 [1896]), vol.1, p.400.

61 Alison, *Europe,* p.140.

of them surrendered despite outnumbering the total Franco-Polish force. Further defeats followed and Rome returned to the control of the republicans. As Alison put it: 'eighteen thousand veterans had driven before them forty thousand men, splendidly dressed and abundantly equipped, but utterly destitute of the discipline and courage requisite to obtain success in war.'[62]

Mack withdrew to a strong position on the Volturno river with all its crossing points covered by artillery and supported by the walled city of Capua. He threatened to allow the guns of Capua to fire on any of his men that fled their position. The French attack, led by future *Maréchal* Etienne Macdonald, was thrown back with great loss.[63] Mack however had now lost confidence in his men completely and became aware of a revolt amongst Francophile elements in the Neapolitan nobility who even attempted to poison him.[64] The French, having been repulsed before Capua, were attacked by Neapolitan peasants and bandits who rose in revolt and waged a murderous proto-guerrilla war against the invader but Mack did not dare to exploit his unexpected fortune.[65]

The King slipped away to Sicily and Mack was left to surrender Naples to the French. No resistance had been offered by the Neapolitans but they were so enraged by Mack agreeing to pay 10 million Francs that he had to flee for his life to the French camp.[66] On his arrival at his enemy's headquarters, Mack declared; 'you see a commander who, in order to escape a mob let loose and the daggers of his own men, has been compelled to take advantage of the armistice concluded by you ... and ... to ask for leave to pass on my way back to the dominion of my master.'[67] Mack said his defeat was due 'as much to commanders of whom no one could have been made into officers, as to men no one could have made soldiers.'[68]

Although he had been promised free passage to Austria, the French reneged on this and Mack, having been defeated utterly in his first independent command, found himself a prisoner of the French.[69] Having been sent to Paris under guard Mack met Napoleon Bonaparte (who was by that point First Consul of France) and the French leader left this, rather low, opinion of him:

> Mack is one of the most mediocre men I have ever met in my life. Full of conceit and vanity, he considers himself fit to do anything. He is nothing now; but I should like to see him some day opposed to one of our good Generals: he would see fine things! He is very self confident, and that is all. He is one of the most incapable men possible; and, in addition, he is unlucky.[70]

62 Alison, *Europe,* p.141.
63 Gramm, *Mack,* p.239 & Thiebault, *Memoirs,* p.430.
64 Gramm, *Mack,* pp.237 & 241.
65 M. Broers, *Napoleon's Other War, Bandits, Rebels and their Pursuers in the Age of Revolutions* (Oxford: Peter Lang, 2010), pp.66–67.
66 A. F. Becke, 'General Mack', *Royal United Services Institution Journal,* 66:462 (1921), p.261.
67 Thiebault, *Memoirs,* p.433.
68 Thiebault, *Memoirs,* p.434.
69 Chisholm (ed), 'Mack von Leiberich, Karl'.
70 Becke, *Mack,* p.262.

Unfortunately for Mack this was not to be their last meeting, nor was it the last example of his misfortune.

Mack was not exchanged, which suggests that Bonaparte may have considered him to be a threat of some sort after all, and he had to escape Paris in disguise and make his way back to Vienna on his own initiative in 1800. On his return it seems that his reputation in his own country (or with the Emperor at least) remained high and when Thugut's ministry came to an end in 1801 the way was clear for him to return to the army. In 1805, with the support of the pro-war party in Vienna, he was appointed quartermaster-general of the Austrian army.

Mack, as usual, threw himself into his new role with enthusiasm and, despite his continued ill-health, began to reform the army. The nineteenth century soldier and historian Frederick Maude (unlike many others) sees much to admire in Mack; pointing to his 'unexampled rise from obscurity ... his great personal courage, and his devouring energy and determination.' However, Maude's belief that Mack had the 'affection and esteem' of the Austrian generals must be questioned, certainly in light of the events at Tourcoing, and Maude admits that Mack had fallen out with the Archduke Charles and they had clashed on at least two occasions.[71]

One of Mack's reforms was an ill-advised attempt to emulate what he thought was the essence of French success; living off the land. One of the cornerstones of Bonaparte's lightening campaigns in Italy (as well as elsewhere) had been the use of foraging to lessen the need for cumbersome supply lines. In making the Austrians live off the land however, Mack was missing the fact this 'innovation' was something of a double-edged sword which came with numerous negatives. Firstly, it only worked if your army was able to forage enough to subsist upon. Secondly, it set the populace against you. Thirdly, it was detrimental to the army's discipline and cohesion. Fourthly, it was especially hard on the army's horses which required specialist fodder.

Even under the best circumstances, living off the land was ill-advised, which was why most armies (including the French) had developed at least a rudimentary commissariat by the end of the eighteenth century, but the Austrians were not even any good at it. The historian Christopher Duffy wrote that 'the Austrians merely wandered in an amiable fashion over the countryside' and Maude said that the Austrians were just too nice; regarding the country folk as 'irresponsible victims of very cruel circumstances.'[72] Finally; Mack did not actually get rid of the officer's baggage, so he sacrificed all the above and gained almost nothing in terms of speed. Also, his troops spent most of the campaign hungry with attendant impact on their morale and they were often too widely dispersed, scavenging, to be able to concentrate against French attacks.[73]

In addition to this self-inflicted difficulty, Mack had some serious issues with unity of command. The chief impediment in this area was the young Archduke Ferdinand who was nominally in charge of the army but had been told by the

71 Maude, *Ulm,* p.37.

72 C. Duffy, *Austerlitz 1805* (London: Cassell, 1999 [1977]), pp.28–29; Maude, *Ulm,* pp.74–75.

73 Duffy, *Austerlitz,* p.29.

Emperor to abide by Mack's advice.[74] Mack's position as commander was therefore unofficial and vague so his authority could be undermined from all sides.[75] The two men were destined to get along badly and Ferdinand second guessed and countermanded almost every instruction that Mack issued. As it was almost invariably the case that the other generals sided with the Archduke, by the end of the campaign they were outright insubordinate and the Archduke impossible to deal with.[76]

Mack therefore entered the campaign at somewhat of a disadvantage. He was to add to the problems of a dispirited army and disunited command the issue of underestimating his enemy. There is much debate as to why Mack marched his army at breakneck speed into Bavaria at the start of the campaign but it seems from his own writings that he felt the position on the River Inn was the safest and gave him the most room (in front of Vienna) to recover his army in case things went wrong.[77] The Archduke (correctly as it turned out) believed that this move was over hasty and would put the army in great danger of being surrounded and destroyed before the Russians could arrive to support it. Mack assured him (and everyone else) that the French could not possibly move from Boulogne to Munich that quickly and would not be able to deploy their entire 150,000 men. He was wrong on both counts.

Maude makes much of the fact that in that day and age a march of that distance should have been impossible at that speed and that Mack was basing his estimate on the speed and manner in which the Austrian army moved.[78] The fact that Ferdinand had thought this move to be dangerous in fact shows that perhaps he was right to resent having to obey Mack. In the end the Archduke declared that 'having been deprived of all initiative, he refused henceforth to accept any responsibility.'[79]

As the French closed in Mack received faulty intelligence and misread a situation that unravelled so quickly that he could not keep pace with it. Operational inflexibility had been a hallmark of his career throughout and at Ulm he refused to believe that he had been humbugged and that his only recourse was retreat. At Haslach on 11 October, Mack made some gains, but Ferdinand had gone off in a huff and did not support his attack, nor did Mack feel he could order His Imperial Highness to come to his aid but hoped, in vain, that one of the other generals with him might suggest it. Mack sought to take advantage of his slight success by breaking out of the encircling French towards Ratisbon where he hoped to link up with the Russians. However, one of his subordinates, Werneck, perhaps emboldened by Ferdinand's behaviour, refused, claiming his troops were exhausted. Mack denied this vehemently and called the notion 'notorious' as the troops were all well rested. Mack complained; 'FML Werneck opposed my proposition with altogether improper violence before the Prince, and his Imperial Highness tolerated his protests.'[80] Unable to march, Mack concentrated his remaining troops around Ulm itself.

74 Maude, *Ulm,* p.131.
75 Chisholm (ed.), 'Mack Von Leiberich, Carl'.
76 Becke, *Mack,* p.263.
77 Maude, *Ulm,* pp.74–75.
78 Maude, *Ulm,* pp.76–77.
79 Maude, *Ulm,* p.132.
80 Maude, *Ulm,* p.136.

Mack would not now move from his position at Ulm; he considered it strategically vital and did not want to appear to abandon either the army in Italy (under Archduke Charles) or the Russians. Again, he was wrong in this. It could be that his continued ill-health had sapped his reasoning, or that the speed of the French advance had undermined his ability to think straight. Mack had always been methodical and working in such a way took time. Time that his opponent was not allowing him.

The march to Ulm had been hard on the French too; the Comte de Segur who accompanied Napoleon wrote that 'on every side our soldiers were running about in disarray. Some were in search of food. Others were shooting hares.' He paints a chaotic scene of bad roads and dying draft animals; the reality of French mobility.[81] In the midst of this chaos (on 13 October) a staff error sent parts of the French army in the wrong direction and this, coupled with a rumour that the British had landed in Boulogne led Mack to believe that they were in fact in retreat and he began immediately to draw up plans for a pursuit. This, misplaced optimism on Mack's part, has led many since to paint him as delusional, one historian presented us with this (almost certainly apocryphal) image:

> There is one picture of Mack during these operations that will ever remain as a proof of his readiness to twist facts so that they might mean what he desired. On 15th October, whilst the fighting was in progress for the heights to the north-west of the Fortress, Mack dragged himself along the ramparts leaning on the arm of his valet. The Austrian Commander was dressed in a blue frock coat and he wore a nightcap under his cocked hat. The firing was heavy and near at hand. Nevertheless, he kept on assuring anyone who would listen to him that the assault was merely a feint and that the French Army was already in full retreat. This amazing statement was made whilst the most convincing proofs to the contrary were being given. For it was delivered to the accompaniment of crashing chimneys and cascading tiles from the roofs of the neighbouring houses, with the besieging hosts close around the walls of Ulm, and an entire army shut up within the fortress itself.[82]

How long Mack actually believed the French were in retreat is not known and for some time he believed that he was helping the strategic situation by simply remaining where he was; drawing Napoleon away from the Russians. At this point the Austrians in Ulm could see the situation was hopeless and a staff officer, *Major* Abele, suggested that this was the last chance to break out; begging Mack to march to the Tyrol. Mack took this suggestion badly; 'he screamed and shouted, behaving in a way that was truly insane. In his fury he advanced on me in a threatening manner, and I feared that I was about to suffer violence at his hands.'[83]

The Archduke Ferdinand and some of the generals (including Werneck) then abandoned Ulm and, despite not allowing Mack to break out, attempted to escape

81 Duffy, *Austerlitz,* p.48.
82 Becke, *Mack,* p.262.
83 Duffy, *Austerlitz,* p.49.

themselves, leaving him and his army to their fate. On 15 October, Ney stormed over the bridge at Elchingen forcing the Austrians to cram into the city of Ulm. There had not been any food for some time and now there was barely standing room. Mack came to his senses and agreed to capitulate. On 20 October 1805 the Austrian army marched out of Ulm to lay down its arms. It was a grim day for Europe and a catastrophic one for the 'unfortunate' General Mack as he now called himself, and as history would come to know him.

Mack had indeed been 'unfortunate' but also he had been bested, perhaps a victim of the arrogance and self-belief which had propelled him to the command of one of the most conservative and rigidly hierarchical institutions in history; the Austrian Army. Christopher Duffy wrote of him:

> We have in Mack the first of the nineteenth-century neo-Napoleonic commanders, the kind of man who believed generalship consisted of grand cure-all strategies, ceaseless undirected activity, and dashing off orders peppered with urgent phrases. He took up scheme after scheme, carried it halfway to execution, then abandoned it altogether.[84]

Mack faced a court martial for his actions and in 1807 he was stripped of his rank and titles, and confined in a fortress for two years. At the end of the war Mack was rehabilitated at Prince Schwarzenberg's request, and given back his rank of *feldmarschalleutnant* and pension. He died in St Pölten on 22 October 1828.[85]

To conclude, we must ask; what was wrong with Mack's method of waging war? Was he just 'unfortunate' to be opposed to one of history's pre-eminent generals? Certainly, there seems to have been a lot to praise Mack for; he was a meticulous staff officer, an innovator, and an aggressive tactician at a time in history when caution and low risk manoeuvring dominated military thinking. Unfortunately, none of this was enough. Mack was a man of ideas but not of practicalities. His plans looked well enough on the maps he poured over and his dispositions were detailed but he seems to have been oblivious to potential obstacles such as geography, distance, or the actions of the enemy. The latter proved to be especially his undoing when fighting the forces of the French Republic whose leaders did not even know the rules and certainly did not allow their actions to be governed by them. Also, on paper he had at his disposal a superb instrument; on the battlefield the Imperial and Royal Army of Austria was superior to its enemy in every way, except in numbers. However, it was not a very flexible instrument; it could not march as far, or as fast as the French and it was tied to its supply lines whereas the republicans were happy to pillage the countryside (and in the early days in fact had little option) and did not mind upsetting the local peasantry. Change was difficult and came slowly, and Mack was opposed in almost everything he did by a conservative officer corps who considered him an upstart, and at various times by government ministers who opposed his strategic view. Mack knew what he wanted to do with the Austrian Army but it seemed

84 Duffy, *Austerlitz*, p.47.
85 D. Smith, 'Biographical Essay'.

determined to prevent him from doing it. Without change, Mack was never going to be able to achieve what he hoped to.

However, the man himself did not seem to see that the instrument he had been given could not do what he wanted it to do. This was as much the case with the Neapolitan army as it was with the Austrian; throughout his career Mack was incapable of seeing that he was wrong and had to adapt to his circumstances. Sir John Fortescue in summing up Mack wrote that; 'he made no allowance for the possible failure of any one of his combinations through unforeseen contingencies or accidents of any description, Mack's actions were rarely successful and always hazardous.'[86] In his defence it might be added that he was not alone in this and many of his ideas (like marching in widely separated columns) were used successfully by his contemporaries under different circumstances.

On balance Mack was not the genius he (and many at the time) believed he was; he made many errors and suffered a lot of bad luck but he probably does not deserve the approbation which history has heaped upon his reputation. He was above all an innovative officer at a time when innovation was needed and a commander that sought decisive battle before the theorist Carl von Clausewitz had established its importance.

Bibliography

Alison, A. *History of Europe from the Commencement of the French Revolution to the Restoration of the Bourbons in MDCCCXV* (London: Blackwood & Sons, 1854)

Anon., *An Accurate and Impartial Narrative of the War, by an Officer of the Guards* (London: Cadell & Davies, 1796)

Anon., *Betrachten uber den Feldzug, welchen die Alliirten Armeen in Jahre 1794 in den Niederlanden führen warden* (Prague: Royal Library, 1796)

Aspinall, A., *Later Correspondence of George III* (London: Cambridge University Press, 1963)

Becke, A.F., 'General Mack', *Royal United Services Institution Journal*, 66:462 (1921)

Broers, M., *Napoleon's Other War, Bandits, Rebels and their Pursuers in the Age of Revolutions* (Oxford: Peter Lang, 2010)

Burne, A., *The Grand Old Duke of York* (London: Staples Press, 1949)

Calwell, C., *Military Operations and Maritime Preponderance: Their Relations and Interdependence* (London: William Blackwood & Sons, 1905)

Chisholm, H. (ed.), 'Mack Von Leiberich, Carl,' *Encyclopaedia Britannica*, 1911 <https://en.wikisource.org/wiki/1911_Encyclopædia_Britannica/Mack_von_Leiberich,_Karl>, accessed 26 February 2021.

Von Ditfurth, M., *Die Hessen in den Feldzügen von 1793, 1794 und 1795 in Flandern, Brabant, Holland und Westphalen, ein Beitrag zur hessischen Kriegsgeschichte. Geschichte des Feldzugs von 1793 in Flandern, Erster Band* (Kassel: Bohné, 1839)

86 Fortsecue, *History*, vol.4, p.92.

Dumouriez, C., *La Vie et Les Memoires du Général Dumouriez* (Paris: Bauduin Freres, 1823)

Duffy, C., *Austerlitz 1805* (London: Cassell, 1999 [1977])

Fitzpatrick, W., *Report on the Manuscripts of J.B. Fortescue Esq., preserved at Dropmore* (London: HMSO, 1894)

Fortescue, J., *History of the British Army* (London: Macmillan, 1899)

Gramm, E., *Der unglückliche Mack Aufstieg und Fall des Karl Mack von Leiberich* (Doctoral Dissertation, University of Vienna, 2008)

Le Marchant, D., *Memoirs of the late Major-General Le Marchant* (Uckfield: Naval & Military Press, 2006)

Maude, F.N., *The Ulm Campaign: 1805* (Driffield: Leonaur, 2007)

Minto, Lady, *Life and Letters of Sir Gilbert Elliot First Lord of Minto from 1751 to 1806* (London: Longmans, 1874)

Nicholas, N. *Dispatches and Letters of Vice Admiral Lord Viscount Nelson* (London: Henry Colburn, 1845).

Von Ochs, A. *Biographie des Generals von Ochs, Eine politische-militarisher beitrag zur geschichte des nordamerikanischen und des franzosischen revolutionskrieges, so wie der feldzuge in Spanien, Russland und Deutschland* (Kassel: J.B.Hampe, 1827)

Paget, A. *The Paget Brothers* (London: J Murray, 1918)

Phipps, W., *The Armies of the First French Republic: Volume I The Armée du Nord* (USA: Pickle Partners Publishing, 2011 [1926])

Von Prokesch-Osten, A., *Kleine Schriften: Der Feldzug in den Niederlanden 1793, Dritter Band* (Stuttgart: Hallberger, 1842).

Rothenberg, G., *Napoleon's Great Adversary, Archduke Charles & the Austrian Army 1792-1814* (Staplehurst: Spellmount, 1985)

Smith, D., *The Greenhill Napoleonic Wars Data Book* (London: Greenhill Books, 1998).

Smith, D., 'Biographical Essay', <https://www.napoleon-series.org/research/biographies/Austria/AustrianGenerals/c_AustrianGeneralsM.html>, accessed December 2021

Thiebault, P., *The Memoirs of Baron Thiebault* (Felling: Worley Publications, 1994 [1896])

3

Military Intelligence in Napoleon's Italian Campaigns (1796–1800)

Terry Crowdy

That which historians often attribute to luck, intuition, or even *genius* on the part of a successful general, often turns out instead to be the appreciation of good and timely, secretly-gathered intelligence. The hidden hand of history is rarely admitted, in order to protect the source and, vain creatures that we humans are, no one wants to be accused of having won by *cheating*. There is perhaps nothing worse in defeat than the sickening realisation one has been duped, deceived, strung along, and manipulated by a *common spy*. There is perhaps some consolation in having been beaten by an unparalleled military genius instead. So, when the memoirs and official histories are written, we rarely find much mention of 'the secret part'.

To provide some context, a good example is found in the Second World War. Field Marshal Montgomery of Alamein was quick to credit his victory over Rommel's forces as the result of solid preparation and the indomitable fighting spirit of his soldiers. He admits in his memoirs there was a brilliant system of deception supporting his victory at El Alamein in 1942, with bogus installations, vehicles and signals; but he did not admit (because it was still top secret) the boon of ULTRA, the Allied codename for intercepted Axis signals decrypted at Bletchley Park.[1] When one reappraises Montgomery's generalship, knowing he was secretly receiving detailed transcripts of the German order of battle and even Rommel's after-action reports to Berlin, one can understand his decision-making process more fully. This is not to detract from his reputation, in fact it arguably enhances it, because the ability to properly exploit intelligence is a key factor in good generalship. Nor does this knowledge dilute the worthiness of the brave deeds of the soldiers at the sharp end of conflict (the most honour always falls on the soldiers exposed to enemy fire); but one hopes today no serious commentator would attempt to explain the defeat of Nazi Germany without crediting the impact of signals intelligence and the work of other secret agencies and operations.

---

1 Bernard Law Montgomery, *The Memoirs of Field-Marshal the Viscount Montgomery of Alamein, K.G.* (Cleveland and New York: The World Publishing Company, 1958), pp.110–113.

The example given above does not stand in isolation. All military history, indeed, all of world history is underpinned by the shadowy goings on of what is euphemistically described as 'the world's second oldest profession'. Indeed we find detailed advice on the employment of spies in biblical stories, in Sun Tzu's *Art of War*, and the ancient Indian treatise on statecraft, the *Arthasástra*. The advice contained in the latter was already ancient when it was codified at the time of Alexander the Great.[2] Morally and legally ambiguous, espionage was as necessary in the days of Joshua as it is today. This 'grey history' is endlessly fascinating.

With this in mind, we need to better understand the intelligence services at work during the Napoleonic Wars, and perhaps move away from the mental image of foppish Scarlet Pimpernels in stockings and wigs, prancing from one parlour to the next. The world of secret intelligence gathering was as deadly serious then as it is today. In Napoleon's time, men were hung or shot out of hand if caught engaged in espionage (no spy swaps on the Gliencke Bridge in those days). One young Austrian agent captured outside Mantua in 1796 was famously stripped naked, tied to a bench by army butchers in bloodied aprons and threatened with disembowelment by *Général de division* Alexandre Dumas (father of the great novelist) if he did not admit he had swallowed a secret message wrapped in a wax tablet. The startling memoirs of *Adjudant-général* Jean Landrieux (who headed Napoleon's secret agency in Italy) explain how another Austrian agent was summarily executed by the French in Milan in order to flush out his contacts, or how in broad daylight in a crowded marketplace Venetian agents knifed a French agent to death. The rules of this game were as brutal then as today, with our poisoned umbrella tips or Novichok-laced perfume bottles.

Lessons From History

In this essay we will introduce Napoleon's military intelligence service during his first (1796–1797) and second (1800) campaigns in Italy. Pre-dating the great battles of the First Empire, these campaigns are particularly interesting because they ultimately made the emperor's reputation. Austerlitz might have been a more sophisticated and complete victory, but few of Napoleon's triumphs were as dramatic or consequential as Marengo on 14 June 1800. Before Marengo, the trajectory of Napoleon's 'star' was still in doubt. The victory confirmed his pre-eminence as the greatest (and perhaps luckiest) general of his age. It cemented his political powerbase and, to use the expression of the time, it placed the crown of France on his head.

In both Italian campaigns there was an extensive use of spies and an organised system of intelligence, which for the most part has been ignored for two centuries.

Despite a veritable avalanche of evidence, including primary and rich oral history sources, the importance of secret intelligence has mostly been underplayed. The Prussian soldier and theorist, Carl von Clausewitz dedicated just a single sentence to espionage in his analysis of the campaigns of 1796–1797, describing how the Austrian

2 Terry Crowdy, *The Enemy Within: A History of Espionage* (Oxford: Osprey, 2006), p.27.

commander *Feldzeugmeister* József Alvinczi was said to have been 'falsely informed by a spy of the French retreat on Mantua' before the Battle of Arcole.[3] The Austrians therefore advanced under false assumptions and were soundly beaten. Clausewitz declares his source was Napoleon's own memoirs, but he apparently paid little attention to it. He was far more confident commentor when describing the effect of French artillery on the Austrian columns. If one reads Clausewitz's *Von Krieg* (actually published posthumously in 1832 and compiled by his widow), one comes away with a very poor understanding of the importance of espionage in the Napoleonic period. In the book, Clausewitz appears dismissive of intelligence, cautioning military commanders against believing reports which were for the most part false and the result of man's 'natural timidity' and an inclination to 'magnify the bad'. Instead the commander ought to remain 'firm in reliance on his own better convictions' and 'stand like a rock against which the sea breaks its fury in vain.'[4] Clausewitz is highly regarded by military theorists even today, but alas he perhaps promotes the very system of warfare that arguably brought the Napoleonic empire crashing down, not the one on which its foundations rested. His is ultimately a doctrine of mass slaughter, the sort of military thinking that led Europe to some of the darkest moments in its collective history. Moments like Verdun in 1916. Big battalions, big guns, bold resolution: where is the *art* in that? Not all warfare is kinetic or a matter of logistics. As any pugilist knows, fighting is as much about the art of *not* being hit, of disguising a telling blow, as much as it is about courageously trading punches. When warfare becomes a simple matter of attrition, of two opponents bludgeoning one another relentlessly, then disguise, stealth, movement, and ultimately human life, become irrelevant. Victories won in this fashion tend to be pyrrhic. Perhaps then we have been learning the wrong lessons from Napoleon's campaigns?

His campaigns in Italy are underpinned with an incredible sub-plot of espionage, intrigue, sedition and betrayal. If we open that great pandora's box of secret history we find a colourful cast of revolutionaries, double-agents, provocateurs and wayward desperados; men such as Lhermit, a French escapee from the prison galleys who impersonated a priest and smuggled fake gems in Bergamo prior to being entrusted with a vital, but seemingly-suicidal secret mission (something every other spy had turned down). A surprisingly large volume of evidence exists for their collective activities, but it has never been fully collated. There are untapped goldmines of evidence in the archives in Vienna and Turin. Many of these players in the secret game were the 'patriots' who were the forerunners of Italy's Risorgimento movement. Italian histories have focused on their passion for Italian unity and have largely ignored the role of these men as secret agents and provocateurs. There are also many false trails waiting to lure the historian from the true path. The study of secrets is no easy feat.

3 Carl von Clausewitz, *Der Feldzug von 1796 in Italien* (Berlin: Ferd. Dümmler's Verlagsbuchhandlung, 1858), p.185.

4 Carl von Clausewitz, *On War* (Harmondsworth: Penguin, 1968), pp.162–163.

Napoleon and Italy

It is important to know Napoleon had strong cultural ties to Italy. Corsica had been owned by the Republic of Genoa until 1768, the year before Napoleon's birth. His parents were descended from families of the Italian mainland. The official language of Corsica was Italian, so naturally Napoleone di Buonaparte (his birth name) spoke it. In 1794 Napoleon took part in a secret mission to Genoa, ostensibly negotiating supplies for the army, but really he was examining the military defences along the riviera. So although aged just 26 when he took command of the army of Italy in March 1796, the appointment appears a good fit. That said, and strange as it may seem for a career soldier four years into a war, Napoleon had not taken part in any of the campaigns against enemy field armies at this point. He had seen action, yes, but only in the context of civil war and counter-insurrections.

From the off, Napoleon was a great consumer of intelligence and fortunately for him, there were a great many sources of it. At a tactical level Napoleon had the reports of his light cavalry patrols, officers sent on reconnaissance, the interrogation of prisoners and deserters. There was also captured enemy correspondence and even open-source material such as newspapers published in neutral countries. Writing in St Helena after the wars, Napoleon described the intelligence work of his cavalry commander *Général de division* Henri Stengel in the 1796 campaign. This short passage clearly illustrates the process of intelligence-gathering when the French army arrived in a town:

> *Général* Stengel, an Alsatian, was an excellent hussar officer; ... he was a true outpost general. Two or three days before his death, when he was the first to enter Lesegno, the commander-in-chief arrived there a few hours later, and, whatever he needed, everything was ready: the defiles, the fords had been reconnoitred, guides were assured, the parish priest and the postmaster had been questioned, the inhabitants had already been questioned, spies were sent in several directions, letters from the post office seized and those which had military information translated and analysed.[5]

As an aside, Stengel was somewhat less effusive in his opinion of Napoleon. Wounded by 22 sword cuts at the battle of Mondovi (21 April 1796) because Napoleon ordered him to make a charge against enemy cavalry outnumbering him ten-to-one, Stengel is reported to have said on his deathbed: 'Beware the hate of this miserable little Corsican, my friends. He wanted me killed and he succeeded.'[6]

In terms of secret intelligence, in 1796 Napoleon inherited a complete system of espionage from his predecessor *Général de division* Barthélemy Schèrer. The most active spies were networks of Italian revolutionaries. With their local knowledge, they could probe beyond enemy lines into the country of Piedmont and to

5 H. Plon and J. Dumaine (eds), *Correspondance de Napoléon Ier: Publiée par ordre de L'empereur Napoléon III* (Paris: H. Plon, J. Dumaine, 1870), vol.XXIX, pp.89–90.

6 Léonce Grasilier (ed.), *Mémoires de l'Adjudant-General Jean Landrieux* (Paris: Nouvelle Libraririe Parisienne, 1893), p.56.

Milan. However, Napoleon also needed intelligence on the movement of any enemy reserves from beyond the alps. To obtain long-range intelligence he used the French diplomatic mission in Venice to send agents into the strategically important city of Mantua, up the Trento valley in the direction of Innsbruck, and into the Adriatic port of Trieste. He used diplomats in Basel, Switzerland to watch Austrian troop movements in southern Germany. Those in Genoa collected intelligence on British naval movements in and out of Livorno (Leghorn). In short there was a mass of intelligence being picked up locally as well as strategic intelligence coming in from afar. Even the voracious Napoleon did not have time to read everything, so how was this intelligence collected, analysed and disseminated?

The Organisation of Intelligence

Intelligence is ultimately a function of staff work. To better understand this statement, let us consult the works of Paul Thiébault (1769–1846), who served as a staff officer in the Army of Italy from 1795–1800. Thiébault published his first manual for staff officers (*Manuel des adjudans généraux*) in 1800. The first draft of this book was written in Padua in September 1797. It was written during a period of house arrest; Thiébault had been instructed to produce 400 fake copies of *Le Moniteur* newspaper, with the text of a key article changed, and to deliver the copies by dawn. He was two hours late on the deadline, hence his incarceration. The manual was produced because Thiébault had witnessed a great deal of chaotic staff work in the Army of Italy, so it perhaps describes an ideal situation rather than an analysis what actually occurred, but as a contemporary document, written in the theatre of operations, by a staff officer, it is invaluable. In 1813 Thiébault returned to the subject of staff work, publishing his *Manuel Général du service des États-majors généraux et divisionnares dans les armées*. This second book elaborates on the function of staff officers in even greater detail.

On the subject of intelligence, Thiébault's first manual describes how it is collected and recorded at divisional level, then at army headquarters level. Each *général de division* had a chief of staff, ranking as a *colonel*, but called an *adjudant-général*. This officer was required to maintain a system of registers dealing with everything from daily orders, correspondence, the states of the division, court martials, reports and movements and so on. Register 10 covered la partie secrète (the secret part) and contained:

1) The instructions given to spies.
2) The reports made by them.
3) Intelligence from local inhabitants.
4) The reports of officers charged with discoveries and reconnaissance missions.
5) Topographical reports provided by engineer officers and others.[7]

7 Paul Thiébault, *Manuel des adjudans-généraux et des adjoints employés dans les états-majors-divisionnaires des armées* (Paris: Magimel, 1800), p.54.

At army level, the chief of staff to the commanding general was responsible for collating the work of all the divisional staff officers. The army staff was organised into five bureaus: 1) the general office of the army chief of staff; 2) provisioning, remounts, transport, distributions, forage, etc.; 3) pay, contributions, accounts, secret expenditure; 4) the 'secret part', spies, guides and the exchange of prisoners; 5) topographical matters. The chiefs of the last four bureaus would daily communicate with the chief of the first bureau to ensure the appropriate information was disseminated efficiently.[8]

Having confirmed the structure of secret and general intelligence gathering, Thiébault elaborates further on the function of the partie secrète. The short chapter is reproduced here in full, because it demonstrates the extent to which secret intelligence gathering was considered an essential part of a chief of staff's activities:

> On campaign above all, espionage, in other words, the secret part, forms an essential branch of the work of a chief of staff. It is a delicate thing to organize this service. You must have enough spies to always have them in the field. Their choice is difficult, because it is important that they are reliable, taken from among men of the same opinion, who do not know each other, lest they listen to each other and concert their answers. A wise precaution is to choose them from among the men who have the most to complain about the party against which they are employed; nothing should be neglected to interest them in the cause they serve. To excite them to serve well, they are given a small salary when they do not learn anything of interest, and large rewards when they bring important, verified advice. Everything that has been promised to them must be given to them exactly. We must bind the ambitious by the promise of what flatters them, those who are timid by threats, those who love money by pecuniary rewards.
>
> One can also temporarily secure the property and families of those who have them. Finally, we must know how to take advantage of all the weaknesses that we can discover in them, and be convinced that without this, we will have no real authority over them, and that we will not obtain any information if we do not make fear and hope act appropriately.
>
> Let us finish by saying on this chapter, that in terms of espionage, the main object is to manage to deceive the enemy about what he wants to know, and to discover what is in his interests to hide.[9]

Thiébault returned to the management of espionage in his 1813 staff officer manual, dedicating nearly seven pages to the subject. He opens his discussion on secret intelligence with the following: 'We name the 'secret part' everything relating to espionage. Nothing is more important in an army than the organization of this service.'[10] Students of Clausewitz may care to ponder this last remark.

8 Thiébault, *Manuel des adjudans-généraux*, pp.32–33.
9 Thiébault, *Manuel des adjudans-généraux*, pp.124–125.
10 Paul Thiébault, *Manuel général du service des états-majors généraux et divisionnaires dans les armées* (Paris: Magimel, 1813), p.95.

Thiébault elaborated on the type of people suitable for employment as spies. He identified five classes of them. The first were those with a complaint against the opposing government. Normally well-educated and holding positions which allowed them to make accurate judgments, Thiébault believed every effort ought to be made to discover these people, and to provide them with all the guarantees they required. The second class of spy were the patriotic sort who spied out of a sense of duty. They would slip into enemy territory on some pretext, often disguised, and ought to be rewarded with honours more than money. The third class, were the most numerous and contained:

> Monks and priests; conniving, gallant, or even impassioned women; people who have some favour to obtain from the government; people who made bad deals, or who, corrupt in their opinion, do not have any other honest means to exist in the world; officers of the enemy army, who having debts, or who enjoy gambling or ostentation, do not have the means of supporting their lifestyle, to fulfil their engagements, or to satisfy their tastes: the majority of these people without principles, that is to say, without honour, will sacrifice their country to their debauchery, just as they sacrificed themselves: Their greed will triumph over all; they will always go to the highest bidder and one will usually need only gold to learn from them everything that is in their capacity to discover. Women and priests, especially in Catholic countries, have often given the most useful intelligence, for the double reason that they have the means that no one else has, and that in general they are not mistrusted.[11]

The fourth class were professional spies who would serve both armies in order to double their pay. Double agents were always the most complex cases and might find themselves attempting to play fair with both camps, never delivering an outright lie. In Thiébault's opinion it was therefore necessary to manage these spies extremely carefully, never allowing them to circulate around the general staff and the army and to monitor those they communicated with. These spies should always be questioned separately, and the interviewer had to play an elaborate game of bluff, pretending to be interested in the things of no importance, and appearing disinterested in the things which were most crucial. There is an incredible example of one of these double agents at work in 1800, and we will introduce Carlo Gioelli later, but for now, Thiébault concluded these spies ought only to be used at the most vital moments, and with the greatest caution.

The final, fifth class of spy were those coerced into espionage by fear. One might simply send someone on a mission with his family and goods held hostage. Typically these spies belonged to the peasantry and were poorly educated. Merchants who had passed through enemy territory might also be arrested and threatened. Although these sources were easy to obtain, their lack of technical knowledge, and the fact they were usually terrified by their interrogators, made these spies poor sources of

11 Thiébault, *Manuel général du service*, p.96.

intelligence. They would often just simply tell the interrogator whatever they thought would please him and keep them out of trouble. This was flattery, not intelligence.

Having recruited one's spy, what did you ask them to find out? Thiébault helpfully lists 11 subjects of interest, which we can summarise below:

1) The headquarters of the enemy commander-in-chief and divisional generals.
2) The location, names and characters of the enemy generals.
3) The location and strength of the artillery parks and cavalry reserve.
4) The names and strength of each corps, its nationality and the number of guns.
5) If the enemy is concentrating or dividing his troops.
6) The measures taken for provisions, transportation and for hospitals.
7 How their troops are nourished, clothed, paid; their morale; how many are sick; the prevalent diseases; the mortality rate etc.
8) If the enemy moves his troops by day or night, by masses, corps or in detachments.
9) The reinforcements the enemy expects.
10) If military reviews are inspections or field manoeuvres.
11) Are fortifications are being built and how many workmen are involved.[12]

In addition to spies, enemy soldiers might also provide useful intelligence, but Thiébault noted prisoners of war were far less likely to reveal secrets than enemy deserters, although the former might be useful in corroborating other intelligence reports. The verification of intelligence was crucial. It was as perilous then as it is today to act only on a single intelligence source. Thiébault cautioned staff officers to always compare the reports of several spies (who were unknown to each other) and against other available intelligence. Where the report of a single spy had to be relied upon, the spy was to be detained until such time as the report could be checked. Meanwhile the spy was to be left under no illusion that his life depended on the accuracy of his report.

The Secret Bureau

The system described by Thiébault above appears to be limited to the gathering, dissemination and analysis of intelligence only. What about the other clandestine activities we might label 'Black Ops' today? Sedition, surveillance, black propaganda, bribery and extortion, it all went on in 1790s Italy, so much so that Napoleon formed a special bureau secret to carry out these nefarious activities. Unlike Thiébault's system, where intelligence was collected by each division and fed back to the army headquarters, this secret bureau was a central agency, reporting directly to Napoleon. The bureau secret was set up soon after Napoleon captured Milan in

12 Thiébault, *Manuel général du service*, pp.99–100.

May 1796. It was under the command of cavalry officer Jean Landrieux who held the staff appointment of *adjutant-général*. Landrieux was a curious appointment. He and Napoleon's aide-de-camp, Joachim Murat, hated each other, having served in the light cavalry together and gone to quite extraordinary lengths to denounce each other at the height of the Terror. Murat was lucky not to be sent to the guillotine, having been first portrayed by Landrieux as a nobleman (he was not), then as an ardent Jacobin revolutionary (which for a time he was). As head of the *bureau secret* Landrieux's mission was to place agents everywhere: in the enemy army and in the French army too. Agents were to infiltrate Naples, Rome, Florence, Turin, Venice, Vienna and even Paris; Napoleon believed with some justification his own government was spying on him. Landrieux was instructed to report directly to Napoleon, something he did several times a day.[13]

Landrieux divided the secret bureau's work into two departments. One dealt with general military matters while the other was for political affairs. The latter included the surveillance of conquered territories and the repression of political opponents. Landrieux described a committee or council of 'high police' he formed for this purpose. Unknown to most of the army, it met late at night outside the Milan opera house because the generals involved in it were free from their normal duties at this time. Landrieux called it l'assemblée nocturne.[14]

On the military front Landrieux would send officers out to deliberately get themselves captured and taken behind enemy lines where they could spy on the opponent's camps. At the time captive officers were afforded a great deal of respect and were often quickly exchanged. Landrieux instructed his officers not to request an exchange until they had something useful to report. When they had gathered sufficient intelligence, they would insert a pre agreed codeword into one of their letters. When Landrieux saw this secret signal (it was usually a mention of 'the cartel'), he would arrange for the captive to be swapped with a captured Austrian officer of similar rank.[15]

Landrieux's agents also pulled off some useful stunts on behalf of the French army. In his memoirs he describes one daring mission undertaken by the agent Nicolini from Brescia that led to the capture of Crema from Venice in March 1797. Leaving a force of 500 grenadiers hidden in the darkness behind them, in the dead of night Nicolini and a compatriot arrived outside the city dressed in the uniform of Venetian couriers, carrying post-whips and with red leather satchels over their shoulders. When challenged they pompously announced they were carrying urgent messages for the governor of Crema and that the city gates should be opened to them. At first the sentries were suspicious, a Venetian courier had only recently arrived, but then Nicolini offered a bribe. One of the sentries quietly removed the keys from the guardroom without waking his superiors (who would have wanted a cut of the money), and then unlocked the postern gate. Nicolini rushed the sentries

13 Grasilier (ed.), *Landrieux*, pp.107–111.
14 Grasilier (ed.), *Landrieux*, p.199.
15 Grasilier (ed.), *Landrieux*, p.111.

and overpowered them. The grenadiers charged and the guardsmen were massacred in their bunks. Men like Nicolini were extremely useful.[16]

In Search of the Rivoli Spy

One of the key battles of Napoleon's first Italian campaign was Rivoli (13–14 January 1797). This decisive battle saw the Austrians give up their attempts to relieve the fortress city of Mantua, in effect abandoning Italy to the French. The French base of operations was the city of Verona, while the Austrians were located to the north at Trento. There were various routes the Austrians might have taken to reach Mantua, and the mountainous terrain (plus the formidable obstacle of Lake Garda) made it difficult for the French to move their forces laterally. It was vital that the French knew well in advance where the main Austrian attack was going to fall. As it turned out, the main weight of attack fell against *Général de division* Barthélemy Joubert who was posted at Rivoli on the Adige River. Shortly after the battle he wrote to his father and included the following paragraph bemoaning his lack of money:

> I only receive gratuities for espionage and my table. I employ them so well that today I have no money, and I asked Bonaparte for 1,500 livres to meet my expenses and renew my carriages. I gave my last ten louis [gold sovereigns] to a spy, the one who warned me of the time, the number and the place [of the attack], the one who perhaps made me save the army.[17]

This is an interesting admission; Joubert was forewarned of the Austrian attack by a spy, and he believed this foreknowledge 'saved the army'. Perhaps, but Napoleon has a slightly different take on things. In his memoirs written in St Helena he claims he was alerted to Alzinzy's attack 'by his agents in Venice.'[18] Napoleon was in Bologna at the time he received this warning, and it allowed him to return to Verona in time to meet the offensive. Although Napoleon did have a spy network run by the French diplomats in the city of Venice, it is important to remember Verona was then part of the state of Venice, and the spies he was referring to were likely the ones based there.

The story is taken up by the famous Italian historian, Carlo Botta (1766–1837). In Verona was a man; a sympathiser of the French, who Botta describes as 'an old friend of Alvinci' (The Austrian commander). This unnamed Italian apparently travelled up to Trento to visit Alvinczi and spent three days there, during which he found a means of copying the entire Austrian battle plan. He returned to Verona and presented the plans to Pico, a Piedmontese exile working for the French as an 'explorer of the enemy's military operations'. Pico then handed the plans to Napoleon, at the same time as this letters from Joubert arrived stating it was clear

16 Grasilier (ed.), *Landrieux*, pp.324–326.
17 Edmond Chevrier, *Le Général Joubert. Étude sur sa Vie, Fragments de sa Correspondance Inédite* (Bourg-en-Bresse: Martin-Borrier, 1860), p.92.
18 Plon & Dumaine (eds), *Correspondance de Napoléon*, vol.XXIX, pp.89–90.

the main Austrian force was against him.[19] This account is intriguing, because it implies there was a second agent at work other than the one Joubert paid his last 10 gold Louis to. Time to pick Botta's account apart.

Where did Botta get his information from? The author was a close friend of and actively corresponded with the Piedmontese lawyer turned revolutionary, Angelo Pico. This man is one of the most fascinating characters of the first campaign in Italy, and even figured on the periphery of the second. In 1794 there was a botched coup in Turin against the ruling King of Sardinia by a group of Piedmontese lawyers and doctors who were in league with the French chargé d'affairs at Genoa, Jean Tilly. Alas, the brilliantly perfidious British were spying on Tilly, uncovered the plot and informed Turin. There were arrests, two of the plotters were executed (they were hanged, burned, their ashes scattered, and their goods confiscated, so no earthly trace of them would remain). Some of the plotters got away and fled to French territory. Botta and Pico were among these political refugees, the latter being hanged in effigy. Pico joined forces with the French and started out as an agent of *Général de division* André Masséna in 1795. By January 1797 Pico was something of a spymaster, reporting directly to Napoleon, running agents in all directions, probing the Austrian forces and also destabilising the neutral Republic of Venice (at Easter 1797 Pico provoked an uprising against the French garrison in Verona, providing Napoleon an excuse to invade Venice). So, we can safely assume Botta was told the Rivoli spy story by Pico himself.

Is Pico trustworthy? To a point. We see elements of mischief and devilry in his letters, and it is highly likely he provided his friend Botta with a colourful interpretation of the facts. What were the chances of there being an 'old friend' of Alvinczi in Verona (Transylvanian-born, Alvinczi was in his sixties and had not served in Italy prior to the end of 1796), an 'old friend' who spontaneously knew where to find the Austrian commander, was sufficiently well known to be accepted into his quarters, to be shown copies of his battle plans, and to have the wit and motivation to copy these plans and then smuggle them back through French lines. This 'old friend' then just happened to know the Piedmontese Pico was the very man who could place these reports before Napoleon's eyes. Quite how this 'old friend' knew Napoleon was greatly concerned about the forthcoming Austrian advance in the first place is yet another unanswered question. The very phrase 'old friend' is also intriguing. Was this something a euphemism on the part of Pico?

There is an anonymous memoir by an homme d'état (man of state) that claims Pico was sent into Alvinczi's headquarters by Bonaparte shortly before the Battle of Arcole the previous November.[20] When Botta said Alvinczi was met by 'an old friend from Verona', perhaps Pico was mischievously revealing he left Verona to go back and visit Alvinczi a second time (this same anonymous memoir describes Pico as one of Napoleon's most intelligent and active secret agents). Or was there another highly talented spy at work either reporting to Pico, or of a similar stature also reporting to Napoleon directly?

19 Carlo Botta, *Storia d'Italia dal 1789 al 1814* (Italy: Libro Ottavo, 1824), vol.2, pp.129–130.
20 Anon., *Mémoires tires des papiers d'un homme d'état* ... (Paris: Michaud, 1831), vol.4, p.68

Researching Napoleon's Italian campaigns 100 years after the event, the identity of his unknown agent attracted the attention of the author Edouard Gachot. He identified a second master spy, one who rivalled Pico's zeal in his service of Bonaparte.[21] Gachot names this spy as Francesco Toli. Let us read Gachot's account of the intelligence reaching Napoleon before the battle:

> A letter to Wurmser, taken from a spy, gave General Augereau some of Alvinzy's plans. Bonaparte was warned on 10 January. Although it had been announced that his poor health no longer permitted him any effort, he quickly went to the Adige, to give the divisional commanders precise orders. Having promised his soldiers victory and rewards, he received in Verona, at the Praetorian Palace, Toli who, having arrived from Trent as an emissary of Alvinzy, sold him Weyrother's plans.
>
> 'Go back to Roveredo. Go tell the Austrian general that Bonaparte is busy in Bologna, constituting a Cispadane Republic, that Joubert and Massena barely have 10,000 men to oppose him, and that the French are demoralized. Junot, give this boy fifty louis.'
>
> 'And I will make Alvinzy pay?'
>
> 'A false report sells for the highest possible price.'
>
> 'If my role is revealed to him?'
>
> 'Are you afraid of risks? Every profession has them. Well, Alvinzy will have you shot. Do not fear this execution. I will be waiting for you tomorrow at the Rivoli presbytery.'
>
> 'See you tomorrow, general.'
>
> The benevolence accorded him by Bonaparte moved Toli, an Italian who had suffered in Borghetto, where he was a peddler, from Austrian domination. He left on Friday morning, disguised as a peasant.[22]

This is all very interesting. Not only is Napoleon receiving intelligence, but he is also using the spy for deception purposes, planting false intelligence on his opponent. The spy, a double agent, is naturally concerned with the risks involved, but the reward is a double payday if he holds his nerve.

The Art of Espionage

The account of Rivoli was not the first time the spy Toli appeared in one of Gachot's works. Édouard Gachot (1862–1945) wrote extensively about the Italian campaigns, and at first glance his books are filled with incredible detail, much of it gleaned from his own travels in Switzerland and Italy in the 1890s. Alas his easy prose lacks sufficient footnotes. In 1899 Gachot's *La deuxième campagne d'Italie (1800)* was published. An important part of his account described the adventures of the spy Toli

21 Edouard Gachot, *La premier campagne d'Italie (1795 à 1798): Historie militaire de Masséna* (Paris: Perrin & Cie., 1901), p.170.

22 Gachot, *La premier campagne d'Italie*, pp.210–211.

in the build-up to the Battle of Marengo. A veritable Napoleonic James Bond, we have stories of Toli climbing the Alps, wearing disguises, and surviving close shaves with death. Where did Gachot get such spectacular source material?

There is an editorial piece in the 1898 *Revue du Foyer* of Lyon. It reports an interview with Gachot fresh back from his travels in Switzerland and Italy researching the 1800 Marengo campaign. One ought to note this interview took place around the time of the infamous *Affaire Dreyfus*, where a Jewish French officer was falsely accused of espionage. In the prelude to the interview, the editor remarks, 'We just discovered the name of a spy. What can reassure us about the consequences of this discovery is that this spy is not an Israelite and that we have been looking for him for a hundred years. So, he is Italian. … Where did Mr. Gachot get this information from?' A transcript of the interview follows:

Gachot: How did I find the name of the spy and an indication of the role he played during the campaign of 1800? I had searched in vain in the war archives for the name of the Italian who, on 30 July 1796, warned General Bonaparte that Wurmser, leaving Trent, was going by skilful manoeuvres to relieve Mantua. Before me, historians had searched too, unsuccessfully. But, to document my work, while consulting papers at the Bernardin Monks of Martigny, I found a note written by the hand of Father Luder, provost of the community in 1800. 'General Bonaparte shut in on May 18 with a certain François Toli, whom he had known since 1796; he's a spy.'

Editor: And that seemed sufficient to you to establish …

Gachot: Sorry, that was only vague information for me. Eight days later, in Aosta, recommended by a person, and I can name Mr Lanier, who owns a number of works of the Academic Society of the Duchy of Aosta, I discovered between a relation of the siege of Bard by Olivero and 'Notes by Father Berenfall', a small booklet, *l'art de l'espionnage* written by the Citizen Francesco Tolli and printed in Milan in 1807, by Monteni. Now, in these memoirs, Toli recounts that, born in Verona, he enlisted in the Austrian army and was used for intelligence by Wurmser's staff when Davidowitch brutally hit him for not having been having accounted for the French march on Brescia. The spy, humiliated, resolved to take revenge by revealing to Bonaparte the plans drawn up by Wurmser; then, having fallen in love with boundless admiration for the conqueror, he remained in his pay until the end of the operations; he recounts all his interviews with Bonaparte.

Editor: The pamphlet must be in the libraries of Milan?

Gachot: One has not been able to find out yet. Only twenty copies were printed: at least, that is the indication written on the back of the cover. However, in Milan, I found in a letter from General Dominique Pino, that Toli was serving the French, a letter addressed to Melzi d'Eril, where the general complained that 'Bonaparte received in his presence a spy, Francesco Toli, who had tricked Wurmser and who was deceiving Mr Melas. This letter was from the Bari collection, in 1894.

Editor: And you conclude?

Gachot: That François Toli was the most active spy, if not the most faithful among those which Bonaparte used in Italy.[23]

This interview is extremely useful, because it reveals Gachot's sources. While researching Napoleon's famous 1800 passage over the Great St Bernard Pass, Gachot claims to have found, by chance, a note from the provost of the monastery (Luder) naming the spy, and then a booklet written by this spy called *l'art de l'espionnage*. This autobiographical work was published in 1807 in Milan with a print run of just 20 copies. There was then a letter by Pino in Milan. Do we believe Gachot?

In more than 20 years of searching, I have found no corroborating evidence for a spy called Toli, Tolli, or even Noli (all spellings Gachot uses), even with the power of internet search engines to trawl through massive catalogues and collections such as Gallica, Google Books or the Internet Archive – research tools Gachot could never have dreamt of. Nor has anyone located Gachot's declared primary source for the spy, *l'art de l'espionnage*. All mentions of Toli in printed sources available today ultimately have Gachot as the source. We know Gachot studied the documents in the French war archives (today the Service Historique de Défense) and he also studied *Maréchal* Masséna's papers (today at the French Archives Nationales). Masséna's papers have some of the general's correspondence with Pico in 1795–1796. The war archives also contain a mountain of intelligence reports, including some by Pico, along with interesting documents by Schèrer revealing the intelligence service he established prior to Napoleon taking command of the army in 1796. Thus far no mention of a spy called Toli has been found in these reports. Alain Montarras, who in 2014 published an excellent study on intelligence during the 1790s (*Le général Bonaparte et le renseignement*), charitably concludes there were all sorts of spies at work who did not hold official ranks like Pico (he held the rank of captain). One of these may have been called Toli.[24]

As for this 'note de Luder' that Gachot says he found in Switzerland, proving the spy Toli met Napoleon, I went in search of it. I corresponded with the archivist at the St Bernard monastery in 2018. I set out Gachot's claim and asked if I could come and look through the archives myself. The archivist thought I was slightly mad but said I could visit them in June when the snows no longer blocked the pass. I studied all the Napoleonic vintage documents held by the monks. I saw some notes written by the hand of Luder, but nothing that named a spy called Francesco Toli. There was an anonymous account by a monk, which said Bonaparte ordered some movements at Martigny to confuse enemy spies, but that was it. In fact the same account said Napoleon arrived at Martigny and locked himself in a room *and saw no one*. So, no pamphlet and no note. And there are significant inconsistencies, not only in the spelling of the name. In his newspaper interview, Gachot says the spy was born in Verona and enlisted in the Austrian Army. In the Rivoli account the spy is a peddler from Borghetto. How could Gachot have become so confused? Everything

23 J. Perroud, *La Revue du Foyer* (Lyon: X. Jervain, 1898), pp.76–77.

24 Alain Montarras, *Le général Bonaparte et le renseignement: la période révolutionnaire et la première campagne d'Italie* (Paris: Éditions SPM, 2014), p.133.

now depends on the letter from Pino; but if it does exist, I already suspect what it will say. At best the letter will make a reference to Bonaparte meeting a spy, but it is extremely unlikely it will name names; and even if does, it is even less likely the spy will be called Toli.

In my experience researching this subject, the key figures in the world of espionage leave traces. It is very much like hearing a stone dropped into a pond. You might not see the object enter the pond, but you hear it, and as you glance towards the source of the sound, you see the ripples. When you see the ripples, you can usually pinpoint the central point of impact, and should you wish to go in search of the object, you at least know where to begin looking. It is also true that the bigger the impact, the greater the splash and the larger the ripples (welcome to the detective work of spy-hunting). We know about agent Pico, but there seems to have been another significant figure too. There are plenty of ripples in the pond indicating someone else was active – there are a host of minor spies already uncovered, but we are looking for a high-level double agent. My working hypothesis is Gachot saw all these ripples too, and correctly guessed there was another master spy with a similar importance to Pico. Frustrated he could not put a name to the man, I believe Gachot invented Toli as a literary device to represent the work of these spies (and to spin a good yarn in the process).

The Marengo Spy

In our pond full of ripples, the largest of them splashed down in 1829 with the publication of the fourth volume of Louis Antoine Fauvelet de Bourrienne's *Memoires de Napoléon*. There are many criticisms of the memoirs of Napoleon's private secretary during the Consulate, indeed a book has been written of them, and Bourrienne's detractors are at pains to point out the books were compiled by a ghost writer (the same accusation could be levelled at footballer David Beckham, but that did not stop half a million people purchasing his autobiography). One of the people who purchased this literary sensation (Bourrienne's, not Beckham's) was the Austrian *Feldmarschallleutnant* Joseph von Stutterheim, who had been a staff officer in Italy at the time of Marengo. One can imagine him spitting out his coffee when he read Bourrienne's account of a spy, sent by the Austrians to Napoleon's headquarters, but who then took Napoleon's pay and betrayed them. Then, with a wry smile, Stutterheim suddenly knew why Marengo had gone so badly wrong for the Austrians. 'That sly Italian,' he concluded. What was it he read? The full account from Bourrienne is below:

> The first consul passed six days at Milan. On the second day, a spy, who had served us very well in the first and admirable campaigns in Italy, was announced. The first consul recollected him and ordered him to be shown into his cabinet.
>
> 'Here you are,' he exclaimed. 'So, you have not been shot yet?'
>
> 'General,' replied the spy, 'when the war recommenced, I determined to serve the Austrians, because you were far from Europe. I always follow

> the fortunate; but the truth is, I am tired of the trade. I wish to have done with it, and to get enough to enable me to retire. I have been sent to your lines by General Melas, and I can render you an important service. I will give an exact account of the force and the position of all the enemy's corps, and the names of their commanders. I can tell you the situation in which Alessandria now is. You know me: I will not deceive you; but, I must carry back some report to my general. You are strong enough to give me some true intelligence, which I can communicate to him.'
>
> 'Oh! as to that,' resumed the first consul, 'the enemy is welcome to know my forces, and my positions, provided I know his, and he be ignorant of my plans. You shall be satisfied; but do not deceive me: I will give you a thousand Louis, if you serve me well.'
>
> I then wrote down, from the dictation of the spy, the names of the corps, their amount, their positions, and the names of the generals commanding them. The first consul stuck pins in the map to mark his plans on places, respecting which he received information from the spy. We also learned that Alessandria was without provisions, that Melas was far from expecting a siege, that many of his troops were sick, and that he lacked medicines. The Major-Général Berthier was ordered to give him a nearly accurate statement of our positions. The information given by this man, of whom the first consul had nothing but praise in his first campaigns, was found so faithful and served him so well, that on his return from Marengo he ordered me to pay him the agreed price. The spy told him that Melas had been enchanted by the way he had served him in this circumstance, and he had been well rewarded. He told us he was able to bid adieu to his villainous trade. The first consul looked upon this small event as one of the favours of his good fortune.[25]

The key thing in this account, which does not appear to have been disputed in any of the counter claims against Bourrienne, is that this unnamed spy had served Napoleon very well in the first campaigns not just at Marengo. Napoleon clearly remembered this man, was jovial with him, and lavished him with money (compare Joubert's 'last ten Louis' to the thousand golden Louis Napoleon paid this man). This sum of money was far in excess of what the Austrians were paying him. Then think of the situation for a moment. The man is a double spy, who admits he is working for the Austrian commander, Melas, but who is able to walk into Napoleon's quarters in Milan and offer him a deal. Read Alvinczi for Melas. Is this not the same modus operandi as our Rivoli spy? It's incredible really. High level double agents able to pass from one headquarters to the other like some secret courier, or backchannel in modern parlance.

Further, we know Bourrienne's spy is not Angelo Pico, because he and Napoleon fell out in 1797 and by 1800 Pico was working for Masséna in Genoa. With sources not available to Gachot a century ago, we can even name this man with a high

25 Louis Antoine Fauvelet de Bourrienne, *Mémoires de M. de Bourrienne, ministre d'état sur Napoléon* (Paris: Chez Ladvocat, 1829), vol.4, pp.105–107.

degree of certainty. Although his research was extensive, Gachot was unlucky his book predated by a few years the works of his contemporary, Hermann Hüffer, the great complier of Austrian documentation on the Italian campaigns. If Gachot had studied Hüffer in detail (as my colleague David Hollins did more than 20 years ago now), then he would have come across the story of a certain Carlo Gioelli.[26]

The real Marengo spy is a fantastically complicated character.[27] When you know what you are looking for, he appears in many accounts, and each time his back story changes slightly, depending on his audience. He was from Piedmont, near Alba, the land of hazelnuts, white truffles and Barolo wine. In 1799 he found himself *chef de la correspondance secrète* for *Général de division* MacDonald's Army of Naples. In effect he was the army's chief intelligence officer, a position of great trust and importance. Fans of John Le Carré's *Tinker Tailor Soldier Spy*, or students of the case of British intelligence officer and Soviet mole, Kim Philby, will know the terrible damage that a rogue senior intelligence officer can inflict. Gioelli was no exception. He started secretly working for the Austrians during the siege of Mantua in June 1799 and from that point not a single important message did not find its way into Austrian hands. The commander of Mantua (a certain Foissac-Latour) was baffled no relief came to him despite his repeated pleas for help (Gioelli was passing his letters to the Austrians). Gioelli stole the French battle plans before the Battle of Genola on 4 November, and as his pièce de resistance, he betrayed the French garrison at Cuneo in December, tricking the French commander into surrendering, even though the guns of the relief columns could be heard in the distance. The calamitous performance of the French in 1799 is far easier to understand when this level of treachery is exposed. Two major fortresses and a battle lost directly because of this most dangerous enemy within.

After betraying Cuneo, Gioelli refused to go back to the French Army of Italy. People had begun to suspect him, and he must have guessed he was effectively blown by the scale of his treachery. The Austrians decided to keep him on as a talent scout and a trainer of future agents. All this changed when Napoleon's Army of the Reserve made its dramatic crossing of the Alps in May 1800. Although Napoleon had caught them off guard (the Austrians knew Napoleon was coming over the Alps but suspected he would first march on Turin or Genoa, not Milan), the Austrians were still very powerful. Masséna's starving army under siege and on the verge of surrender in Genoa, and the Austrians had cleared the Italian riviera of French troops, pushing them back beyond the River Var. The Austrians needed to know exactly what they were dealing with, so they sent Gioelli to Milan to find out the size of the newly arrived French army. This is the interview described by Bourrienne above.

When Gioelli returned to Melas's headquarters the intelligence provided by the spy had an explosive effect. The Austrians learned the French had crossed the St

26 Gioelli is pronounced something like 'Joy-elly'. It is a variation of Gioielli (jewel), and also sometimes spelt Giovelli or Giojelli.

27 The story of this spy is discussed in greater detail in Terry Crowdy, *Marengo: The Victory That Placed the Crown of France on Napoleon's Head* (Barnsley: Pen & Sword Military, 2018), p.117.

Gotthard Pass as well as the St Bernard Pass, and the French were moving troops from the German theatre of operations into Milan. From a position of strength, the Austrians now saw themselves surrounded and about to be cut off from their lines of communication. A mad scramble ensued with orders for the imperial army to abandon all its operations and concentrate at Alessandria. A portion of the forces besieging Genoa were directed to the city of Piacenza to safeguard the bridge across the River Po there, without which Melas would be trapped in northeast Italy. The groundwork for the battles of Montebello and Marengo had been done.

The Austrian and French forces clashed at Montebello on 9 June. It was a classic encounter battle with the two forces effectively blundering into one another and the fate of the battle swaying this way and that as more troops arrived on either side. In the end the French prevailed and the Austrians retreated in the direction of Alessandria to join the main part of the army. For the purposes of this essay, the important part is a second meeting between Gioelli and Napoleon which occurred just after the battle. The Austrians wanted to know where the French were and how many troops had crossed the Po and were blocking their escape route. This time Napoleon also had questions for the spy. He wanted to know if the imperial army had concentrated, specifically the location of the troops previously on the Var and at Genoa. Most crucially, Napoleon wanted to know if the imperial army wanted to cross the Po? Napoleon needed to know on which bank of this mighty river he needed to locate the bulk of his forces.

Gioelli's handler was the Austrian chief of staff, *Generalmajor* Anton Zach. A separate essay could be written about Zach's unpopularity in Melas's army, but having had this superstar spy working for him since the previous summer, Zach had a succession of wins to his name. No one could deny his track record over the previous year. But increasingly isolated and blamed for the perilous predicament of the Austrian army, now surrounded and cut off from home, Zach made one last play, gambling everything on the spy who had never failed him.

The game of roulette rose to popularity in the salons of 1790s Paris. It is often called the *devil's game*, and true enough, the numbers on the wheel (0-36) do add up to 666 – the so-called number of the beast. The peril of the roulette wheel (which then had both a 0 and a 00) is that a seemingly 50/50 bet between red and black only has a 47.4% chance of winning. The odds on a single number winning are just 37 to 1. By placing complete trust in his spy, a single spy, a single source of intelligence, a single point of failure, the odds were increasingly stacked against Zach. Like a player stood at the roulette wheel, if he won, he would win big; but if he lost, the losses would be irredeemable.

On Friday 13 June (perhaps not a luckiest day to stake everything on a spin of the wheel), Zach began drafting the imperial army's battle plans. The Austrians had concentrated their forces at Alessandria as planned. They needed to lure Napoleon's army onto the enormous flat plain between Alessandria and Tortona, a plain bordered by the river Bormida in the west, the Po to the north, the Scrivia to the east, and the Apennine mountains to the south. This plain would allow the Austrians to bring to bear their superior number of guns and cavalry. The lure was the spy Gioelli. Zach provided the spy with a fake order of march for the imperial army that he was to take to Napoleon. It showed troops marching up from Genoa to Alessandria and then the whole imperial army crossing the Po at the town of Casale before making a run in the direction of Milan. Gioelli was instructed to tell Napoleon he could catch the Austrian army in the act of crossing the river by marching through Sale to the north of the plain. This ruse was (on paper at least) brilliant. It played to Napoleon's biggest fear, namely the Austrians might escape him and drag the campaign into an interminable game of cat and mouse. In fact, if Napoleon did march on Sale, it would be the French army caught in a trap, with the Austrians converging on this town in a pincer movement. Brilliant.

On the afternoon of 13 June, Gioelli arrived back in Zach's headquarters and told him the news. Napoleon had swallowed the bait. The main force of French troops was now marching on Sale, while a portion had been sent south to intercept the fictious troop movement said to be arriving from Genoa. Zach was ecstatic. He started walking around his headquarters shouting at the top of his voice: 'This time we have this Bonaparte!'[28]

Napoleon did indeed interview the spy that day. He was shown the fake movement orders. We do not know if Gioelli outright told Napoleon the plans were fake, but he may have covered himself by telling Napoleon he had been instructed to hand over these plans. The spy's intelligence left Napoleon in something of a pickle. If the Austrians were planning to fight, why was the army not camped in the middle of the plain, ranged in battle order with its guns in batteries and swarms of cavalry in advance and on the wings of the formidable infantry? Napoleon's cavalry patrols were reporting the plain was mostly empty. Napoleon also had scouts opposite Casale and although the imperials were present on the other side of the river, there was nothing to indicate a major river crossing was about to take place. Why was the spy telling him to march to Sale? What were the Austrians trying to trick him into? You can now see the genius of Napoleon in weighing up *all* the intelligence, not just the report of a single double agent.

While Zach was leaping around his headquarters like a man possessed, Napoleon did two things on the afternoon of 13 June. He sent *Lieutenant-général* Louis Desaix south with an infantry division and some cavalry to investigate the road to Genoa. By the early hours of the morning, this column confirmed that no Austrians were marching up the road from Genoa. His second decision was to order *Lieutenant-général* Victor to advance across the middle of the plain straight at Alessandria to see what the Austrians would do in response. Victor clashed with the Austrian forward posts at a little hamlet called Marengo and drove them to the banks of the River Bormida where the Austrians had a heavily fortified bridgehead. Even as French cannonballs began raining down on the Austrian camp that evening, Zach ignored pleas to change his orders. The spy had told him the French were at Sale, and that is what he continued to believe. Twenty-four hours later, Zach was a prisoner of war, and the imperial army was wrecked, having been shot to pieces trying to recapture that little hamlet called Marengo, the critical strategic pinch-point on the road network in that area. For all his brilliant ruses and deceptions, Zach had forgotten the most basic requirements of a military operation in Italy: secure the

28 Crowdy, *Marengo*, p.117.

road network. It is a testament to the bravery of the Austrian officers and soldiers that they almost won the battle despite Zach's shenanigans. Indeed, Napoleon was so dumbfounded that the Austrians attacked on 14 June having ceded all the strategically important ground the day before, he was convinced the attack was a feint, a trick, and did not arrive on the battlefield himself until noon.

Conclusion

This essay is just a short glimpse into a much larger, murkier subject. We have not even discussed in any detail how Napoleon used a variety of spies and agent-provocateurs to destabilise and ultimately conquer the state of Venice in 1797, and we have only touched upon the exploits of Angelo Pico. However, by now it should be apparent secret intelligence played an important part in Napoleon's early career.

One crucial question remains to be answered in this essay – are Gioelli and Toli the same person? Was Gioelli the Rivoli spy? It is certainly possible. In 1799 and 1800 we see Gioelli able to pass from one headquarters to the other, bartering and selling secrets to both parties. The modus operandi is largely the same. He was clearly an important, well-connected person to become MacDonald's chief of secret correspondence. He was undoubtedly very clever, and a very convincing liar when he needed to be. He was a professional spy – the heels of his boots were hollow for carrying concealed messages. What had Gioelli done to be placed in such an important position of trust? What did Gioelli do in 1796 and 1797 for Napoleon to remember him so clearly in 1800? Or are Gioelli and Toli completely different men? Did Gachot really find a small pamphlet with a print run of just 20 copies: does *l'art de l'espionnage* really exist? Is it there on a shelf in a private collection in Aosta, still waiting to be found? If not, where did Gachot really get his information from? Was it just a piece of well researched fiction after all?

We may never know the full truth, but there is certainly more evidence waiting to be discovered, perhaps not in Paris, but certainly in Turin, Verona and Vienna. The Rivoli spy (or spies) must finally be found. The investigation begins.

Bibliography

Anon., *Mémoires tires des papiers d'un homme d'état …* (Paris: Michaud, 1831)
Botta, Carlo, *Storia d'Italia dal 1789 al 1814* (Italy: Libro Ottavo, 1824)
Bourrienne, Louis Antoine Fauvelet de, *Mémoires de M. de Bourrienne, ministre d'état sur Napoléon* (Paris: Chez Ladvocat, 1829)
Chevrier, Edmond, *Le Général Joubert. Étude Sur Sa Vie, Fragments De Sa Correspondance Inédite* (Bourg-en-Bresse: Martin-Borrier, 1860)
Clausewitz, Carl von, *Der Feldzug von 1796 in Italien* (Berlin: Ferd. Dümmler's Verlagsbuchhandlung, 1858)
Clausewitz, Carl von, *On War* (Harmondsworth: Penguin, 1968)
Crowdy, Terry, *Marengo: The Victory That Placed the Crown of France on Napoleon's Head* (Barnsley: Pen & Sword Military, 2018)

Crowdy, Terry, *The Enemy Within: A History of Espionage* (Oxford: Osprey, 2006)

Gachot, Edouard, *La premier campagne d'Italie (1795 à 1798): Historie militaire de Masséna* (Paris: Perrin & Cie., 1901)

Grasilier, Léonce (ed.), *Mémoires de l'Adjudant-General Jean Landrieux* (Paris: Nouvelle Libraririe Parisienne, 1893)

Montarras, Alain, *Le général Bonaparte et le renseignement: la période révolutionnaire et la première campagne d'Italie* (Paris: Éditions SPM, 2014)

Montgomery, Bernard Law, *The Memoirs of Field-Marshal the Viscount Montgomery of Alamein, K.G.* (Cleveland and New York: The World Publishing Company, 1958)

Plon, H., & Dumaine, J. (eds), *Correspondance de Napoléon Ier: Publiée par ordre de L'empereur Napoléon III* (Paris: H. Plon, J. Dumaine, 1870)

Thiébault, Paul, *Manuel des adjudans-généraux et des adjoints employés dans les états-majors-divisionnaires des armées* (Paris: Magimel, 1800)

Thiébault, Paul, *Manuel général du service des états-majors généraux et divisionnaires dans les armées* (Paris: Magimel, 1813)

4

General Mikhail Kutuzov and the Allied Headquarters on the Eve of the Battle of Austerlitz

Alexander Mikaberidze

As the month of November 1805 came to an end, the mood in the Allied headquarters at Olmutz, a small town in Moravia, was jubilant. Three months into the War of the Third Coalition, the strategic situation was beginning to favour the Russo-Austrian allies. Although the Austrian army was routed at Ulm, the Russian army, commanded by *General ot infanterii* Mikhail Kutuzov, avoided Napoleon's envelopments and made it to Olmutz, where Russian and Austrian reinforcements were now assembling. Archduke Charles with a force as large as the combined Russo-Austrian army, had already crossed the Julian Alps into Hungary, where he was preparing to take up the offensive against Napoleon.

The arrival of both Russian and Austrian sovereigns promised to boost the Allied war effort, for it seemed to ensure political and military unity. The youthful Russian emperor – Alexander was about to celebrate his twenty-eighth birthday on 23 December– had arrived after a quick but memorable visit to the Prussian court in Berlin. He was able to convince Prussian King Frederick Wilhelm III to sign the Treaty of Potsdam and promise to support the coalition if Napoleon did not accept Prussian mediation, which seemed all but certain, considering the steep concessions the Allies expected from the French; within weeks, Prussia could commit over 100,000 troops for the Allied cause. The Anglo-Swedish army was, meanwhile, ready to march from Hanover into Holland, which was largely undefended, while an Anglo-Russian expedition was finishing its preparations for the invasion of Naples. The Allies could thus hope to field over a quarter million men for the next phase of the war.

Napoleon, threatened on all sides, seemed on the defensive, his army weakened – barely 50,000 men were in the vicinity of Brunn – and at the end of his logistical tether. The situation worried many French officers and soldiers. 'In ten years of fighting,' remembered a French general, 'many of our officers had been risking their lives in one battle or another. The thought of making their wills had never occurred to them. Now they started to make them.'[1] Rumours of anxiety in the ranks of the French army had reached the Allied camp, reinforcing the growing belief in Napoleon's vulnerability. Some were convinced that the French emperor was about to be enclosed between converging Allied forces and destroyed.

Such sentiments bred overconfidence. The Allies, in the words of a modern historian, 'began to think in terms of vast combination of hundreds of thousands of troops acting in a coordinated fashion over hundreds of miles of separation.'[2] Opinions as to what strategy to pursue were 'very much divided,' observed *Generalmajor* Karl Wilhelm von Stutterheim, who commanded an Austrian cavalry brigade in 1805.[3] Alexander and Francis agreed to keep Kutuzov in charge of the combined Allied army, which could muster some 68,000 Russian and 15,000 Austrian troops at Olmutz, but they disagreed with his strategic assessments. The Russian general led a group of senior officers who urged the sovereigns to not engage the French in battle. To borrow Clausewitz's later-day phrase, he believed that 'time allowed to pass unused accumulates to the credit of the defender who reaps where he did not sow.'[4] Kutuzov argued that it was in Napoleon's interest to fight since the longer his Grande Armée remained far away from France, the weaker it would get. Kutuzov pointed out the advantages of remaining in the highlands of Moravia, where the army was bivouacked on an elevated position from where it was possible to survey the area for miles around. The front was covered by a river while the Allies could use the wide valleys behind them to conceal the reserves. Having seen French operational mobility in action in the previous few weeks, Kutuzov was concerned about Napoleon's ability to concentrate his forces and outmanoeuvre his opponents. Coalition warfare posed inherent challenges of coordinating goals and actions of allied forces, which is never an easy task, and Kutuzov was worried that upon leaving the safety of the Olmutz ramparts, the Allied army would be vulnerable to an enemy counterstrike. Hence, instead of giving battle, he argued that a simple delay of the operations would in a very short time have constrained Napoleon to withdraw due to the double necessity of concentrating his troops and preserving his supply and communication lines. For the Allies, it was crucial to gain a few more weeks, during which their reinforcements would arrive and the Prussians would enter the war, tilting the scales decidedly into the Allies' favour. The time thus gained would, by itself, equate to a decisive victory. And if Napoleon chose to attack the Allies before then, Kutuzov was ready to fall back even further east. 'We could retreat farther into Galicia,' he remarked. 'For I intend to bury the French bones there.'[5]

Neither Francis nor Alexander heeded this counsel. The Kaiser, still reeling from the disaster at Ulm and the loss of Vienna, yearned for the calm of his palace, now occupied by the French, and hoped to bring the campaign to a quick and victorious

1 Paul Thiébault, *Mémoires du général Baron Thiébault* (Paris: Plon, 1894), vol.III, p.439.

2 For a judicious analysis see Frederick W. Kagan, *The End of the Old Order. Napoleon and Europe 1801-1805* (New York: Da Capo, 2006), pp.550–559.

3 Karl von Stutterheim, *La Bataille d'Austerlitz, par un militaire témoin de la journée du 2 décembre 1805* (Paris: Fain, 1806), p.14.

4 Michael I. Handel (ed.), *Clausewitz and Modern Strategy* (London: Frank Cass, 1986), p.139.

5 I. Butovskii, *Pervaya voina imperatora Aleksandra I s Napoleonom I v 1805 godu* (St Petersburg: Voennaya tipografiya, 1858), p.37.

conclusion; he was little inclined to listen to any advice that prolonged the occupation of his realm, particularly when the overall strategic picture seemed to favour the Allies. Alexander was even more susceptible to such wishful thinking. This was his first war and he longed for the laurels of victory. Surrounding him was a group of young noblemen who lauded his talents as a military leader and urged him to lead the army against Napoleon. Few of them had experienced the grim realities of war before and remained oblivious to the hardship that the army had endured. 'It has been twenty-six days since we left Braunau, yet we are still living in open air,' a sullen *General-leitenant* Dmitry Dokhturov told his wife in late November. 'Our poor officers and soldiers, without shoes and bread, are all in wretched condition. Looking at them is simply heartbreaking...'[6] Another Russian officer remembered that 'Even our commanders were dressed in ill-assorted, even comic attire.'[7] Observing the arrival of Alexander and his brilliant entourage, *General-leitenant* Louis Alexandre Andrault de Langeron and other officers were 'surprised by the deep silence and sombre mood' of the fatigued troops as they dolefully greeted the emperor.[8]

Such details escaped the attention of the toadies who surrounded the czar. They relished the prospects of military glory and, despite knowing little about war and strategy, claimed to understand the military situation better than the military commanders. Among them was *General-leitenant* Aleksey Arakcheyev, a martinet renowned for his fondness for spit-and-polish marching and the severity with which he treated his subordinates. However, he had never taken part in a war; when offered the command of a column at Austerlitz, he refused it on the plea that he had bad nerves.[9] The rest of the imperial suite was equally young and overconfident. Probably the most influential of them was Peter Dolgorukov, a scion of a distinguished Russian family of princes, born with a deep sense of power and privilege. He was enrolled in the elite Life Guard Izmailovskii Regiment at the tender age of just three months and began actual service as a 15-year old captain, quickly rising through the ranks due to the family connections. At 21, he was already a *general-major* and adjutant-general to Emperor Paul. His meteoric rise only accelerated after Alexander ascended the Russian throne in 1801. The young czar became very fond of Dolgorukov, who espoused hawkish views in foreign policy and wanted Russia to be more assertive in Europe. In 1804–1805, he was one of the architects of the Russian

6 Dmitri Dokhturov to his wife, in *Russkii arkhiv* 1(1874), p.1904.

7 Alexander Mikaberidze (ed., trans.), *The Czar's General. The Memoirs of a Russian General in the Napoleonic Wars* (Welwyn Garden City: Ravenhall Books, 2005), p.50. On the problems with supplies see Stutterheim, *La Bataille d'Austerlitz*, pp.32–34.

8 Louis Alexandre Andrault de Langeron, *Journal inedit de la campagne de 1805* (Paris: La Vouivre, 1998), pp.24–25; Nikolai Shil'der, *Imperator Aleksandr pervyi. Ego zhizn' i tsarstvovanie* (St Petersburg: A.S. Suvorin, 1897), vol.II, pp.133–134, 283. Bavarian diplomat Olry described Grand Duke Constantine demanding his guard units to move by parade marches from St Petersburg to Olmütz. He estimated that the Guard Corps lost 2,000 men as a result. See Olry's correspondence in *Istoricheskii Vestnik*, 147 (1917): p.435.

9 Theodor von Bernhardi (ed.), *Denkwürdigkeiten aus dem Leben des Kaiserl. russ. Generals von der der Infanterie Carl Friedrich Grafen von Toll* (Leipzig: Otto Wigand, 1856), vol.I, p.151; Shil'der, *Alexander*, vol.II, pp.138–139.

confrontation with Napoleon and carried out several diplomatic missions, including one to sway the Hohenzollern court to join the Third Coalition. Accompanying the czar to Olmutz, Dolgorukov extolled the rearguard actions at Lambach, Amstetten, Durrenstein and Hollabrun as great Russian victories and spoke with profound contempt of the Austrians, who had allowed themselves to be defeated at Ulm. Any success Napoleon had achieved so far was, in his opinion, due to the imbecility of the Austrians.

Anti-Austrian sentiments remained high among the Russian officers, who continued to complain about logistical problems that the army experienced due to inadequate provisioning. Even the czar had to admit, in a letter to the Prussian king, that the Allied camp at Olmutz was 'neither well provisioned nor in an [adequate] state of defence.'[10] The extent of Allied difficulties can be gleaned from the progressively worsening relations between the Russian and Austrian officers, with accusations of cowardice and timidity flying back and forth. Russians alleged that some Austrian officers had been bribed by the French. Kutuzov went as far as to suspect at least one Austrian officer of outright spying for the enemy.[11]

Kutuzov's insistence on pragmatic retreat was too much for Alexander to swallow. He was the first Russian sovereign to command an army in battle since Peter the Great. He had no intentions to this show his back to Napoleon. Indeed, the czar was determined to march forward and confront the enemy. His advisors argued that the lack of movement by Napoleon indicated timidity and weakness; victory seemed within grasp. 'In vain did Kutuzov, [Pavel] Suchtelen, Buxhöwden, Prince Karl zu Schwarzenberg, Prince Johann Lichtenstein and other Austrian generals oppose such an absurd project,' commented *General-leitenant* Langeron. 'Emperor Alexander desired a battle and so it was decided.'[12]

Had Kutuzov been left to follow his own judgment, he would have adopted a Fabian approach to the war – avoiding major actions and wearing the enemy down by attrition and harassment. But he could not exercise his authority freely. Alexander and Francis formally appointed him as the commander-in-chief of the combined Allied forces, but their very presence inexorably constrained the general, who also had to deal with a group of supercilious officers who – full of ardour, courage, and illusions – influenced the emperors and foretold glorious new conquests over the French. These men increasingly marginalized and ridiculed Kutuzov for his insistence on discretion. Here was an old man, clearly past his prime, almost blind in one

10 Alexander to Frederick Wilhelm of Prussia, 19 November 1805, in Paul Bailleu (ed.), *Briefwechsel könig Friedrich Wilhelm's III und der königin Luise mit kaiser Alexander I* (Leipzig: S. Hirzel, 1900), p.84. To alleviate food shortages, Kutuzov suggested spreading the army over the wider area and billeting units in the villages around Olmutz 'in such a manner as to be able to reassemble the army within twenty four hours.' His advice, however, was not considered. Langeron, *Journal inédit de la campagne de 1805*, p.27.

11 In his letter Kutuzov claimed that the Austrian 'imperial-royal police has determined that *Rotmistr* de Winzell of the de Bussy Regiment is employed by the enemy to spy on the Russian army.' Inzov to Dokhturov; Kutuzov to Prince Liechtenstein, 12/24 November 1805, Lithuanian State Historical Archives: f. 378, op. 13, d. 213, part 1, l. 196.

12 Alexander Langeron, 'Mémoires du Comte de Langeron,' in *Nouvelle Revue Rétrospective* (January–June 1895): p.290.

eye, corpulent, and struggling to stay in the saddle; to them, he was more famous for his obsequious behaviour at the court and agility with a coffeepot – Kutuzov infamously served freshly brewed coffee to the Russian empress' favourite in bed – than he was for three decades of military service. They called him 'General Dawdler' [*général Lambin*] and spread rumours that Kutuzov had lost his mind during the retreat.[13] Emperor Alexander had little regard for old veterans like Kutuzov, observed *General-leitenant* Langeron, who witnessed what had transpired in the Allied headquarters. 'He received them rarely and spoke to them little. Instead, the emperor reserved all his favours for five or six young favourites who were his adjutants. He gave himself over to a familiarity with them that was humiliating for the old generals, who saw their bearing and manners ridiculed by all these children whose influence extended to everything.'[14]

It has been long argued that Kutuzov was too obsequious to raise his voice in protest; that despite his intelligence and experience, he shied away from openly confronting Alexander and instead choose to acquiesce to his wishes, even when he knew that they were wrong. 'Kutuzov was far too good of a courtier to assert his opinion seriously and emphatically,' alleged one Russian officer; he 'found it convenient to be silent,' charged another officer,[15] while still another thought that the commander, facing ridicule and 'left without power and any consideration, should have quit but chose to stay.'[16] Russian court historian Alexander Mikhailovskii-Danilevskii drew an unfavourable contrast between Kutuzov's acquiescence and the combativeness of *Generalissimo* Alexander Suvorov, who, in 1799–1800, repeatedly clashed with the Hofkriegsrat over the planning and direction of the Allied war efforts. Others spoke of the moral failing to stand firm for his beliefs, of 'the lack of sufficient civic courage to tell the whole truth' to the young czar.[17] Even a Soviet historian had to admit in his otherwise hagiographical biography of the field marshal that he backed down too easily. 'He lacked the courage to oppose his opinion to that of two Emperors, their suites, the court of Vienna, and the Austrian generals. But this weakness was not evidence of Kutuzov's ambition or perfidy. It was an expression of his personal tragedy.'[18]

There is some validity to the criticism. Contemporaries frequently remarked on Kutuzov's 'timorous character and courtier-like habits'[19] and that 'one could

13 Langeron, 'Mémoires du Comte de Langeron,' p.290; Butovskii, *Pervaya voina imperatora Aleksandra I s Napoleonom I v 1805 godu*, p.37.
14 Langeron, *Journal inedit de la campagne de 1805*, p.26.
15 Toll, *Denkwürdigkeiten*, vol.I, p.142.
16 Toll, *Denkwürdigkeiten*, vol.I, pp.141–142; Langeron, *Journal inedit de la campagne de 1805*, p.31.
17 I. Heisman's entry on Kutuzov in *Russkii biograficheskii slovar'*, vol.IX, p.650; Heinrich Leer, *Podrobnyi konspekt voiny 1805 goda. Austerlitskaya operatsiya* (St Petersburg: Tip. V. Bezobrazova, 1888), pp.57–58.
18 M. Bragin, *Feldmarshal Kutuzov* (Moscow, 1942), p.86. A similar opinion is voiced in many other publications, most recently in Oleg Sokolov, *Bitva trekh imperatorov. Napoleon, Rossiya i Evropa, 1799-1805 gg.* (St Petersburg: Piter, 2019), pp.426–427.
19 Adam Gielgud (ed.), *Memoirs of Prince Adam Czartoryski and his correspondence with Alexander I…* (London: Remington, 1888), vol.II, p.103

not have more wit and less character' than him.[20] Throughout his life, Kutuzov operated within a deeply entrenched patronage culture, one that had shaped his character and manners; he had learned to fit himself within its received roles and expectations. Forcefully raising his voice of protest against the Emperor, who held supreme military command was simply unfeasible. Drawing parallels with Suvorov seems wrongheaded. Kutuzov faced a situation that was entirely different from the previous Coalition War. In 1799, Suvorov was the hero of Rymnik and Izmail whose prestige stood much higher than Kutuzov's in 1805, and who therefore enjoyed a far greater degree of independence; he could afford to quarrel with an Austrian military council that was hundreds of miles away. Kutuzov had to contend with not just one but two emperors who were constantly breathing down his neck.

At the very heart of this matter lay Alexander's character. The czar was driven by the need to prove himself a great commander and to match the exploits of 'the hero of the century,' as Napoleon was being called.[21] But Alexander was also self-aware enough to know that it would not be prudent for him to assume direct command of the army. He did the next best thing: keeping the veteran around as a nominal commander and depriving him of actual decision-making authority. This arrangement gave the czar power over the army while also shielded him from any blowback. If a decisive victory over Napoleon was achieved, it would be attributed to the czar's sagacious leadership; and in the event of a setback, Alexander could avoid personal responsibility by shifting the blame. Kutuzov thus found himself 'without power and respect,' aptly noted a Russian general.[22] Openly confronting an all-powerful sovereign would have changed nothing and Kutuzov knew all too well what disagreeing with a ruler could entail in Russia. In spite of his brilliance and fame, even Suvorov was hounded and disgraced. Nor was resigning an option, both because the czar could simply refuse to accept it and because Kutuzov's own sense of duty and responsibility would not allow him simply to abandon the troops on the eve of the battle.

Yet as long as Alexander remained with the army, there was little Kutuzov could do to change plans or countermand orders. He was not the only one to grasp the gravity of the situation. Adam Czartoryski, the czar's influential advisor on all foreign matters, was equally exasperated to see that Alexander 'would not believe what we continually repeated to him, that his presence would prevent Kutuzov from exercising any real authority over the movements of the army.' Czartoryski acknowledged that Kutuzov was not admitted to the councils of war and that 'his advice was certainly not listened to.'[23]

Contrary to prevailing views, Kutuzov did try to convince the czar of the error of the strategy that he and the Kaiser had approved. 'I was young and inexperienced,' Alexander later noted plaintively. 'Kutuzov should have dissuaded me from undertaking the battle.' This is a canard. Kutuzov repeatedly did try to warn him; Alexander simply would not listen to his advice. When the general asked to be involved in the

20 Langeron, *Journal inedit de la campagne de 1805,* p.8.
21 Toll, *Denkwürdigkeiten*, vol.I, p.142.
22 Langeron, *Journal inedit de la campagne de 1805,* p.31.
23 Czartoryski, *Memoirs*, vol.II, pp.103, 106.

planning, the Emperor bluntly told him, 'That is none of your business.'[24] When Kutuzov pressed the matter and urged the czar to reconsider launching offensive, Alexander doubted his courage – fighting the French was 'not the same as trouncing those absconding Turks and Poles, and now your bravery is suddenly waning.' This must have been maddening to Kutuzov, but he kept his calm. 'Your Majesty, henceforth you should command the army as you please,' he simply replied. 'You know full well that I am no coward. I refuse to fight as a general and will instead serve as a soldier.'[25] Therein lies the answer to Kutuzov's perceived reticence and indifference. Repeatedly mocked and humiliated, he was consigned to handling the mundane issues of supplies (and incompetent commissars), unit deployment and discipline. He haplessly witnessed the unfolding of a planning disaster whose architects were men half his age and possessing little of his experience or foresight.[26]

Ignoring Kutuzov's advice, Emperor Alexander listened instead to his Austrian allies who, in the words of one diplomat, 'took over the control of the war, did everything their way … and reserved the right to draft the plans.'[27] The most influential of these was *Generalmajor* Franz von Weyrother, who had assumed the position of the chief of staff of the Austro-Russian army.[28] A fortuitous series of events placed this 50-year old officer – 'the very opposite of Kutuzov,' as one Austrian historian described him[29] – in such a powerful position. Born in Vienna, Weyrother had served in the Austrian army for the better part of 30 years. After Austria became embroiled in the War of the First Coalition, he served as a staff officer first in the Rhineland and then Italy, gradually advancing through the ranks but never really distinguishing himself. At least not in a positive way. His plan for the Austrian offensive against a young Bonaparte led to a divided and disjointed advance of the Austrian army and a crushing defeat at Rivoli in January 1797. His fortunes somewhat recovered during *Generalissimo* Suvorov's campaign in Italy, which earned Weyrother promotion to *oberst*. However, many Russian officers, including Bagration and Miloradovich, were convinced that Weyrother's ineptitude and misconduct cost them so dearly during the crossing of the Alps in the autumn of 1799.[30] The new campaign against France in 1800 confirmed Weyrother's liabilities. Sent to the Rhineland, he drafted a

24 Langeron, *Mémoires*, p.290.

25 I. Fedyukin (ed.), *Zapiski* (Moscow: Novoe literaturnoe obozrenie, 1997), pp.168–169.

26 Kutuzov's numerous letters and orders are in the Lithuanian State Historical Archives: f. 378, op. 13, delos. 213 (part 1), 285 and 312. A handful of these documents has been published in Liubomir Beskrovnyi (ed.), *M.I. Kutuzov: Sbornik dokumentov* (Moscow: Voenizdat, 1950), vol.II, pp.189–198.

27 Joseph de Maistre to King Victor Emmanuel I of Sardinia, 19/31 January 1806, in *Russkii arkhiv* 6 (1871), p.73.

28 Toll, *Denkwürdigkeiten*, vol.I, p.141.

29 Clemens d'Elpidio Janetschek, *Die Schlacht bei Austerlitz: 2. December 1805* (Brunn: Päpstliche Benedictiner-Buchdruckerei, 1898), p.70.

30 For interesting details on Weyrother's role and the continued infighting between Austrian officers see letters written by British master spy William Wickham in *The Correspondence of the Right Honourable William Wickham* (London: Richard Bentley, 1870), vol.II, pp.260, 270–271, 278, 306–308, 323, 391. For a critical discussion see Otto Hartmann, *Der Antheil der Russen am Feldzug von 1799 in der Schweiz: Ein Beitrag zur Geschichte dieses Feldzugs und zyr Kritik seiner Geschichtschreiber* (Zurich: A. Munk, 1892), pp.84–88, 138, 161, 168.

convoluted plan for an offensive against the French that led to yet another Austrian debacle, this time at Hohenlinden, effectively ending Austria's involvement in the War of the Second Coalition.

Weyrother nonetheless continued to enjoy support and protection at the Habsburg court, which employed him during the War of the Third Coalition in 1805. Promoted to *generalmajor*, he was assigned to the Army of Podolsk, where he served as a quartermaster until the death of Johan Heinrich von Schmitt, Kutuzov's chief of staff, at the battle of Krems-Durrenstein on 11 November, 1805. Despite lacking Schmitt's talent and experience, Weyrother was appointed as his replacement. While his appointment might look baffling, given that so many Russian officers remembered his ineptitude, he clearly possessed the necessary people skills, convincing the Kaiser that his prior service with the Russians had actually made him better aware of how to work with them. Weyrother, also gained Emperor Alexander's confidence in short period of time.[31] 'He won the Russians over by enduring their arrogance and flattering their vanity,' scoffed a nineteenth century German military historian. 'In many respects he resembled Mack, being like him a learned *doctrinär* who came up with plans without the necessary consideration of real circumstances.'[32] However, what mattered most was that the Austrian's call for an offensive appealed to Alexander who, in the words of an eyewitness, 'seemed to be confident of a victory that would place him one stroke above the man who as yet had no equal, if any rival, on the battlefield.'[33]

On 24 November, the Allies made the decision to leave Olmutz and advance toward Brunn, where they intended to roll Napoleon's right flank, isolate him from Vienna and the logistical lines, and then push him into the mountains of Bohemia, where they would destroy him.[34] The Allied sovereigns ordered the army to depart 'as if on the parade grounds,' with ranks and files lined up and marching in step.[35]

* * *

31 Toll, *Denkwürdigkeiten*, vol.I, p.141. In the eyes of Langeron, Weyrother was 'callous, rude, insolent, convinced of his own merit and carrying self-esteem to the most disturbing excess. He had all the faults of an upstart…' Langeron, *Journal inédit de la campagne de 1805*, p.28.

32 Wilhelm Rustow, *Der Krieg von 1805 in Deutschland und Italien* (Frauenfeld: Verlags-Comptoir, 1853), p.325; Czartoryski, *Memoirs*, vol.II, p.102. A similar characterisation in Toll, *Denkwürdigkeiten*, vol.I, p.141.

33 Langeron, *Journal inédit de la campagne de 1805*, p.28; Collectif (ed.), *Austerlitz raconté par les Témoins de la Bataille des Trois Empereurs* (Geneva: Éditions de Crémille, 1969), p.147.

34 Rustow, *Der Krieg von 1805*, p.336; Toll, *Denkwürdigkeiten*, vol.I, p.144. Kutuzov made arrangements to supply the army with two-days' worth of provisions – 'at least three pounds of meat per soldier, and, similarly, an appropriate ration of bread,' – on November 24–25 in preparations for the army's departure on the 26th. However, he was unable to get sufficient supplies and the departure date was therefore postponed by a day. See Kutuzov's orders of November 24–26 in Lithuanian State Historical Archives: f. 378, op. 13, d. 285 l.78; Ibid., d. 311, 272b; Kutuzov to Lieven, 13/25 November 1805, in *M.I. Kutuzov: Sbornik dokumentov*, vol.II, p.199.

35 Toll, *Denkwürdigkeiten*, vol.I, pp.144–145.

Napoleon understood perfectly well the dangerous situation he was in. Throughout the past three months of the campaign one of his most exasperating problems had been Kutuzov, whose strategy of avoiding pitched battles in favour of a war of attrition and indirection had again and again frustrated the French emperor. After destroying the Austrian army at Ulm, Napoleon clearly expected to defeat the Russians in a series of quick strikes and enveloping manoeuvres, all of which Kutuzov had thwarted.

After establishing his headquarters at Brunn, Napoleon observed with growing anxiety the rapidly changing situation on the continent. Some 400 miles away from Paris, he was confronted with the myriad challenges of managing an empire and commanding an army scattered over a vast area in Germany and Italy. The Grande Armée was fatigued by the strenuous marches from the Atlantic coast to the heart of Moravia; strategic consumption and battles against the Austrians and Russians had significantly reduced its overall numbers and now it had about a third of the army's original strength. Confounding these problems, he received news of the Battle of Trafalgar, where on 21 October, 1805, the British Royal Navy destroyed much of the French fleet.[36]

Napoleon was conscious that a Russian force was threatening the electorate of Hanover while a British expedition had landed at Stade in the Hanoverian dominion. The Swedes were ready to advance toward the Elbe, the Prussians to Franconia and additional Prussian forces were gathering in Silesia to bring immediate succour to the Austro-Russian army. The arrival of the Prussian envoy at the French headquarters with the ultimatum of Prussia, as agreed on in the Treaty of Potsdam, underscored how fraught with danger the situation had become for the French. So long the Allies remained on the defensive, as Kutuzov had urged, Napoleon could not hope to obtain a quick military resolution to the war, and each passing day worsened his situation.[37]

Napoleon therefore avidly sought a diplomatic way out of this conundrum while he could still speak from position of relative strength. 'I wish to make peace promptly' he told his foreign minister, instructing him to offer moderate conditions to the Austrians. He then dispatched one of his trusted generals, *Général de division* Anne-Jean-Marie-René Savary, to the Allies, ostensibly to deliver a complimentary letter to Emperor Alexander but in reality, 'to take notice of what was going on around him' and to probe for any diplomatic openings.[38]

Informed of the arrival of the French envoy at the Cossack outposts, Kutuzov made sure Savary could not observe much by delaying his arrival until after sunset. 'Kutuzov was lodged in the suburbs of Olmutz,' Savary wrote Napoleon. 'Everything was packing at his house and I saw plainly that he was preparing to follow the movement of his army.' Kutuzov told the Frenchman that Emperor Alexander was sound asleep in the fortress of Olmutz and offered to personally deliver Napoleon's missive

36 Philippe-Paul comte de Ségur, *Histoire et mémoires* (Paris: Firmin Didot Frères, 1873), vol.II, pp.445–446.

37 Rustow, *Der Krieg von 1805*, pp.345–346.

38 Claude-François Baron de Méneval, *Memoirs illustrating the history of Napoleon from 1802 to 1815* (New York: D. Appleton and Company, 1894,) vol.I, p.399.

in due time. However, the Frenchman declined, insisting that he had orders to deliver it himself. He thus waited for a considerable amount of time in an anteroom among a number of young Russian officers. Savary, a shrewd man who would soon become Napoleon's minister of police, took the opportunity to converse with these officers, whom he found ardently declaiming the ambition of the French emperor and full of confidence of their success in combat. He took note that 'all the Russian youth of the highest quality were eager for battle … They all made much the same kind of calculations as the maid with her pail of milk.'

Around 10 o'clock in the morning, a commotion in the street announced the Russian emperor's approach. Alexander stopped in front of Kutuzov's house and alighted to talk to the French envoy, who seemed smitten by the Russian ruler. 'Nature had done much for him, and it would have been difficult to find a model so perfect and so graceful,' Savary later observed. The czar –who spoke 'the French language in all its purity, without foreign accent and always using its elegant academic expressions'– assured Savary of his good will towards France and his respect for Napoleon. 'He has long been the object of my admiration,' the Emperor told him. 'I have no wish to be his enemy, any more than that of France.' And yet here they were in the fields of Moravia fighting a war. Alexander pointed out that it was Napoleon's growing imperial ambitions that caused him to embark on this path. France had pursued policies that had given European powers 'a just cause of disquietude for their independence,' he told Savary. 'You are already a nation so strong of yourselves, by your union under the same laws, by the uniformity of your habits and your language, that you naturally inspire terror. What need have you to be continually aggrandizing yourselves?'[39]

At the close of the conversation Alexander presented Savary with a written reply to Napoleon's letter – addressed not to the Emperor of the French but to the Head of the French government – and ordered to have him escorted back to the advanced posts.[40] Savary was unable to achieve what Napoleon had wanted but his mission was not a complete failure, producing a wealth of valuable information on the prevailing mood at the allied headquarters and the mindset of Emperor Alexander. Among other things Napoleon learned that the prudent Kutuzov was being sidelined and that Alexander was 'surrounded by twenty scamps' who pushed him to attack. He greeted the news of the Allied advance with great joy, confident that these scamps would bring about Alexander's downfall, particularly now that the Russians no longer had 'a first rate general' in charge. They would assume that the French supply and communication lines ran through Vienna and would therefore seek to

39 Anne-Jean-Marie-René Savary, *Mémoires du duc de Rovigo écrits de sa main, pour servia à l'histoire de l'Empereur Napoleon* (Paris: Colburn, 1828), vol.I, Part 2, pp.113–123.

40 It is noteworthy that, in his letter, Napoleon deliberately tried to cultivate the Allied perception of his weakness by addressing the czar as 'Sire' rather than 'Mon frère' as it was customary for royal sovereigns and he had been doing in correspondence with the rulers of Bavaria and Wurttemberg. He knew well that such details would not go unnoticed at the Allied camp. See Michel Kerautret and Gabriel Madec (eds), *Correspondance Générale* (Paris: Fayard, 2008), vol.V, pp.866, 874–875.

disrupt them.[41] This was exactly what Napoleon hoped the Allies would do. He was now resolved to launch a decisive counterstroke.[42]

* * *

On 27 November, the Allied army had left its encampment and marched in five columns southward.[43] Kutuzov must have been deeply frustrated, for he had voiced his objections at the councils of war on 24 and 27 November and had failed to convince the Emperors to reconsider strategy. Now the army was on the move, though the troops still lacked essential supplies despite his best efforts to secure at least two-days' worth of provisions. Kutuzov lamented the fact that the army had 'only half a day's worth of bread' which caused misery among his soldiers and delayed the start of the offensive by a whole day.[44]

Rarely had a commander-in-chief of an army wielded so little command as Kutuzov in November 1805. Once the Allied offensive had commenced, he primary dealt with matters of transports and supplies; none of his letters discuss planning or wider strategy, a clear sign of the extent to which he had been side-lined. The Allied plan of operations was, in fact, the creation of Weyrother. It was complex and dense, with dispositions so puzzling that, when the hour of advance came, many column commanders had not yet sufficiently understood their orders, a portent of the problems to come.[45] *General-leitenant* Langeron, leading one of the columns, fumed that his men had to march 'over very bad roads washed away by the autumnal rains... in very short days, with insufficient supplies and no way to distribute them.' Weyrother kept sending out new orders that further complicated matters. A Russian officer bewailed 'incredible confusion that reigned everywhere, with daily changes that had no place and no reason, not even a pretext.'[46]

41 Note A on Kutuzov's report in Anon., *Campagnes de la Grande Armée et de l'Armée d'Italie en l'an XIV* (1805) (Paris: Librairie Economique, 1806), p.96.

42 Napoleon to Frederick II, Elector of Wurttemberg, 5 December 1805, in Kerautret and Madec (eds), *Correspondance Générale*, vol.V, p.875; Ségur, *Histoire et mémoires*, vol. II, pp.446–447. Also see Jean Lambert Colin, 'Campagne de 1805 en Allemagne,' *Revue d'histoire 76* (1907), pp.61–68; Sokolov, *Bitva trekh imperatorov*, pp.422–423.

43 Kutuzov's Orders to the Army, 14–15/26–27 November 1805, Lithuanian State Historical Archives: f. 378, op. 13, d. 285, l. 75, 82; Disposition for the Offensive Operations of the Allied Forces, 14/26 November 1805, Lithuanian State Historical Archives: f. 378, op. 13, d. 213, part 1, l. 208-215. Also see A copy of the disposition at RGVIA, f. 846, op. 16, d. 3174, l. 13-18b; General Uvarov's documents in Ibid., f. 846, op. 16, d. 3154, l.1-1b; Langeron, *Journal inedit de la campagne de 1805*, p.31; Rustow, *Der Krieg von 1805*, pp.348–349; Mikhailovskii-Danilevskii, *Opisanie pervoi voiny... v 1805 godu* (St Petersburg: Tip. Shtaba Otdel'nago Korpusa Vnutrennei Strazhi, 1844), pp.159–161.

44 The offensive was planned for 26 November but was postponed because the army lacked sufficient supplies and additional time was needed to translated dispositions. Kutuzov to Lieven, 13/25 November 1805, in *M.I. Kutuzov: Sbornik dokumentov*, vol.II, p.199. Also see Stutterheim, *La Bataille d'Austerlitz*, p.35.

45 Stutterheim, *La Bataille d'Austerlitz*, p.35.

46 Yermolov, *The Czar's General*, p.56; Langeron, *Journal inedit de la campagne de 1805*, pp.31–32.

Bagration, newly promoted to a *general-leitenant*, spearheaded the Allied movement from Olmutz to Wischau, where his advance guard encountered French outposts on 28 November.[47] Emperor Alexander accompanied the vanguard and received his baptism by fire that day. At first, he found the sight of cavalry charges, the smell of gunpowder, and the din of battle exhilarating and cheered the Allied victory over the small French rearguard. His mood changed when he toured the aftermath of the battle and saw first-hand the carnage of war, the dead corpses strewn on the plain and the wounded men bleeding and begging for help. The sight made him so sick that he retired to the rear and refused to eat for the rest of the day.[48] As the French pulled back to Raussnitz, where a strong reserve awaited them, Bagration launched a forceful pursuit, engaged the enemy, and took possession of the town. 'Everything turned in favour of the arms of His Imperial Majesty,' reported Bagration with a clear sense of bravado.[49]

The Allied victories at Wischau and Raussnitz – partly orchestrated by Napoleon, who had intentionally deployed a small advance guard to bait the enemy – persuaded many at Allied headquarters that the French were indeed weak. Alexey Yermolov remembered that 'there was a rumour, which everyone believed, that the enemy was in full retreat.'[50] The Allies were increasingly convinced that Napoleon would not risk the fate of a battle in front of Brunn and would flee upon seeing the Allied army approaching. After the action at Wischau, 'this *hope* became the prevailing *opinion* at the headquarters,' remarked *Generalmajor* Stutterheim.[51] Like many of his comrades, Ivan Zhirkevich, a young artillery lieutenant, was euphoric after hearing the news of Bagration's victories. 'It seemed to us that we were going straight to Paris!'[52] The Allies thus resumed their advance high in spirits – and almost completely ignorant of their enemy's strength, location, or intentions.

In the last days of November Napoleon made another last-minute attempt to negotiate with Alexander. He instructed Savary to return to the Russian headquarters with an offer of an armistice and direct negotiations between emperors. On 29 November, Alexander was pleasantly surprised to see Savary presenting himself once again. He welcomed the offer to negotiate, which he read as a clear sign that Napoleon was in a weak position. He declined personal interview with the French

47 Disposition for Offensive towards Wischau, [not dated] circa 28 November 1805, RGVIA: f. 846 op. 16, d. 3174, l. 3-5.

48 Mikhailovskii-Danilevskii, *Opisanie pervoi voiny… v 1805 godu*, pp.160–161; Shil'der, *Alexander*, vol.II, p.135.

49 Bagration to Kutuzov, 16/28 November 1805, Lithuanian State Historical Archives: f. 378, op. 13, d. 213, part 1, l. 491-492.

50 Yermolov, *The Czar's General*, p.57.

51 Stutterheim, *La Bataille d'Austerlitz*, p.44. A well-informed participant later pointed out that 'it was here that Emperor Alexander and his advisers were in fault. They imagined that Napoleon was in a dangerous position, and that he was on the point of retreating. The French outposts had an appearance of hesitation and timidity which nourished these illusions, and reports came at every moment from our outposts announcing an imminent movement of the French army to the rear.' Czartoryski, *Memoirs*, vol.II, pp.104–105. See also Rustow, *Der Krieg von 1805*, pp.349–350.

52 Ivan Zhirkevich, 'Zapiski Ivana Stepanovicha Zhirkevicha, 1789-1848,' in *Russkaya starina* 2 (1874): p.218.

leader, claiming a prior 'appointment with the Emperor of Germany,' but sent his aide-de-camp, Prince Dolgorukov to the French camp.[53]

Napoleon took care to not give the Russian envoy the same opportunity to make observations that Savary had had in the Allied camp. He greeted the prince at the entrance to the French cantonments, where Dolgorukov was allowed to see only what Napoleon wanted him to witness: weary French troops falling back on all points, crowded, timid and seemingly disheartened. The French emperor was annoyed that so young a man should be sent on such an important mission. And his irritation only grew when the Russian presented the terms. The czar would consider negotiating peace only if the French withdrew from all conquered territories, Dolgorukov haughtily declared. Napoleon was expected to give up Belgium, Holland, and Switzerland and surrender the 'Iron Crown' of Lombardy (Italy). Taken aback by the sheer arrogance of such demands, Napoleon snapped that he would yield nothing, not even if the Russians were encamped on the heights of Montmartre. 'The Emperor will never desert his allies,' retorted Dolgorukov, to which Napoleon replied, according to Savary's memoirs, 'Then we must fight.'[54] The meeting ended in just 15 minutes. Napoleon later confided to the elector of Wurttemberg that he had been annoyed by this Russian 'coxcomb,' who had spoken to him 'as he would speak to a boyar whom he was about to send to Siberia' He said the young Dolgorukov 'mistook my moderation for fear, an error that I encouraged for military reasons and which brought about the decisive battle.'[55]

Dolgorukov returned to the Allied headquarters convinced that the French army was in a pitiable state and that Napoleon was weak and easy to defeat. 'He trembled of fear in front of me,' Dolgorukov said of Napoleon.' Even our advance guard would be sufficient to defeat him.'[56] Later that evening a council of war was convened. Dolgorukov reported on his meeting with Napoleon and urged attacking at once. Kutuzov objected. Time was on the side of Allies, he pointed out. He advised the Emperor to postpone offensive and wait for reinforcements. Dolgorukov apparently sniggered hearing this. 'What are you laughing at, young man?' Kutuzov snarled at him. 'Maybe you think that I am a coward and fear a battle? My age and wounds speak for themselves.' Witnesses recalled that he stormed out of the meeting.[57] Dolgorukov, noting that the czar seemed deep in thought, told him, 'If Your Majesty retreats, Napoleon will consider all of us cowards.' Alexander responded, 'Cowards? Then, it is better for us to die.'[58] At midnight, the army was ordered to proceed to the

53 Savary, *Mémoires,* vol.I, Part 2, pp.110–124. Also see Modest Bogdanovich, *Istoriya tsarstvovaniya imperatora Aleksandra I i Rossii v ego vremya* (St Petersburg: Tip. F. Sushinskogo, 1869), vol.II, pp.46–47, 50–52.

54 Savary, *Mémoires,* vol.I, Part 2, pp.127–128; Ségur, *Histoire et mémoires,* vol.II, pp.448–449; Mikhailovskii-Danilevskii, *Opisanie pervoi voiny... v 1805 godu,* pp.163–165.

55 Napoleon to Frederick II, Elector of Wurttemberg, 5 December 1805, in Kerautret and Madec (eds), *Correspondance Générale,* vol.V, p.875.

56 Langeron, *Journal inedit de la campagne de 1805,* p.30.

57 Sergey Glinka, *Zapiski Sergeya Nikolayevicha Glinki* (St Petersburg: Russkaya starina, 1895), p.152.

58 Additional Bulletin, 31 December 1805, 'Correspondence of Olry', in *Istoricheskii Vestnik,* 147 (1917): pp.460–461. Olry mentions that Prince Bagration, who, in the words of one

small village of Austerlitz (Slavkov u Brna), 15 miles east of Brunn. Underscoring the extent to which Kutuzov was detached from command, the new order did not even bear his signature.[59]

The meeting with the Russian envoy convinced Napoleon that he could not hope to reach an understanding with the czar. He shifted his focus to a military resolution, for which eventuality he had been preparing for some time. He had carefully observed the enemy movements. *Maréchaux* Murat, Lannes, and Soult received orders to fall back to Brunn while keeping a dense cavalry screen; Bernadotte was recalled from Bohemia, while Davout was told to come up with all imaginable haste from Vienna. *Maréchal* Mortier was left behind with his corps – still recovering from drubbing it received at Durrenstein – to secure Vienna. In this way Napoleon could expect to have 56,000 within 24 hours of the Allied offensive, 70,000 within two days, 80,000 in three days and 90,000 by the fourth day.[60] Time was clearly of the essence.

The Allies showed no sense of urgency. Their movements were slow and vacillating, taking two days to cover the 15 miles separating Wischau from Austerlitz. *Generalmajor* Stutterheim, not privy to the internal dynamics of the Allied headquarters, blamed Kutuzov for giving confusing marching orders. He was right about the confounding movements on 29–30 November, but wrong about the culprit – Kutuzov had no power to change the disposition that was drafted by Weyrother and approved by the czar and the kaiser. Carl Friedrich von Toll, serving in the Russian headquarters, had a much better view of the situation. He noted that 'the very peculiar strategic manoeuvres performed under Weyrother's direction' had squandered valuable time.[61] Instead of building on the success gained at Wischau and Raussnitz, the Allies dithered, shifting their forces several miles to the left and reshuffling their columns.[62] 'We made short marches,' described a Russian officer, 'but they were so confusing that we rarely completed them before ten o'clock in the evening or even midnight because the columns always crossed each other's path, in some cases as much as several times, and wasted time waiting for others.'[63]

The mishandling of the advance gave Napoleon an opportunity. He spent the whole of these days on horseback, receiving a constant stream of reports about the enemy's movements. He grasped the significance of the Allied sluggishness. Had they attacked on 30 November or even 1 December, the battle would have turned out very differently, given that Napoleon's reinforcements would not have arrived in time. The delays gave him time to refine his plans. He increasingly focused his attention on the Pratzen plateau – an almost two-mile-long ridge that overlooked the wide rolling plains between Austerlitz and Brunn. He decided to allow the Allies

---

diplomat, 'loved to fish in murky waters,' and was present at the meeting.

59 Disposition for the Offensive to Austerlitz, 12:00 a.m., 18/30 November 1805, Lithuanian State Historical Archives: f. 378, op. 13, d. 213, part 1, l. 200. The order was issued by Duty General Inzov.

60 Michel de Lombarès, "Devant Austerlitz,' sur les traces de la pensée de l'Empereur,' *Revue Historique de l'Armée*, 3 (1947): pp.41–43.

61 Toll, *Denkwürdigkeiten*, vol.I, p.148.

62 Langeron, *Journal inedit de la campagne de 1805*, p.32.

63 Yermolov, *The Czar's General*, p.56.

to occupy this position in order to convince them of his weakness and then intended to lure them into attacking his right wing. He correctly assumed that in attempting such a manoeuvre the Allies would shift most of their forces to the left, weakening their centre to reinforce their main attack around the villages of Telnitz and Sokolnitz in the south. Two-thirds of the French army, meanwhile would be in the north, concealed by the regular early morning fog and ready to break through the weakened Allied right flank and centre with a decisive assault, and conducting an envelopment to cut their line of retreat.[64] Napoleon had earlier told his generals by holding the Pratzen heights, he would be assured of 'an ordinary battle' but that was not what he wanted. He chose to abandon the heights to the enemy and deliberately expose his right wing back. If the Allies dared to descend from the heights in an attempt to envelop his flank, 'they will surely be beaten, without a hope of success!'[65] As the month of December dawned, Napoleon, holding true to his dictum to 'never interfere with an enemy while he was making a mistake,' watched the dark and massy columns of the Allied troops moving into position on the Pratzen plateau, clearly intending to turn his right flank. This was precisely what he had hoped for.[66]

* * *

On 1 December, the Russians and Austrians – in large numbers but still lacking essential supplies[67] – passed through the village of Austerlitz and climbed the slopes to the Pratzen plateau. That the French had surrendered such crucial ground added to the impression of weakness that Napoleon so carefully cultivated. Many in the Allied headquarters drew contrast between his bold operations against the Austrians at the start of the war and the seemingly more subdued and defensive posturing now. By nightfall, some 80,000 Russian and Austrian troops had taken up their positions on the rolling plains west of Austerlitz. The first three columns – of Generals Dokhturov, Langeron, and Ignacy Prszebyszewski – reached the Pratzen plateau. The fourth, under Austrian *Feldzeugmeister* Johann Karl von Kolovrat-Krakowsky, was behind them, while the main cavalry force, designated as the fifth column and commanded by Prince Liechtenstein, halted even farther to the rear. Bagration, still in charge of the advance guard, bivouacked his forces around Posoritz and formed the extreme right flank of the Allied position. The Russian Imperial Guard was

64 For discussion of Napoleon's evolving plan of battle see Colin, 'La Campagne de 1805 en Allemagne,' *Revue d'histoire* 77 (1907): pp.303–309; Robert Goetz, *1805. Austerlitz. Napoleon and the Destruction of the Third Coalition* (London: Greenhill Books, 2005), pp.92–96, 106–110, 112–113, 117–118; Sokolov, *Bitva trekh imperatorov*, pp.446–449; Ian Castle, *Austerlitz: Napoleon and The Eagles of Europe* (Barnsley: Pen&Sword, 2005), chapter 13.

65 Ségur, *Histoire et Mémoires*, vol.II, pp.451–452.

66 Colin, 'La Campagne de 1805 en Allemagne,' pp.300–302.

67 'My men are suffering greatly, for it is already second day that they do not have meat and only a little of bread. Horses remain without forage.' reported Bagration to Kutuzov on November 30. Lithuanian State Historical Archives: f. 378, op. 13, d. 213, part 1, l. 535.

positioned in front of Austerlitz itself. Kutuzov and the army headquarters were lodged at the nearby village of Křižanovice.[68]

There was no moon the night of 2 December and the thick fog made movement difficult.[69] Around midnight Prince Peter Volkonskii summoned all column commanders to the council of war held in the large drawing room of a local nobleman's house, where the Allied headquarters was set up. Here gathered Kutuzov, Weyrother, and all but one column commanders – Bagration sent word that he could not arrive in time. Kutuzov welcomed the officers and curtly told them that they would attack the current enemy positions at 7:00 a.m. the following morning.[70] Weyrother then took over the council. Because he had previously gone over the terrain on several occasions, he had already drafted a plan, which Emperor Alexander had approved, and now presented it to senior Allied officers.[71] Reading rapidly and indistinctly, Weyrother ran through a litany of unfamiliar geographic names and manoeuvres, but it was at least clear that he envisioned three columns – over 40,000 men led by Dokhturov, Langeron, and Ignacy Przybyszewski, under overall command of Buxhöwden – descending from the Pratzen Heights to launch a flanking manoeuvre across the Goldbach stream to overwhelm the weak French right flank and drive it northward, severing Napoleon's line of retreat to Vienna. As this attack was underway, additional forces – the fourth and fifth columns – would come down the plateau to support the left-wing columns, while Prince Bagration, in charge of the advance guard and forming the Allied right flank, would serve as a pivot around which the rest of army would swivel.[72]

Standing in front of a large and detailed map, Weyrother read 'his dispositions in a loud tone and with a boasting air, which announced in him the intimate persuasion of his own merit and that of our incompetence,' remembered a Russian participant. The Austrian 'resembled a form-master in a high-school reading a lesson to the young pupils,' griped *General-leitenant* Langeron.[73] The officers struggled to make sense of the complex dispositions; their confidence in Weyrother, as shaky as it already was, was further undercut when Austrian *Oberst* Ferdinand Bubna von Littitz, upon hearing Weyrother bragging that that he knew the terrain around Austerlitz very

68 Disposition for the Offensive to Austerlitz, [not dated] circa 30 November 1805, RGVIA: f. 846 op. 16, d. 3174, l. 48-49; Disposition for Offensive to Menin and Sokolnice, [not dated] circa 1 December 1805, RGVIA: f. 846 op. 16, d. 3174, l. 47-47b. Also see Mikhailovskii-Danilevskii, *Opisanie pervoi voiny... v 1805 godu,* pp.165–170; Rustow, *Der Krieg von 1805,* pp.356–359; Langeron, *Journal inédit de la campagne de 1805*, p.41; Colin, 'La Campagne de 1805 en Allemagne,' p.291; Michel de Lombarès, 'Devant Austerlitz, sur les traces de la pensée de l'Empereur,' *Revue Historique de l'Armée* 3 (1947): p.47.

69 Jean-Baptiste-Antoine-Marcelin Baron de Marbot, trans. Arthur J. Butler, *The Memoirs of Baron de Marbot, Late Lieutenant General in the French Army* (New York: Longmans, 1903), vol.I, p.160.

70 Mikhailovskii-Danilevskii, *Opisanie pervoi voiny... v 1805 godu,* p.174.

71 Czartoryski, *Memoirs*, p.106.

72 Disposition for Attack, [not dated] circa 2 December 1805, RGVIA: f. 846 op. 16, d. 3117/1, ll. 50-53. Also see, Disposition for Attack on the Enemy Position Behind Slapanitz and Sokolnitz on 20 November [2 December] 1805, RGVIA: f. 846, op. 16, d. 3113, l. 1-3; Stutterheim, *La Bataille d'Austerlitz*, pp.67–75.

73 Langeron, *Journal inedit de la campagne de 1805*, pp.33–34.

well because he had been on maneuverers there, remarked, 'Let's hope you will not make the same mistakes as at last year's manoeuvres.'[74] Dokhturov (who days earlier in a letter to his wife had beseeched 'the Almighty of only one thing – to get me out of here alive'[75]) remained taciturn throughout the meeting, stooping over the outspread map, and diligently examining the dispositions. According to Langeron, Buxhöwden seemed not to listen or understand a word of what Weyrother was saying; Miloradovich, unusually sombre and subdued, remained silent. Kutuzov sat quietly in a low armchair. He had already seen Weyrother's plan and disapproved of it. Some had overheard him yelling, 'I cannot consent to this. This is Napoleon's plan!'[76] Others heard him tell Prince Peter Volkonskii that he did not want to fight and had been forced to sign off on the plan, though he was convinced that it 'will not be to our benefit.' He felt had had no choice except to comply.[77] Now he sat with his eyes closed, tired of voicing his opposition when 'his advice was certainly not listened to,' as Czartoryski ruefully observed.[78] Weyrother's droning lulled him into a sleep. The sight, which was subsequently described in virtually every book written on Austerlitz – with various degrees of drama[79] – reflected the depth of Kutuzov's misery and resignation.

The basic idea of turning an enemy flank was simple and appropriate. Weyrother's strategy, however, was based on limited information, made too many false assumptions and conveyed orders in such convoluted manner that six weeks after the battle was over Kaiser Francis admitted to the Russian ambassador, 'You might be surprised to hear that even at this time, I still do not yet comprehend this battle plan.'[80] Weyrother treated Napoleon in a remarkably cavalier fashion, which prompted a contemporary Prussian military thinker to observe that 'the Allies adopted the plan of action against an enemy army they had not seen yet, assumed it was in the

74 Mikhailovskii-Danilevskii, *Opisanie pervoi voiny... v 1805 godu*, p.175.
75 Dmitri Dokhturov to his wife, in *Russkii arkhiv* 1(1874), p.1904.
76 Glinka, *Zapiski*, p.153.
77 Val'kovich and A. Kapitonov (ed.), *Fel'dmarshal Kutuzov: dokumenty, dnevniki, vospominaniya*, p.316.
78 Czartoryski, *Memoirs*, p.106.
79 French historian Claude Manceron imagined the following scene, almost all of it fictional: 'There he was, lying rather than sitting in a huge portable armchair, hollowed out by his heavy frame, which accompanied him everywhere... To his left, dispatched were piled on a great oak table, where he tolerated only one candlestick with three candles. He did not want it to be seen that he was asleep. He was drunk. He usually overcame his annoyance with some girls: he had three in his baggage-train and would undoubtedly have sent for them all together, in accordance with the habits attributed to him for ten years on great occasions, if his wagons had not remained near Olmutz. Fortunately, his personal berlin contained immediate relief: the armchair, the fur-lined coat for his knees, the icon of the Virgin of Kazan, and a supply of highly fortified Crimean wine, a sort of liqueur, two bottles of which had been poured out for him before supper. He reacted by giving sketchy salutes to the messengers who came to bring him news, and smiled and grunted without anyone knowing why or what he was trying to say.' *Austerlitz: The Story of a Battle*, translated by George Unwin (London: George Allen & Unwin, 1966), p.180
80 Count Razumovskii's letter of 22 January 1806, cited in Mikhailovskii-Danilevskii, *Opisanie pervoi voiny... v 1805 godu*, p.212.

positions it never occupied, and expected it to remain as idle as the border posts.'[81] The topography of the battlefield was not fully taken into account and neither were the difficulties of the terrain dotted with vineyards, ditches, garden walls, and other obstacles – through which the Austro-Russian left wing had to move.[82] The reserve force, comprising of the Russian Imperial Guard under Emperor Alexander's brother Grand Duke Constantine, was both inadequate and badly situated behind the Pratzen heights.[83] Weyrother, although in charge of an army numerically superior to Napoleon's, had divided the Allied force into what were practically three disconnected sections, of which two – the right flank and centre – were too weak to contain any offensive movement by the enemy. The possibility of counterattack was not even contemplated.

When Weyrother finished his 'peroration,' Langeron, if we are to believe his own claims, was the only one to question the Austrian's assumptions. 'All this sounds good,' he supposedly asked, 'but what will we do if the enemy attacks us?' Weyrother scoffed in response. Had he not just explained that Napoleon was weak and vulnerable? Why otherwise would he have abandoned the Pratzen heights? Given that the French had not already attacked, it was obvious that they were keen on avoiding battle. The Allies could not afford 'allowing so good an opportunity to escape of destroying the French army and dealing Napoleon a decisive and fatal blow.'[84] As the two officers began to debate, Kutuzov awakened from his slumber and cast a weary look at the assembled generals, reminding them of the lateness of the hour and urging them to get some rest before the battle.

The council ended around three o'clock in the morning. Kutuzov felt compelled to make a final effort to change Emperor Alexander's mind. Having been previously rebuffed and knowing that the czar would not listen to him, he went to *Oberhofmarschall* Nikolai Tolstoy who enjoyed Alexander's confidence. 'His Majesty intends to fight a battle, but you must dissuade him from it, because we are almost certain to lose the battle tomorrow,' Kutuzov candidly told him, according to Toll. But 'the hot-tempered' Tolstoy 'got annoyed' at being awakened so late at night and snapped, 'My function is to dabble with sauces and roasts, yours is war, so deal with it.'[85] Kutuzov returned to the headquarters where he watched as the adjutants made copies of the disposition, which ran for several closely written sheets. They struggled to make sense of the complicated German narrative, which many Russian regimental commanders could not read. In their rush to complete a translation, the

81 Adam Dietrich Heinrich Bulow, *Der Feldzug von 1805 militärisch-politisch betrachtet von dem Verfasser des Geistes des neuern Kriegssystems* (Leipzig: privately published, 1806), vol.II, pp.65–66.

82 For interesting discussion see Toll, *Denkwürdigkeiten*, vol.I, pp.152–153.

83 For detailed criticism see Rustow, *Der Krieg von 1805*, pp.360–363.

84 Langeron, *Journal inedit de la campagne de 1805*, pp.33–34; Czartoryski, *Memoirs*, p.105. Czartoryski goes to note that 'everything in the French army seemed to announce a resolution to attempt a retreat. It was therefore decided to advance, in order to take advantage of this disposition of the enemy.' Also see Toll, *Denkwürdigkeiten*, vol.I, pp.155–156.

85 Joseph de Maistre to Chevalier de Rossi, 3 January 1807, in *Oeuvres complètes de J. de Maistre*, vol.X, p.291. Also see *Russkii arkhiv*, 6 (1871), p.91.

officers misread or misinterpreted some passages, so that, according to some, the Russian version was even more confusing.[86]

Not until around six o'clock in the morning – an hour before the scheduled attack – were the orders sent to the units scattered across the vast battlefield. There was hardly enough time for local commanders to read and understand what was expected of them. Young artillery officer Alexei Yermolov recalled seeing 'a disposition written on several sheets of paper, crowded with difficult names of villages, lakes, streams and distances and heights. We were not permitted to make a copy because it had to be read by a good many other commanders and there were only a few copies available. I must confess that when I heard it read out, I understood very little of what was intended. The only thing I comprehended was that we were to attack in the morning.'[87] Some commanders did not even receive orders and remained in total ignorance of the plan. When Alexander visited the fourth column shortly before the sunrise, he discovered that some units were still resting. 'Are your muskets loaded?' the czar asked *General-major* Berg, who commanded the Malorossiiskii Grenadier Regiment. Surprised by this question, Berg replied that they were not, as he had not yet received any instructions. Only after Alexander personally ordered him did Berg learn that the battle was about to commence. Three miles to the north, Prince Bagration was among the last to receive a copy of the disposition and, after quickly perusing it, and, according to Mikhailovskii-Danilevskii, gloomily told his Austrian colleagues, 'We will be defeated tomorrow.'[88]

Select Bibliography

Anon., *Campagnes de la Grande Armée et de l'Armée d'Italie en l'an XIV (1805)* (Paris: Librairie Economique, 1806)

Bailleu, Paul (ed.), *Briefwechsel könig Friedrich Wilhelm's III und der königin Luise mit kaiser Alexander I* (Leipzig: S. Hirzel, 1900)

Bernhardi, Theodor von (ed.), *Denkwürdigkeiten aus dem Leben des Kaiserl. russ. Generals von der der Infanterie Carl Friedrich Grafen von Toll* (Leipzig: Otto Wigand, 1856)

Beskrovnyi, Liubomir (ed.), *M.I. Kutuzov: Sbornik dokumentov* (Moscow: Voenizdat, 1950)

Bogdanovich, Modest, *Istoriya tsarstvovaniya imperatora Aleksandra I i Rossii v ego vremya* (St Petersburg: Tip. F. Sushinskogo, 1869)

86 Toll, *Denkwürdigkeiten*, vol.I, p.156.

87 Yermolov, *The Czar's General*, p.57; Langeron, *Journal inedit de la campagne de 1805*, pp.33–34; Colin, 'Campagne de 1805 en Allemagne,' pp.324–325; Mikhailovskii-Danilevskii, *Opisanie pervoi voiny… v 1805 godu*, p.175; Shil'der, *Alexander*, vol.II, p.138.

88 Mikhailovskii-Danilevskii, *Opisanie pervoi voiny… v 1805 godu*, p.196. For Bagration's criticism of the plan see Toll, *Denkwürdigkeiten*, vol.I, p.157. Prince Czartoryski described an interesting incident: 'Someone remarked that the following day [2 December] was Monday, a day regarded as unlucky in Russia. As the Emperor was passing over a grassy mound his horse slipped and fell, and he was thrown out of the saddle. Although the accident was not serious, it was regarded by some people as a bad omen.' Czartoryski, *Memoirs*, p.106.

Butovskii, I, *Pervaya voina imperatora Aleksandra I s Napoleonom I v 1805 godu* (St Petersburg: Voennaya tipografiya, 1858)

Castle, Ian, *Austerlitz: Napoleon and The Eagles of Europe* (Barnsley: Pen & Sword, 2005)

Colin, Jean Lambert, 'Campagne de 1805 en Allemagne,' *Revue d'histoire* 76 (1907), pp.53–105; 77 (1907), pp.272–325

Collectif (ed.), *Austerlitz raconté par les Témoins de la Bataille des Trois Empereurs* (Geneva: Éditions de Crémille 1969)

Duffy, Christopher, *Austerlitz, 1805* (London: Seely Service, 1977)

Gielgud, Adam (ed.), *Memoirs of Prince Adam Czartoryski and his correspondence with Alexander I...* (London: Remington, 1888)

Glinka, Sergey, *Zapiski Sergeya Nikolayevicha Glinki* (St Petersburg: Russkaya starina, 1895)

Goetz, Robert, *1805, Austerlitz. Napoleon and the Destruction of the Third Coalition* (London: Greenhill Books, 2005)

Janetschek, Clemens d'Elpidio, *Die Schlacht bei Austerlitz: 2. December 1805* (Brunn: Päpstliche Benedictiner-Buchdruckerei, 1898)

Kagan, Frederick W., *The End of the Old Order. Napoleon and Europe 1801-1805* (New York: Da Capo, 2006)

Kerautret, Michel, and Gabriel Madec (eds), *Correspondance Générale de Napoléon* (Paris: Fayard, 2008)

Langeron, Louis Alexandre Andrault de, *Journal inedit de la campagne de 1805* (Paris: La Vouivre, 1998)

Mikaberidze Alexander (ed., trans.), *The Czar's General. The Memoirs of a Russian General in the Napoleonic Wars* (Welwyn Garden City: Ravenhall Books, 2005)

Mikhailovskii-Danilevskii, Alexander, *Opisanie pervoi voiny Imperatora Aleksandra s Napoleonom v 1805 godu* (St Petersburg: Tip. Shtaba Otdel'nago Korpusa Vnutrennei Strazhi, 1844)

Rustow, Wilhelm, *Der Krieg von 1805 in Deutschland und Italien* (Frauenfeld: Verlags-Comptoir, 1853)

Savary, Anne-Jean-Marie-René, *Mémoires du duc de Rovigo écrits de sa main, pour servia à l'histoire de l'Empereur Napoleon* (Paris: Colburn, 1828)

Shil'der, Nikolai, *Imperator Aleksandr pervyi. Ego zhizn' i tsarstvovanie* (St Petersburg: A.S. Suvorin, 1897)

Sokolov, Oleg, *Bitva trekh imperatorov. Napoleon, Rossiya i Evropa, 1799-1805 gg* (St Petersburg: Piter, 2019)

Stutterheim, Karl von, *La Bataille d'Austerlitz, par un militaire témoin de la journée du 2 décembre 1805* (Paris: Fain, 1806)

Thiébault, Paul, *Mémoires du général Baron Thiébault* (Paris: Plon, 1894)

Thiers, Adolphe, *Histoire du Consulat et de l'Empire* (Paris: Paulin, 1847)

Zhirkevich, Ivan, 'Zapiski 1789-1848 gg', in *Russkaya starina*, 2 (1874), pp.207–244

5

The Raising of the White Cockade Regiments, 1794–1802

Alistair Nichols

On 1 February 1793 the French Republic declared war on Britain and it quickly became clear that it was to be a very different conflict than those previously fought between the forces of the two rival monarchs, and their cabinets, during the last century. The British Government soon came to the decision that European peace could only be achieved through the fall of the regime that held power in France and considered the most effective means of achieving this was by supporting internal counter-revolutionary movements. On 17 April 1794 Henry Dundas, the Home Secretary and a leading figure in the development of war policy, addressed this in a speech to the House of Commons, asking what better way was there than,

> … making use of the means which were the most closely connected with the object? … to employ great bodies of the unfortunate sufferers, of different ranks, who had been driven from their country, from their families, from their property, … as principals, as well as auxiliaries, in restoring the peace of Europe. … such men would erect the standard of exiled religion, oppressed virtue, and expatriated loyalty.[1]

His speech was made during the third reading of a bill '… to enable Subjects of France to enlist as Soldiers in Regiments to serve on the Continent of Europe, and in certain other Places; and to enable His [Britannic] Majesty to grant Commissions to Subjects of France, to serve and receive Pay as Officers in such Regiments, or as Engineers, under certain Restrictions' which was enacted on 9 May.

Frenchmen, particularly former officers of the army and navy, had emigrated as the Revolution progressed, driven from their posts by violence and threats, or considering themselves no longer able to live under the changing constitution. As the war had progressed some had come to serve in the armies of the coalition against France, those that served in that of Britain, for example in the Loyal

1 William Cobbett (ed.), *The Parliamentary History of England, from the earliest period to the year 1803* (London: T.C. Hansard, 1818), vol.XXXI, pp.411–414.

Emigrant Regiment, wore the British Army's black cockade, but the units that were now authorised were to be distinguished by the use of the white cockade and other symbols of the French Bourbon monarchy.

A variety of units were raised under the Act including by the Baron de Montalembert and M. de Charmilly for service in Haïti; the five corps commanded by Allonville, Léon, Quiefdeville, du Trésor and Williamson of volunteers who were intended to form the officer cadres for troops raised in France; the French Emigrant Artillery, a half-battalion commanded by Rotalier, and a corps of engineer officers. It is the line regiments, envisaged to be perhaps 12 in number, which were raised under the Act that are the subject of this chapter.

Their formation and deployment were governed by the act itself, consisting of five sections, the attached Articles of War, with 11 sections, which were printed in both English and French, and the regulations consisting of 28 articles.[2] These last being agreed, on 22 August 1794, with the Duc d'Harcourt, the London representative of the French Regent, the Comte de Provence, the elder of Louis XVI's two brothers, who had taken on this role after the latter's execution on 21 January 1793, and who was uncle to the uncrowned boy king Louis XVII – kept in prison by the republicans until his death aged just 10 years old. The regiments, collectively, became known as the French Corps or, more commonly, the White Cockade Corps. Their service was restricted to 'any part of the Continent of Europe, or in the [Channel Islands] … or in any Part of the Dominions of his late Most Christian Majesty' and both officers and men were to take a simple oath to 'be faithful, and bear true Allegiance to His Majesty King George, and that I will serve him honestly and faithfully in Defence of His Person, Crown, and Dignity, against all His Enemies or Opposers whatsoever' as well as obey orders.[3]

The white cockade regiments were raised to aid and support armed opponents of the current regime in France but by the summer of 1794 the only regions where such an intervention could be realistically considered were Brittany and the Vendée. They remained the last areas in arms against the French Convention as well as open to the opportunity of being accessed and sustained from the sea. The Comte d'Artois, Louis XVI's youngest brother who had taken responsibility for counter-revolutionary activity in these parts of France, was closely involved in the formation of the regiments and the nomination of the *colonels*.

Letters of service were issued in the name of King George III to eight French émigrés as regimental *colonels*, dated 1 August 1794.[4] The regiments took the name of their *colonel* as a scheme to use the names 'of the great Provinces & favourite Regts of the French Army' had been abandoned because too many problems arose in allocating these titles.[5] In the corps, officers of equal rank took their seniority from

2 Examples are kept in the National Archives, Kew (TNA): WO 24/1112 and HO 42/41.
3 TNA: WO 24/1112 and HO 42/41: Section 1 of the Act and Section 1, Articles 1 and 2, of the Articles of War.
4 TNA: HO 51/147.
5 British Library (BL): Add MS 37850: list of issues discussed by Artois and Woodford, October 1794.

that they had held in the French army on 1 July 1789.[6] The ranking of the regiments matched that of their *colonels*, most of whom were *maréchaux de camp*, entitled to command more than one regiment, as brigadier.

Table 5.1: White Cockade Regiments raised 1 August 1794

No.	*Colonel*	Rank on 1 July 1789
1	Jean-François-Thérèse-Louis de Beaumont Marquis d'Autichamp	*Maréchal de camp* 1 March 1780
2	Charles-Hyacinthe-Joseph du Houx Comte de Vioménil	*Maréchal de camp* 1 March 1780
3	Eugène-Eustache Comte de Béthisy (or Béthizy) de Mézières	*Maréchal de camp* 5 December 1781
4	Anne-Alexandre-Marie-Sulpice-Joseph de Montmorency Duc de Laval	*Maréchal de camp* 1 January 1784
5	Victurien-Jean-Baptiste-Marie de Rochechouart Duc de Mortemart	*Maréchal de camp* 9 March 1788
6	Armand-Charles-Augustin de la Croix Duc de Castries	*Maréchal de camp* 9 March 1788
7	Louis-Marie-René-Ambroise Marquis du Dresnay	*Colonel* (*maréchal de camp* 1791)
8	Louis-Charles Le Cat Comte d'Hervilly	*Colonel* (*maréchal de camp* 13 November 1791)

All the regiments were to be of infantry and were to have the same structure, despite some indications that there may have been some consideration, at the earliest stages, of raising the Régiment d'Autichamp as cavalry. Their establishments were:

Staff (*état-major*) – *colonel, lieutenant-colonel, major, quartier maître trésorier* (quartermaster with rank of *lieutenant*), two *aides-majors* (*capitaines*), two *sous-aides majors* (*lieutenants*), *ingénieur* (engineer with rank of *lieutenant*), two *adjudants* (*sous-lieutenants*), *aumônier* (chaplain), *chirurgien major* (surgeon major), two *aides-majors* (assistants) = 15

Staff, other ranks (*petit état-major*) – *tambour major* (drum major), *caporal tambour* (corporal drummer), *maitre tailleur* (master tailor), *maitre armurier* (master armourer), *maitre cordonnier* (master shoemaker) = 5

Each Company – *capitaine*, two *lieutenants*, two *sous-lieutenants*, *sergent major, fourrier*, three *sergents*, six *caporaux*, 72 *soldats*, *tambour* = 89

Each Battalion – one company of *grenadiers* and eight of *fusiliers* = 801; two battalions = 1,602

Artillery detachment – a *lieutenant*, two *sergents*, four *caporaux*, 28 *canonniers* (gunners) = 35

Total for the regiment = 1,657[7]

6 TNA: WO 24/1112 and HO 42/41: Articles of War, Section VIII (I).

7 TNA: WO 24/1112 and HO 42/41: Formation table attached to the regulations.

Article 22 of the Regulations stated, 'The Uniform will be red lined with white, white waistcoat and breeches, without any decoration than the distinctive marks of rank. The cockade will be white, the flags white with three golden fleurs-de-lys.' The regiments were distinguished by the following facing colours:

> Autichamp – sky blue
> Vioménil – white
> Béthisy – light yellow
> Montmorency-Laval – yellow
> Castries – light green
> Dresnay – dark green
> Mortemart – black
> Hervilly – 'ventre de biche' (doe's belly, light tan colour).[8]

The administration of the white cockade regiments fell to the War Office, under the direction of William Windham MP, as of July 1794 the newly-appointed Secretary at War.[9] A new Foreign Department was formed and on 13 September 1794 the *colonels* were informed that Emperor John Alexander Woodford had been appointed 'Chief Inspector and Commissary General of Musters' to supervise the recruitment and payment of the new units, assisted, in time, by five 'Regimental Inspectors.'[10] However, the expense of the French Corps was borne by the Foreign Office, on the secret service account, meaning that both departments were concerned in its administration.

Steps were immediately taken to begin raising the regiments:

> LONDON, August 14 – The Duke de Laval, the Duke de Mortimar [sic], and the Count de Hervilly, Colonels of the three new regiments of French Emigrants, in the pay of our Government, were yesterday presented to the King, in their uniforms; as were also the Count de Laval, brother to the Duke; and also a son of the Duke. They will set off in a few days, with the officers of the other French corps, to form their regiments on the Continent, and are to embark on board a British frigate.[11]

This urgency was required as these *colonels* were, according to their letters of service, to have 'completed' their regiments by 1 December, 'The Sum, which will wanted for Levy Money and Subsistence of them in that period, will be about thirty five thousand Pounds, of which eleven thousand four hundred must be issued immediately.'[12] Later two further senior French officers were issued with letters of service to raise

8 TNA: WO 24/1112: Article 22, Règlements.

9 R.G. Thorne 'WINDHAM, William (1750–1810) of Felbrigg Hall, Norf,' <http://www.historyofparliamentonline.org/volume/1790-1820/member/windham-william-1750-1810>, accessed 30 November 2021.

10 TNA: WO 4/154 and 65/167; Woodford had been bestowed with his impressive first name as Emperor had been his mother's maiden name.

11 *The Leeds Intelligencer*, 18 August 1794.

12 TNA: WO 4/154: Windham to Treasury 17 August 1794.

regiments. One was 72-year-old Victor-François Duc de Broglie, *maréchal de France* since 16 December 1759, King George III having reportedly made the appointment '... without any solicitation ... a flattering homage paid to the virtues and talents of the above illustrious soldier.'[13] Due to Broglie's age his son, Auguste-Joseph de Broglie, Prince de Revel, was to take effective control of the regiment as *colonel commandant*. The other letter went to the naval officer, Jean-Charles Comte d'Hector, *lieutenant général des armées navales*. There are indications that his regiment might have been intended to be a 'Corps of Cannoneers of the Marine'[14] and this may explain why, although it had otherwise, initially, the same establishment as the other regiments, it was not to have an artillery detachment. This was soon, however, not a distinction as these detachments were also dropped from the other regiments, that of Hervilly being disbanded on 28 December 1794, as was the post of engineer on the regimental staffs.[15] It was stipulated that Hector's officers were 'to be exclusively selected from belonging to the Royal Navy of France, ...'[16] This led to the regiment being known, alternatively, as Royal Marine and the adoption of related symbols such as the officers' white metal uniform buttons being, 'stamped with an anchor and 3 fleurs-de-lys.'[17] The regimental facing colours were violet for Broglie and iron grey for Hector.[18]

The letters of service were delivered to Broglie and Hector on 11 and 22 October 1794, respectively.[19] However they were ante-dated to 1 August, an 'Indulgence, granted expressly and solely as a Mark of personal attention' to ensure that the precedence of their regiments matched the *colonels*' seniority in the French service.[20] This, of course, meant the other regiments were re-numbered and an extant belt plate for the Régiment d'Hervilly, now in the Musée de l'armée at Paris, appears to have been manufactured before this change as it bears, with the legend 'HERVILLY' above a central fleur-de-lys, the number '8'.[21]

It had been originally envisaged that recruitment for the regiments would take place in Flanders, immediately behind the battlefront and where there were many deserters, prisoners and émigrés of all classes. However, by the time the bill had made its way through Parliament the tide of war was turning against the allies and then, following the Battle of Fleurus on 26 June 1794, they were in retreat towards the United Provinces (the Netherlands) and the Rhine. Article 23 of the Regulations stated that: 'The English Government will try to obtain all necessary facilities so that the Recruiters of the different Corps can engage in Brabant, the Palatinate, the

13 *The Kentish Weekly Post*, 19 September 1794.
14 *The Kentish Gazette*, 30 September 1794.
15 Vicomte Robert Grouvel, *Les corps de troupes de l'émigration française* (Paris: Les Éditions de La Sabretache, 1957–1964), vol.I, p.125.
16 TNA: WO 6/131: Henry Dundas to Lord Amherst 16 October 1794.
17 Vicomte de Gouzillon de Bélizal, 'Journal et Lettres d'un Émigré', *Revue de Bretagne*, vol. XXVII, January–February 1902, p.98.
18 Grouvel, *Les corps*, vol.I, pp.103, 137.
19 TNA: WO 4/154, Broglie, and WO 4/155, Hector.
20 TNA: WO 4/155: Windham to Hector 4 December 1794.
21 'Plaque de baudrier du régiment d'Hervilly', <https://art.rmngp.fr/fr/library/artworks/plaque-de-baudrier-du-regiment-d-hervilly_laiton_1795>, accessed 14 November 2021.

Electorate of Trier and on all the borders of France deserters from the troops of the line or peasants, who wish to serve in the different Corps.'[22]

Even this was difficult as the Rhineland princes raised objections and difficulties, fearing repercussions from the advancing French republicans which only added to their pervading antipathy towards the émigrés. On 7 October 1794, Woodford reported that only two depots were established, Vioménil at Dillenburg in Nassau, deeper into Germany, and Autichamp at Deventer, in the Dutch province of Overijssel. The Régiment de Castries which had had to quit Cologne, with 150 recruits, was refused entry to Osnabrück and, when Woodford encountered it, it was marching towards the Netherlands 'with the Duc de Castries at their head, himself on foot,' he instructed it to halt immediately.[23] Woodford was on his way to Düsseldorf where the other *colonels* had established themselves nearby but before he got there they were scattered by the republican advance. On 9 October he reached Wesel where, as he informed the Duke of York, British commander in the Netherlands, he 'met the Duke de Mortemart with the Officers & Recruits of his Corps, old Knights of St Louis carrying their own baggage & knapsacks knee deep in these miry roads, refused shelter or covering for the night or the morrow.'[24] Writing to seek help in finding temporary depots for the regiments in the Netherlands, he sent another letter to the British Ambassador at The Hague which was even more impassioned. He was successful as depots were eventually found in the Netherlands for the following regiments: Castries at Enschede, on the German frontier; Mortemart at Doetinchem then Almelo; Béthisy at Montfoort, west of Utrecht, and Broglie was likely, so Woodford thought, to be placed at Zwolle. However, French republican forces soon invaded the United Provinces bringing about the ancient republic's collapse and forced the British to retreat into Germany at the end of January 1795 so the depots, except for that of the Régiment de Vioménil which was unaffected, were established in the small princedom of Waldeck, in and around Pyrmont.

It had not been envisaged, when the bill was drafted, that any white cockade regiment would be stationed in Britain. In recognition of Parliament's traditional distrust of foreign troops in the country, Section II of the Act only permitted troops raised under its auspices to land if it had been 'deemed necessary or expedient to bring [them] … to any Port or Place in *Great Britain*, for the Purpose of Rendezvous, or with a View to Operations Abroad …' in which case they could land 'for Health and Exercise … Provided always, That such Troops so landed shall not be marched into the Country to any Distance greater than Five Miles from the Sea Coast.' If any did land both Houses of Parliament, if sitting, had to be informed within 14 days and, if not, within the same period, of the commencement of the next sitting. Furthermore, Section III stipulated, 'That there shall never be at any One Time'

22 This repeated the stipulations of Article 3 which included that the men had to be at least 5 feet 5 inches (1.65 metres) tall and had been passed, as fit, by a surgeon.

23 BL: Add MS 37850: Woodford to William Windham 7 October 1794.

24 BL: Add MS 37850: Woodford to Duke of York and Lord St Helens, both of 9 October 1794.

more than 5,000 'Persons who shall have been enlisted under the Authority of this Act' in the Kingdom.[25]

Nevertheless, Régiments d'Hector, du Dresnay and d'Hervilly were almost exclusively raised in England, stretching, or even breaching, what was permitted by the Act. Apparently in recognition of this, the regiments were forbidden from wearing the white cockade while in Britain. This measure, from the lack of comment in the letters and memoirs of those in the regiments, appears to have been uncontroversial, indeed only one officer mentioned it, and this was in passing when he described a detachment of the Régiment d'Hector leaving the depot with white cockades in their pockets.[26]

Each of these regiments had distinctive features, Hector's, with its naval officers, was to be raised 'from among the Sailors now Prisoners of War in this Country and the Crews of the French Ships which were brought away from Toulon who may be willing to engage in this Service.'[27] The latter had arrived as a result of the allies' brief occupation, British and Spanish naval squadrons having entered the port, on 28 August 1793, on the invitation of royalists who had seized control. After a siege the allies were defeated and the last of the British ships left the harbour on 19 December; with them sailed 15 French navy ships, with French crews, and the first of these, the *Pompée*, *Puissant* and *Arethuse*, arrived at Spithead, the anchorage off Portsmouth, in April 1794. However, the Régiment d'Hector did not obtain many recruits from this source, almost all of the French sailors who wished to enter British service wanted to remain at sea and naval gunners who volunteered were allocated to the artillery.

In 1793 the Marquis du Dresnay had been authorised to organise émigrés, predominantly from Brittany, who had taken refuge on Jersey into a military unit. By November these gentlemen and their servants, about 600 in all, formed into companies and armed, had made sufficient progress in their training to take part in a military exercise involving the island's garrison repelling a mock invasion on 11 May 1794.[28] It had been intended that this corps would be simply converted into one of the new regiments, with the marquis as *colonel*, and 'the Gentlemen now serving in that Corps are to be formed into distinct Companies … [with] their allowance of one Shilling per Diem.'[29] However most of the gentlemen émigrés were not happy to leave Jersey to join such a regiment so they formed the kernel of two of the cadre corps, those of Léon and du Trésor, while others joined the new regiment as officers and NCOs.[30]

The Comte d'Hervilly had been one of the French officers serving with Lord Moira, who commanded the British force intended to support any intervention in

25 TNA: WO 24/1112 and HO 42/41: Act of Parliament concerning enlistment and commissioning of French subjects.
26 Gouzillon de Bélizal, 'Journal et Lettres d'un Émigré', p.105, letter to James Frémaux 30 March 1795.
27 TNA: WO 6/131: 16 October Henry Dundas to Lord Amherst.
28 Anon. (ed.), *Mémoires d'Olivier d'Argens et Correspondances des Généraux* (Paris: Baudouin Frères, 1826) pp.47, 50; TNA: WO 1/175: memorandum of 7 January 1794.
29 TNA: WO 6/131: Henry Dundas to Lord Amherst 10 August 1794.
30 Anon. (ed.), *Olivier d'Argens*, pp.56, 59.

France, and had impressed the general with his activity and 'the universal testimony borne to ... [his] merit ... [and] talents ...'[31] Thus when the three ships arrived from Toulon and were found to have, in addition to their crews, French troops onboard who had fought for the royalists, Moira wrote on 6 May 1794, days before the bill had its final reading, 'If it be determined that d'Hervilly shall have a Corps, it would be eligible that you should privately signify it to him as soon as possible ... that he could immediately nominate three or four Officers ... [to] take charge of the Men who have entered into the Land Service ...'[32] His recommendation was accepted as by 1 June François-Nicolas Junot Comte d'Atilly, later *lieutenant-colonel* of the Régiment d'Hervilly, had formed the men into four companies at Netley Camp near Southampton.[33] Atilly, like many of the regiment's officers had formerly served, during France's passage from absolute monarchy to republic, in the short-lived Garde Constitutionnelle du Roi in which Hervilly had commanded the cavalry.

The newly arrived troops were former National Guardsmen, marines and chasseurs of an independent company as well as three officers, 16 NCOs and 73 men from the Régiment Royal-Louis.[34] Subsequently more men from this last regiment were transferred to the Régiment d'Hervilly as they arrived from the Mediterranean where they had been serving on Corsica or as marines. Formed by combining various army detachments that were at Toulon, the Régiment Royal-Louis had been 'raised in the name and for the service of Louis XVII, approved by Monsieur, Regent of France, ... the first battalion breveted by him with the consent of the coalition powers.'[35] Clothed and organised as French army line infantry, it had in effect been 'the first French Corps formed by England ...'[36] It was apparently to retain this kudos that the Régiment d'Hervilly, the most junior of the new regiments, would often use the name Royal-Louis.

The rest of the recruits, for the Régiment d'Hervilly as well as the other two regiments, were obtained from the various depots in England holding prisoners of war. Anne-René de la Motte de Montmuran, *lieutenant* in the Régiment du Dresnay, a former naval officer and an English speaker, was sent to recruit among the prisoners at Portchester Castle, near Portsmouth. His task was to be difficult, as a local newspaper noted that at Portchester 'an unabated spirit of republicanism seems to pervade the whole mass of light-hearted captives.'[37] With Montmuran were officers from three other regiments, Hervilly's and Hector's, as well as Charmilly's; he described his work in a letter to his sister:

> At the start of the night, all the recruiting officers assemble and enter the courtyard of the prison, then into a guardroom where the goalers bring

31 TNA: WO 1/175: Moira to Nepean 9 June 1794.
32 TNA: WO 1/175: letter of 6 May 1794.
33 BL: Add MS 49088: return 1 June 1794, Netley.
34 TNA: WO 1/175: Return of Officers, Sailors & Seamen on board the French Ships, 27 April 1794.
35 Grouvel, *Les Corps,* vol.I, p.118 , citing *Mémoire du chevalier de Boisgelin.*
36 TNA: WO 1/388: letter, Boisgelin presumably to Dundas, dated 11 December 1794. Boisgelin became *capitaine* in the Régiment d'Hervilly.
37 *The Hampshire Chronicle*, 19 January 1795.

> the prisoners who wish to engage. Then one of the officers of the three first corps says very fine things to try to persuade the men to engage with them; then the officer from M de Charmilly also sells his merchandise by embellishing as much as he can, and he succeeded several times more than us, because the pay of the corps destined for America is much more than ours, ... Every day he takes out a few prisoners. The share is made equally between the three [white cockade] regiments.
>
> You can see that this type of life is not entertaining and is going to become still more tedious beginning from tomorrow. We will spend almost the whole day disguised in the office of one of the commissaries of the prison, who speaks French, and who, under the pretext of asking each prisoner if he received clothes, will pose to them afterwards several questions to learn if they wish to join the royalists; we will pretend to write, and the commissary will ask us in English what we think of the man who he comes to question. After our response, he will have him led to a room assigned for such an opinion. We will have the pleasure to review in this manner about six thousand prisoners; but we thought that this was the means to speed up our recruitment.

Later he was able to tell her that he had 'sent to the regiment a certain number of good men and former soldiers.'[38] Despite Montmuran's efforts the Régiment du Dresnay only received 106 recruits between 24 February and 24 April 1795, 23 were émigrés, 43 came from Portchester and the rest from other depots; just over half of the total were Bretons, while five came from the Caribbean.[39]

Some writers have stated that the émigré officers, particularly the *colonels*, were opposed to the recruitment of prisoners of war, claiming the measure was forced upon them by the British Government, however there is no primary evidence to support this. The nearest thing to such evidence is a letter Grouvel quotes which was purportedly written by Hervilly to Windham on 12 May 1795 in which he complained of the 'great number of republican prisoners incorporated in the regiment of Royal-Louis and in the legions of Hector and du Dresnay ... to accept among us prisoners of whom no one knows the morality, is to introduce an enemy into our ranks ...'[40] However Grouvel, himself, describes its authenticity as doubtful and indeed the language, such as the curious and distinctive terms for the respective units, indicate Hervilly was not its author. What does exist is evidence that the *colonels* wished to get the most men they could from among the prisoners, so in November 1794 Windham responded to a complaint from Hervilly that he could not interfere with the preferential treatment Hector obtained by the Duke of Portland, Secretary of

38 Letters of 26 January and 6 March 1795 reproduced in Charles Robert, *1795 Expédition des Emigres à Quiberon Le Comte d'Artois à l'îsle d'Yeu* (Paris: Lamulle & Poisson, 1899), pp.341–342.

39 TNA: WO 12/11708: seven, all recruited at Chatham, were transferred to the Régiment d'Hector.

40 Grouvel, *Les Corps*, vol.I, p.125. Grouvel does not give his source and despite efforts to do so, no trace of such a letter has been found in Windham's correspondence in the British Library or in that of the War Office in the National Archives.

State at the Home Office, instructing those in charge of the depots, 'to discontinue the Recruiting of the other French Corps from the Prisoners of War, until Count d'Hector had an opportunity of selecting those who were particularly qualified for the service to which his Regiment is destined.'[41] Then on 18 January 1795 Hervilly complained that officers recruiting for Charmilly's regiment had been giving gaolers a guinea for every recruit they obtained, so preventing those who wished to join the white cockade regiments from doing so, and a memorial on a similar theme was submitted by all three colonels in May that year.[42]

Indeed, it appears that many of the officers were quite pleased with the results of the recruitment to the regiments along with their vigilance and efforts to impose discipline. Other measures were also used as *Capitaine* André-Marie Gouzillon Vicomte de Bélizal, of the Régiment d'Hector, described when he wrote to a friend, 'If one can count on outward appearances, a great change to their advantage has occurred in three weeks; that came perhaps through the exemplary punishments that have been inflicted. In this time three émigré priests along with our chaplain preach and hold lectures on religion. All the soldiers and officers attend them twice a day.'[43] *Lieutenant* Magloire Marquis de Coëtlosquet, of the Régiment du Dresnay, formerly an officer in the Gardes Françaises, was impressed with the results, '... we are infinitely satisfied with our soldiers; though they are recruited in the prisons. We have managed to set the thing on an excellent footing; discipline without being hard is severe, morale is good.'[44] *Lieutenant* André-Louis-Lambert Baron Le Charron, of the Régiment d'Hervilly, had been a junior infantry officer before serving in the Garde Constitutionnelle and then the Loyal Emigrants was also content, writing:

> ... our regiment, composed of officers of all arms, all ages, ranks and grades, with in all thirteen hundred soldiers assembled, for the most part unfortunately in the prisons of England, and among them there were many sailors, a type of men very difficult to train to drills and manoeuvres, became, despite these obstacles, and in a few months, by care, activity, justice and the presence of its commander, a model of discipline, subordination and instruction.[45]

However, the number of men raised by the regiments was disappointing, in the summer of 1795, only that of Hervilly was close to being at full strength, 244 officers and men short of establishment, whereas that of Dresnay only had 59 grenadiers and 341 fusiliers while Hector's had 56 grenadiers and 299 fusiliers.[46]

---

41 TNA: WO 4/155: Windham to Hervilly 5 November 1794.

42 TNA: HO 50/386: Hervilly to Grymes 18 January 1795 and Lewis to King 5 May 1795.

43 Gouzillon de Bélizal, 'Journal et Lettres d'un Émigré', pp.105–106, letter to James Frémaux 30 March 1795.

44 Letter to his aunt, Romsey 5 April 1795, in E.M.C., *Deux Victimes de Quiberon* (Vannes: La Foyle, 1895), p.13.

45 André-Louis-Lambert Baron Le Charron, *Expédition de Quiberon, suivie de L'Évasion des Prisons de Vannes* (Paris: Ambroise Dupont et Roret, 1826), pp.127–128.

46 TNA: WO 12/11681, 11708 and 11741.

The men of those regiments recruited on the Continent came from a wider range of sources and nationalities, the wording of the Act (Section 1) that the recruits would be, '… such Persons who were Subjects of his late Most Christian Majesty,' provided the opportunity to enlist Germans as Alsatians. James Poole, inspecting recruits for the Régiment de Vioménil considered that, '… our enlisting the Germans was inconsistent, and involved us in jealousies and misunderstandings with the troops and government of the country. [But following advice] … I was henceforth incapable of refusing in the first instance those whose language was German, but were presented to me as Alsacians [sic].'[47] Officers and NCOs from the white cockade regiments ranged throughout Northern Europe seeking recruits and in Switzerland, for example, their imprudent behaviour gave rise to complaints.[48] Matters were worse for Auguste de Faucompré, a 19-year-old émigré already with three years' service as a volunteer in Dutch service, who at Utrecht had been promised a place as *sergent* in the Régiment de Montmorency-Laval if he brought six recruits. He succeeded in engaging four men but through, according to his father, 'imprudence pardonable by his inexperience and age' two of them were Dutch deserters for which he was arrested and it took some time for Woodford to arrange for his release.[49]

Other recruits were also claimed, perhaps not always justly as deserters, as Poole found, '… the Austrian cavalry sometimes visited us, and claimed their deserters from those I had received as Alsacians, taking, by force, such as they found, and we could not hide away.'[50] There was also direct competition for men from those recruiting for other units in British pay let alone other armies; early on Woodford accused the Dutch of '… trepanning [luring] the few men whom as yet enlisted with the French Corps, which they do in the most barefaced manner & with perfect Impunity & Defiance of all redress.'[51] Recruits became scarcer as the French republicans advanced to 'the left bank of the Rhine; and instead of men coming from the French side, the few who had crossed it, returned to join the successful army.'[52] Recourse was taken to enlisting prisoners, but without the niceties of persuasion that had to be used in England, 'A great many of the French Prisoners who were taken by the Prussians have been sold for a Louis each to the Emigrant Corps'.[53] Poole, at Pyrmont in 1795 saw the results:

> … at this time the desertion was so great, that, in the regiment of Laval, the serjeants had orders every night to take away from the recruits their shoes and most indispensable parts of their dresses, but all to no purpose – and also, that one day being walking round the chateau of Pyrmont, where the

47 James Poole, *A Narrative exposing a variety of Irregular Transactions in one of the Departments of Foreign Corps during the Late War* (London: J. Parson and Son, 1804), p.6.
48 TNA: FO 74/5: letters of 18 and 24 February 1795.
49 BL: Add MS 37859: Faucompré (père) to Windham 22 May 1795.
50 Poole, *Irregular Transactions*, p.9.
51 BL: Add MS 37850: Woodford to Windham 7 October 1794.
52 Poole, *Irregular Transactions*, p.9.
53 TNA: WO 1/171: Craig to Nepean 10 November 1794. The Régiments du Dresnay, d'Hector and d'Hervilly also recruited in Germany but no recruits appear to have joined the regiment from there before the expedition.

> venerable Marshal de Broglie was lodged, and had a guard from one of our regiments of his name, they had posted a centinel [sic], so lately recruited from amongst the French prisoners, that I heard him sing the national airs for near a quarter of an hour, when an officer observing him, got him relieved by another ...[54]

Later that year, a British newspaper carried a report on the Régiments de Castries and de Mortemart, 'Two hundred of the Emigrant soldiers ... have deserted with all their accoutrements. ... Instead of procuring Frenchmen, ... men were picked up from all nations, Dutch, Germans, Danes, &c. the consequence has been desertion and mutiny.'[55]

There was no shortage, on the other hand, of suitable candidates to be officers in all the regiments; the setbacks that most of the émigrés had endured over several years meant that most of the senior NCO posts were also taken up by former officers, simply pleased to earn enough to live on. So, such places, in all the regiments, were filled quickly as if they were at full strength, despite the lack of soldiers. For example, on 1 November 1794 the Régiment de Mortemart had the full complement of officers for its staff, 18 companies and an artillery detachment as well as most of the requisite senior NCOs, *sergents* and above, 183 in all. Nevertheless, the two grenadier companies only had four *caporaux* between them and 10 of the fusilier companies had no other ranks at all, the other six each had on average two *caporals* and 11 *fusiliers* – 83 all told.[56] Due to this sort of surplus *Colonel* d'Hector was authorised, on 1 November 1794, to form the additional naval officers and *élèves de marine* he had into a separate company.[57]

It was authorised that 'The Colonels will nominate the Officers subject nevertheless to the approval or non-approval of His Majesty.'[58] Broadly speaking kinship with the *colonel* seems to have been the overriding qualification for nomination as an officer in all the units, in the Régiment de Montmorency-Laval, for example, the *lieutenant-colonel* as well as three of the *capitaines* were from the *colonel*'s family.[59] Only in the Régiment d'Hervilly was this less apparent with, in addition to those coming from Royal-Louis, several of its officers had formerly served in the Garde Constitutionelle. Victor-Louis-Alexandre Marquis de Toustain Frontebosc, Vioménil's nephew, noted that while his uncle acted with probity, '... the majority of his colleagues sold places to augment their revenues ...'[60] The result was that many hopeful applicants were left disappointed and disillusioned, Comte Pierre-Paul Faydit de Terssac, formerly an infantry *major*, recalled that in September 1794 the *Maréchal* de Broglie placed him, in all good faith, on a list as *capitaine* in his regiment, but when he joined it:

54 Poole, *Irregular Transactions*, p.15.
55 *The Hull Advertiser*, 17 October 1795.
56 BL: Add MS 37858: Régiment de Mortemart 1er novembre.
57 Grouvel, *Les Corps*, vol.I, p.134.
58 TNA: WO 24/1112 and HO 42/41: Regulations, Article 7.
59 Grouvel, *Les Corps*, vol.I, p.94.
60 Marquise de Perry de Nieüil, *Mémoires du Marquis de Toustain 1790–1823* (Paris: Plon, 1933), p.52.

> It did not take me long to realise that there were many intrigues and underhand manoeuvres on the part of all who surrounded the maréchal; the business of nomination to the posts was a mystery and took a long time, because it was continually changed. After several days, Prince Amédée, his son, announced to me that I was placed as lieutenant. I did not hide my great surprise after the genuine promise I had received from the maréchal; I beseeched him to tell his father that it was only the extreme poverty to which I was reduced that made me accept this position in his regiment in order to have bread. The maréchal never spoke of it to me … the people surrounding him ended up making him do what they wanted, and his family was very large. I guessed he was sorry not to do better for me. The Marquis de Boisronoie, attached for years to the maréchal, could only obtain a lieutenancy, which he refused, because he had enough to live on ... It was in March that the maréchal assembled, in Pyrmont, the officers he had appointed to form his regiment. I went on foot to this place ... The maréchal, on my arrival, instructed me to go to Hamburg ... I was very happy to be useful and not to begin again the trade of lieutenant, after having quitted it 34 years ago.[61]

The original intention of the British Government was that all those receiving commissions would have been officers in the French Royal Army on 1 July 1789, recognised as the start of what became the Revolution, and they could not be placed in a higher rank to that they had held in France. However, the wording of the relevant articles, 7 and 8, of the regulations had been interpreted by some of the *colonels* as allowing them to place other men as officers in their regiment. So, on 3 December 1794 Windham wrote to each of the *colonels*, and the Duc d'Harcourt, to find out how each was interpreting the articles, not to enforce any particular position but to ensure that there was consistency across all the regiments. Vioménil, for one had followed the original intention, and so had declined to give his nephew a commission, Toustain having only served since the Revolution, as an officer in the Armée de Condé, the last of the émigré armies raised by Royal Princes in 1791. Doubtless it was after consistency across the regiments was established, following Windham's enquiry, that Toustain received his commission, however he put Vioménil's change of mind down to a more immediate reason, writing, 'My uncle finally consented, doubtless due to pestering from my aunt, to admit me, in the rank of lieutenant, in his regiment, …'[62] The lack of recruits, however, meant that he like so many other officers had little to do, 'My company still not being formed, I had no occupation; except a guard every fortnight.'[63]

61 D. Cau-Durban and F. Pasquier (eds), 'Mémoires du Comte Pierre-Paul Faydit de Terssac, Major d'Artois, Chevalier de Saint-Louis 1736–1820', *Bulletin Périodique de la Société Ariègeoise des Sciences, Lettres & Arts et de la Société des Études du Couserans*, vol.18, No.1, (1901), pp.226–227.

62 Perry de Nieüil, *Mémoires*, p.50.

63 Perry de Nieüil, *Mémoires*, p.55.

Having come, like so many of the officers of the white cockade regiments, from the army commanded by Louis-Joseph de Bourbon, Prince de Condé, which was so often forced to operate within very tight financial constraints, Toustain found the amount of money that was available to pay and equip the new regiments remarkable. He also described the uniform worn by the Régiment de Vioménil, which had white facings:

> The uniform consisted, for the soldier, of a round hat decorated with a blue turban around the body and with a bearskin which, passing over the top, formed the [appearance of a] helmet. A red Austrian-style jacket, white collars, cuffs and lining, white waistcoat and breeches, of woven cloth during the winter and cotton canvas in summer; gaiters of black cloth in winter, of grey canvas in summer. Grey Austrian-style overcoat.
>
> The officers wore the three-cornered hat, the cockade-loop and stiffeners in gold, white plume and cockade, as with the soldier; the full uniform was red, collar, cuff, piping, lining white. The coat buttoned down to the waist, French-style epaulettes of silver like the buttons stamped with a fleur-de-lys. White waistcoat and breeches, American-style boots, white lacquered sword-belt, sword and gold sword-knot, black sash. The officers' undress uniform was a big blue tailcoat, with the collar red and the grey frock coat with white buttons.[64]

The uniform was common across all the regiments, the different facing colours being displayed on the collars and cuffs, and the only significant variation seems to have been the colour of the turban on the hat: contemporary, or near contemporary, illustrations show those of the Régiments de Castries and d'Hervilly as red but for the Régiment de Béthisy white. Woodford had, apparently on his own initiative, had the NCOs of the regiments in Germany provided with coats, similar to those of the officers 'as many of them were Officers in the French Service ...'[65]

The use of black sashes by the officers is noteworthy. Sashes were a common sign of command in European armies and their colour displayed loyalty, generally to nation, those worn by the British, for example, being crimson. Soon after the raising of the regiments had commenced, on Windham's suggestion, King George accorded to 'the French Corps, the black sash, sword knot & cravats to their Colours. ... a pleasing tho' melancholy mark of respect to the memory of his late most Christian Majesty [Louis XVI] ...'[66] Evidence that they were worn across the different regiments, including those raised in England, comes from *Capitaine* Gouzillon de Bélizal, of the Régiment d'Hector, who had his sash, 'black with silver fringes' and a fine sword presented to him by an English family he had been staying with on the eve of his departure to join his regiment at Lymington.[67]

64 Perry de Nieüil, *Mémoires*, p.53.
65 BL: Add MS 37875: Craufurd to Windham 5 June 1795.
66 BL: Add MS 37850: Woodford to Windham 7 October 1794.
67 Gouzillon de Bélizal 'Journal et Lettres d'un Émigré', pp.99–100.

On 26 March 1795, the seven regiments being raised on the Continent, together, had no more than 737 rank and file. The British ministers were keen to use these men in the forthcoming expedition to France, so instructions were issued to draft all these men into the Régiments d'Autichamp and de Vioménil, 'which would then form two Corps of upwards of 600 Men each.' As soon as this had been done, these two regiments were then to be sent to Britain as quickly as possible; they were selected simply because their *colonels*, except for Broglie, were the most senior and the remaining units were to continue recruiting.[68] These measures did not happen among the ever-changing priorities and confusion that surrounded the evacuation of the British forces from the Continent.

On 27 June 1795 the Régiments d'Hector, du Dresnay and d'Hervilly, along with other émigré troops, landed in Brittany and soon secured the Quiberon peninsula. They were there to form a secure bridgehead for the supply and support of insurgents fighting the republican regime, however, within the month, they were utterly defeated. One cause for the failure was the defection of soldiers from the white cockade regiments, chiefly those who had been recruited from republican prisoners while the expedition was in France, rather than those enlisted in England. This led to the decision, dated 24 October, being made to disband the three regiments with their remaining soldiers being drafted into the Loyal Emigrants.[69] However this part of the plan was abandoned as '... these Corps being raised, under an Act of Parliament and on terms entered into by the Secretary of State for Foreign Affairs, place them in a situation different from the other foreign Corps.' Should any such regiment be disbanded the men could only be drafted into another white cockade corps, transferring them to another unit would be another engagement which they could decline, in which case they would have to be returned, not to prison, but to France.[70]

Whilst Britain was withdrawing its forces from the Continent, the country was not abandoning the alliance, so it committed to pay a subsidy to Austria, which continued to fight France. Furthermore, it not only agreed to take over the cost of the Armée de Condé, deployed alongside the Austrians, but also to pay for its expansion and sent Lieutenant Colonel Charles Craufurd to act as commissioner and to liaise with the prince. On 7 July, before the defeat at Quiberon, it was decided that the two most complete white cockade regiments, those of Mortemart and Castries, should be brought to Britain while the remainder would be amalgamated into the Armée de Condé.[71] Orders were issued for the Régiment de Mortemart, now organised as a single battalion, and the Régiment de Castries to march towards Stade on the Elbe, one of the embarkation ports for the British evacuation.[72] They continued to recruit on the way, sending a recruiting party to Hamburg on 7 July with the city's authorities' permission, however three weeks

68 TNA: WO 6/131: Dundas to York 26 March 1795.
69 TNA: WO 4/735: Windham to Woodford 17 September 1795.
70 TNA: WO 4/377: Windham to Brownrigg 23 January 1796.
71 TNA: FO 29/5: Grenville to Charles Craufurd 7 July 1795.
72 TNA: WO 1/173: D. Dundas to H. Dundas 18 July and 2 August 1795; WO 4/292: Windham to Woodford 4 August 1795.

later, its activities were met with violent public opposition.[73] Despite these orders, there was to be no speedy embarkation for the two regiments, as ships were put to other uses, and the corrosive effect of desertion reduced their numbers. Pandering to complaints from French diplomats, the Hamburg authorities excluded all émigrés from the city. It was about this time that an English correspondent visited the camp of the Régiment de Castries :

> … not above one half of them Frenchmen; the rest are Dutch emigrants with some Germans and Swiss. They are now encamped on a sandy hill which overlooks Hamburgh [sic], and all the country on the side of the Elbe; and neither the men nor the officers know how long they are to remain. I went … to see this little camp; it has not the neat and orderly appearance of some that I have seen in England, but the tents are very good, and the soldiers are fine men, and seemed to be in excellent spirits, particularly the French. … [Well received, he] was sorry to see that a similar behaviour was not observed towards the poor peasants, whose curiosity led them to gaze at, perhaps, an unusual scene: they were rudely driven away by the sentinels from the precincts of the camp, with a degree of violence and military tyranny that would never have been suffered in Old England.[74]

On 10 October 1795 the Régiment de Mortemart had 298 and that of Castries 448 other ranks and each had 108 officers, 24 'followers and servants', 48 women and children and 20 horses.[75] Finally, among the last of the British forces to leave Germany, they both sailed in the first two weeks of December for Spithead.[76] On their arrival the remnants of the Régiments d'Hector, du Dresnay and d'Hervilly were drafted into the two regiments: the Régiment d'Hervilly providing 180 men in two companies, one going to each regiment.[77] The soldiers who did not wish to transfer to the Régiments de Mortemart or de Castries but to return to France were to be informed that they 'shall be sent at the expense of Government on board Cartel Ships to Calais as returned prisoners. They must themselves make their story good when they get there.'[78] The two regiments were soon posted to the Channel Islands before, in 1797, being sent to Portugal as part of a force to reinforce Britain's ally. They remained there, without seeing active service, until after the Peace of Amiens when they were brought back to Britain and disbanded on 24 August 1802.

The men of the five regiments that remained in Germany were intended to augment the Armée de Condé, Craufurd suggesting, on 19 June 1795, assuming they were Frenchmen, that they could do so by forming a two battalion regiment

73 *The Chester Courant*, 21 July, and *Saunder's News-Letter*, 14 August 1795.
74 *The Hampshire Chronicle*, 7 September 1795.
75 TNA: WO 1/173: Return of foreign corps still on the Continent.
76 TNA: WO 1/173: D. Dundas to H. Dundas 16 December 1795.
77 Le Charron, *Expédition de Quiberon*, p.115.
78 TNA: WO 4/367: Woodford to Major Grymes 26 October 1795.

under Broglie.[79] In response Woodford, knowing that many of them were Germans, proposed forming two single-battalion regiments, one of Frenchmen to join Condé and the other of Germans for service in the West Indies.[80] After the decision was taken to embark the Régiments de Castries and de Mortemart, the men of the remaining five regiments were to march south to be closer to Condé's army, but this was postponed when news arrived of the defeat at Quiberon so that they could be available to be sent to France as reinforcements.[81] Some additional delays arose as Woodford and Craufurd, while not completely in opposition to each other, had very different views over how the men, and especially the officers, of the white cockade regiments should be treated. In essence Woodford was pressing for advantageous conditions, for instance, for the officers who would be without employment in the new regiment, while Craufurd, supporting the views of the prince, did not want them to be better off than others in the army. So, on that particular issue, he wrote, 'I must remark that it is absolutely impossible the supernumerary officers should be on any other footing in the Condé army than that of serving in his Corps Nobles according to their respective ranks, ... were it otherwise there would be the greatest discontent from so invidious a distinction ...'[82] Craufurd subsequently tried to shift Woodford's view by pointing out, 'A positive specific agreement was made with a certain set of French officers – and it became null of course the moment they failed to fulfil the conditions for which the contracting parties had stipulated. Therefore the keeping them upon pay since has been merely a matter of indulgence.'[83]

To maintain discipline during the transition the white cockade regiments kept their organisation and would only be disbanded on the shores of the Bodensee (Lake Konstanz) in the vicinity of the Armée de Condé. The regiments at Pyrmont left first: Autichamp's on 21 August, Montmorency-Laval's the next day and both Broglie's and Béthisy's on 26 August.[84] The last to leave was the Régiment de Vioménil, marching from Dillenburg on 1 September towards Rottenburg am Neckar.[85] When Woodford issued detailed instructions for the disbanding on 2 October it seems that, by and large, Craufurd's opinions held sway. The men were to either join the Armée de Condé, the prince having discretion how to employ them, or a new regiment, restricted to only serve in Europe, which would be immediately sent to Corsica. Although it seems that it was first proposed to form a second battalion in a black cockade regiment raised by Edward Dillon in Italy which was already serving in Corsica, no such permission was granted. The new regiment was to be commanded by Charles Jerningham, the scion of a distinguished English Roman Catholic family by whom he was known as Chevalier as he had served in the French army rising to the rank of *maréchal de camp* on 20 May 1784.[86]

79 TNA: FO 29/5: Craufurd to Grenville 19 June 1795.
80 TNA: FO 29/5: Craufurd to Grenville 6 July 1795.
81 TNA: FO 29/5: Craufurd to Eden 4 August 1795.
82 BL: Add MS 37875: Craufurd to Woodford 8 July 1795.
83 BL: Add MS 37875: Craufurd to Woodford 19 July 1795.
84 BL: Add MS 37875: Richard Gardiner to Windham 25 August 1795.
85 Perry de Nieüil, *Mémoires*, p.56.
86 TNA: WO 4/367: Woodford to Gardiner (three messages) and Basset (one) 2 October 1795.

It was directed that Jerningham was to recruit the Germans and it was '… not intended to engage any French for the new Regiment or a larger number of Non Commissioned Officers of that nation than are necessary.'[87] The men were not entitled to be discharged, unless unfit for further service, '… as they are to be kept on the same pay & are destined for a Service strictly conformed to the Tenor of the Engagement and Capitulation.'[88] Nevertheless they received a new bounty, for those joining Condé this was 25 shillings for *sergents*, 20 for *caporaux* and 15 for *soldats* and, respectively, 20, 15 and 10 for those joining Jerningham. The latter's men were to be formed into companies, 100 strong with five officers, a *capitaine*, two *lieutenants* and two 'subalterns' selected from the disbanded regiments, Windham having reserved some spaces for named individuals. No staff were to be appointed to the new regiment and the discharged officers received between six and one months' pay depending on their rank, circumstances and future employment. The men were '… to be armed & equipped in the best manner the remains of our stores will admit of.'[89]

Woodford, perhaps a little bitterly, observed that the disbanding of the white cockade regiments in Germany was good news for the Prince de Condé who, '… cannot desire more than the breaking of the Regiments.'[90] They had attracted many officers from his army and indeed been a draw for his men to desert. The men who joined the Armée de Condé were placed in four new regiments, formed as cadres as part of the augmentation, that bore the names of their *colonels*: Bardonnenche, Roquefeuil, Alexandre de Damas and Montesson. Most of the officers who joined, or more correctly, re-joined the prince's army were placed in the noble corps formed of officers and gentlemen. They had been concerned that the welcome they received on their return would at best be lukewarm and Toustain, for one, considered these fears fulfilled when, 'We were presented as a body to Monseigneur, he welcomed us with little grace, which managed to disgust a large part among us.' It was only the efforts of the Duc de Berri, Artois's son, and the Duc d'Enghien, Condé's grandson, that the officers that felt so unwelcome did not leave immediately.[91]

Jerningham's colonelcy, if he was indeed formally appointed, was brief. On 15 October Windham wrote to Woodford to inform him that Dillon had been authorised to have a second battalion and orders had been sent to Richard Gardiner, an inspector who acted as Woodford's deputy, that all the Germans, expected to be about 300, were to be kept for this battalion.[92] The battalion left the Bodensee in December to march to an Italian port where it could embark for Corsica. On 8 January 1796 Dillon wrote to Windham suggesting several ways his two battalions could be brought to some parity, the first being organised like a British unit and the second, now four companies strong, more like a French one.[93] After a march

87 TNA: WO 4/367: Woodford to Gardiner 2 October 1795.
88 TNA: WO 4/367: Strangely Woodford informed Basset that Jerningham had the regiment but told, Gardiner, on the same day, that the command was undecided.
89 TNA: WO 4/367: Woodford to Gardiner 2 October 1795.
90 TNA: WO 4/367: Woodford to Gardiner 15 October 1795.
91 Perry de Nieüil, *Mémoires*, p.58.
92 TNA: WO 4/367: Windham to Woodford and Gardiner 15 October 1795.
93 BL: Add MS 37860: Dillon to Windham 8 January 1796.

of three months, during which more men were recruited than deserted, the troops finally embarked at Civitavecchia, north-west of Rome, and landed at Bastia on 22 April 'between six and seven hundred strong.'[94] The Dillon Regiment served in the Mediterranean, including Egypt and Eastern Spain, throughout the wars until disbanded in 1814.

Controversy

Whenever significant sums of public money are spent on schemes, even if they are well intentioned and planned, that come to no effective result criticism follows. That to raise the white cockade regiments is no exception. However, in this case, the way the money was spent was, at best, questionable.

As has been seen Toustain was impressed by the amount of money that was available for the new regiments and noted that most of the *colonels* made money from selling places in them, observing, 'These regiments were like farms of which the colonels were directors. The clothing, armament, hospitals, recruitment were on their account.'[95] Such arrangements were far from unusual in the era and, without proper scrutiny, could be open to abuse. Unfortunately, there was a belief among the Foreign Department of the War Office, supervising the formation and payment of the regiments, that the process, and their actions, would not be checked. Poole was to claim that Gardiner explained to him, '... that these accounts were never to be subject to a board of controul [sic], being he believed chiefly borne on the article of secret service money ...'[96]

Poole's recollection, however, may have been somewhat clouded by his antipathy to Gardiner, who he considered had taken his place as the senior inspector by false means. Indeed it would seem that Gardiner, through an intermediary, was in April 1795 the first to raise concerns about the how the money was being spent and somewhat contradicts Poole's statement. He made it clear that the regiments were 'two thirds of Germans, called Alsatians, who would desert.' He doubted their effectiveness, even if at full strength, as well as the motives of the émigré officers, writing, 'If any service than what directly lends to their own interest be expected from them, more is expected that they will ever perform.' Nevertheless, his chief concern was the probity of the spending, wishing to see Windham pressed, '... to order me home, with the accounts as delivered in by the different Colonels; that seeing the nature of their contingent charges, he may, while yet there is time, give such directions, as to enable, who ever may have to settle them not to disgrace us before a Board of Controul.'[97]

94 TNA: FO 20/10: Elliot to Palmerston 28 April 1795; it had 45 officers and 729 other ranks on 1 June (WO 1/899).

95 Perry de Nieüil, *Mémoires*, pp.52–53.

96 Poole, *Irregular Transactions*, p.18.

97 BL: Add MS 37875: Catherine Longe to Windham 28 May, enclosing extracts from his letter to her of 29 April 1795.

However appointments to the department were a product of eighteenth century national and local political patronage and friendship, as well as family loyalties, that provided strong links of mutual interest between those who gave the places and those who received them. William Windham had since 1784 been Member of Parliament for Norwich in Norfolk, the county in which his family's seat was situated. He had many admirable features but was often in the shadow of those he admired such as Edmund Burke, his political mentor, for which he had an 'excess of friendship and admiration.'[98] He and Burke were among the Whigs who became disillusioned and then opposed to the progress of the French Revolution, leading him to join Pitt's Government and he became a partisan for the Bourbon cause.

Woodford, 29 years old and from a Lincolnshire family, had been a close friend of Edmund Burke's son, Richard who, also an MP, had died in August 1794, and this did not go unnoticed when his appointment was reported, 'Young Mr Woodford, the friend of the late Mr R. Burke, is appointed to the lucrative situation of inspector general of these emigrant corps.'[99] It was, however, his lack of experience which was remarkable; he had been an infantry captain but, otherwise, '... had not held any other public situation connected with the Army or the War Office.'[100] The inspector, Gardiner, had also been an infantry captain and when appointed was adjutant to the North Lincolnshire Militia, such battalions being bastions of county influence.[101] The Agent, the conduit for payments between the Paymaster General and individuals, did not provide independent oversight as Windham appointed his half-brother, Robert Lukin, to the post on 14 August 1794 without requiring securities as was normal for such a position.[102] Even Jerningham, who had written to Windham asking for a post but would not agree '... to serve in any other inferior [to that rank he held in the French service], unless it was as titular colonel of a regiment ...' may have owed his proposed appointment to such influences as he came from a prominent Norfolk family with close links to the Windhams.[103]

In 1804 Poole, apparently after having tried to seek redress otherwise, published a small book in which he described a number of financial abuses relating to the accounts of the white cockade regiments and the Foreign Department. One example he gave was that of an extraordinary expense of 'some hundred livres ... which an officer recruiting in Holland stated he had lost into the canal at Delft' followed by another, submitted the following month, on behalf of the same officer for 'a still larger sum' which had also met a watery grave, this time in the Zuiderzee. He refused to sanction the payments but subsequently found they had been accepted

98 Quoted by R.G. Thorne, 'WINDHAM, William.'
99 *Hampshire Chronicle*, 6 October 1794.
100 'Report on the Office of the Secretary at War, Foreign Department', *The Seventh Report of the Commissioners of Military Enquiry* (London: House of Commons, 1809), p.11.
101 Poole, *Irregular Transactions*, p.1.
102 *The Seventh Report*, p.14 and 'An Account of the Amount of Sums issued in each year to Robert Lukin Esq an Agent to a Foreign Corps between 1794 and 1801 ...' Anon., *Papers presented to the House of Commons 18th April 1806* (London: House of Commons, 1809), p.24. Windham's mother, Sarah Lukin, née Hicks, was a widow when she married his father.
103 BL: Add MS 37860: Jerningham to Windham, the archivist has dated the letter 2 November 1795 but this is clearly a mistake as this would be after his nomination.

over his head.[104] Others involved the activities of a man known as Charles Devaux who was engaged as an agent for supplies and, according to Poole, was an acquaintance of Gardiner. He had the contract to supply, at government expense, fodder for the horses belonging to the regiments' officers although, as Poole pointed out, almost none had horses, *capitaines* and below simply could not afford to buy one. Nevertheless, this provision was soon provided universally to every officer in the regiments although they could opt to receive a payment in lieu of the rations, the better option if they had no horse. The payment was however worth less than a third of the value of the ration, an arrangement which was, of course, '... very beneficial to the contractor.'[105]

Scrutiny was avoided by accounts being certified by other members of the same department, who in many cases were related by blood or marriage. So Gardiner, who succeeded in Woodford's role abroad before returning to Britain to take up the post of Accountant of the Foreign Department, and as such certified 'Mr Lukin's Account, including his own Expenditure.'[106] With gentle understatement it was later reported that, 'It appears therefore on the whole, that those checks and precautions, which are usually adopted in the cases of Officers entrusted with such large powers in money transactions, were not observed in his case.'[107]

Windham, after a break, finally left office in 1807 by which time parliamentary investigations had commenced. However, Woodford, who had, separately been found to have been selling places in the civil service of the Honourable East India Company, absconded the country in 1809 to avoid answering for his accounts. Although Robert Lukin, whose role as Agent had been taken by his brother James, had to reimburse large sums of money, there was no political appetite to pursue the matters further after Windham's death in 1810. Indeed, Gardiner received a superannuation on 15 August 1815, for his post as First Clerk, when the Foreign Department was reduced.

The money spent in the raising of the white cockade regiments was substantial, the 'Paymaster General of His Majesty's Land Forces' issued £78,900 in 1794 and £482,500 in 1795 to Robert Lukin for 'Levy Money, Subsistence and other Services of sundry Foreign Corps.'[108] On his own account, Lukin paid out a total of just over £163,906 for costs relating to the White Cockade regiments between 1794 and 1796.[109] Poole estimated that as much as £60,000 was spent on the contract to supply fodder alone.[110]

104 Poole, *Irregular Transactions*, pp.7–8.
105 Poole, *Irregular Transactions*, pp.17–22.
106 *The Examiner*, 5 July 1812.
107 *The Seventh Report*, p.12.
108 Anon., *Papers presented to the House of Commons*, p.3.
109 £17,046,224 at estimated values 2020/2021, <https://inflation.iamkate.com/>, accessed March 2021.
110 Poole, *Irregular Transactions*, p.18, equivalent of £6,240,000 (see above).

Table 5.2 – Extracted sums from 'A General Abstract of Payments made by Mr Robert Lukin, on Account of the Foreign corps, …' (to the nearest pound).

Regiment	*1794 & 1795*	*1796*	*Total*
Raised in Britain			
Hector	25,422	11,409	36,840
Dresnay	29,281	6,469	35,750
Hervilly	43,281	247	43,528
Total for regiments raised in Britain			116,119
Raised on the Continent			
Broglie	2,205	740	2,944
Autichamp	587	678	1,265
Viomenil	82	325	407
Bethisy	11	103	115
Montmorency-Laval	1777	203	1,980
Mortemart	1,780	18,834	20,611
Castries	51	20,415	20,465
Total for regiments raised on the Continent			47,787
Grand Total			163,906

Source: Anon., *Papers presented to the House of Commons*, pp.26–27.

These were not the only payments that were made as both Woodford and Gardiner had separate accounts, the former drawing 'from the time of his appointment in August 1794, to the time of his return to England in September 1796, or of his ceasing to receive his allowances as Inspector General in December following' just over £461,159.[111]

The raising of the white cockade regiments was a costly project. When conceived it may have brought some success but the changing tide of war, in Germany and then at Quiberon, put paid to these prospects. Its failure and expense only added to the suspicions, already held by some, of the motivation of the émigrés and the efficacy of supporting their military formations. Unfortunately, the inept, and perhaps even fraudulent, way the project was managed by British officials, along with some émigrés, only fed these doubts. The project was, however, one of a number of measures taken by the British Government to provide support for the French royalists which, finally, bore fruit with the restoration of the Bourbon monarchy in 1814. In the realm of British military affairs, it brought the raising of units under specific capitulations to an end. When the wars started again, after the breach of the Peace of Amiens, foreign units were raised within the British Army itself, their officers receiving King's commissions, albeit temporary ones at first, which clarified and simplified their command but also, more significantly, their administration: their financing coming under regular Parliamentary scrutiny and their officers and men being subject to the army's military justice system.

111 *The Seventh Report*, p.12, equivalent to £47,960,536 (see above).

Bibliography

Archives

British Library (BL)
- Add MS 37842–37935 Windham Papers
- Add MS 49088 Napier Papers

National Archives, Kew (TNA)
- FO 20/10 Sir Gilbert Elliot
- FO 29/5 Colonel C. Craufurd
- FO 74/5 William Wickham
- HO 42/41 Domestic correspondence George III
- HO 50/386 Military correspondence Secretary at War
- HO 51/147 War Office correspondence, miscellaneous
- WO 1/171–175 British Army on the Continent
- WO 1/388 Foreign troops on British pay
- WO 12/11681 Muster books, Régiment d'Hervilly
- WO 12/11708 Muster books, Régiment du Dresnay
- WO 24/1112 Capitulation book
- WO 4/154–155 Secretary at War out letters
- WO 4/367 Foreign Department, inspectors
- WO 4/377 Foreign Department, out letters
- WO 4/735 French Corps out letters
- WO 6/131 Secretary of State for War out letters
- WO 65/167 Army lists, Foreign Corps

Published Material

Anon. (ed.), *Mémoires d'Olivier d'Argens et Correspondances des Généraux* (Paris: Baudouin Frères, 1826)

Anon., *Papers Presented to the House of Commons 18th April 1806* (London: House of Commons, 1809)

Anon., 'Report on the Office of the Secretary at War, Foreign Department', *The Seventh Report of the Commissioners of Military Enquiry* (London: House of Commons, 1809)

Cau-Durban, D., and Pasquier, F. (eds), 'Mémoires du Comte Pierre-Paul Faydit de Terssac, Major d'Artois, Chevalier de Saint-Louis 1736–1820', *Bulletin Périodique de la Société Ariègeoise des Sciences, Lettres & Arts et de la Société des Études du Couserans*, vol.18, No.1, (1901), pp.5–36, 78–96, 148–166 and 209–237

Cobbett, William (ed.), *The Parliamentary History of England, from the Earliest Period to the year 1803* (London: T.C. Hansard, 1818)

E.M.C., *Deux Victimes de Quiberon* (Vannes: La Foyle, 1895)

Gouzillon de Bélizal, Vicomte de, 'Journal et Lettres d'un Émigré', *Revue de Bretagne*, vol.XXVII, January–February 1902, pp.92–113

Grouvel, Vicomte Robert, *Les corps de troupes de l'émigration française* (Paris: Les Éditions de La Sabretache, 1957–1964)

Le Charron, André-Louis-Lambert Baron, *Expédition de Quiberon, suivie de L'Évasion des Prisons de Vannes* (Paris: Ambroise Dupont et Roret, 1826)

Perry de Nieüil, Marquise de, *Mémoires du Marquis de Toustain 1790–1823* (Paris: Plon, 1933)

Poole, James, *A Narrative Exposing a Variety of Irregular Transactions in One of the Departments of Foreign Corps during the Late War* (London: J. Parson and Son, 1804)

Robert, Charles, *1795 Expédition des Emigres à Quiberon Le Comte d'Artois à l'îsle d'Yeu* (Paris: Lamulle & Poisson, 1899)

Roussel, M. de, *Etat militaire de France pour l'année 1790 Trente-deuxième édition* (Paris: Chez Onfroy, 1790)

Online sources

R.G. Thorne 'WINDHAM, William (1750–1810) of Felbrigg Hall, Norf,' <http://www.historyofparliamentonline.org/volume/1790-1820/member/windham-william-1750-1810>, accessed 30 November 2021

'Plaque de baudrier du régiment d'Hervilly', <https://art.rmngp.fr/fr/library/artworks/plaque-de-baudrier-du-regiment-d-hervilly_laiton_1795>, accessed 14 November 2021

6

The House of Orange and the Re-establishment of the Dutch Army, 1810–1814

Mark Edward Hay

This chapter examines the reorganisation of the Dutch army in 1810–1814. The history of the Dutch army of the Revolutionary and Napoleonic era is well known. After the Dutch defeat by Revolutionary France in what has become known as the War of the First Coalition, a rejuvenated Batavian Republic re-entered the Revolutionary wars as a French ally. This marked a beginning of a steady realignment of Dutch geopolitical interests with those of France and a close co-operation with the French armed forces. For example, in 1806–1809 the Dutch army participated in Napoleon's campaigns in northern Germany, and in 1808 the Dutch dispatched a contingent to assist Napoleon in pacifying Spain.[1] The Dutch army also played a key role in defending France's exposed northern flank, most notably in 1799, when an Anglo-Russian force landed at Den Helder, and in 1809, when the British attempted an invasion through Zeeland.[2] The year 1810 is a watershed in Dutch military history. On 9 July 1810, the Kingdom of Holland was annexed to France and the Dutch army was integrated into Napoleon's Grande Armée.[3] From this date, there was no longer an independent Dutch army. Instead, there were only a handful of regiments of the Grande Armée with a Dutch pedigree. As part of the Grande Armée, the Dutch regiments participated in the Russian Campaign of 1812, where they suffered

1 M. van der Hoeven, *Van de Weser tot de Weichsel. Het leger van het Koninkrijk Holland en de Duitse veldtochten van Napoleon, 1806, 1807 en 1809* (Amsterdam: De Bataafsche Leeuw, 1994); J.A. de Moor and H.Ph. Vogel, *Duizend miljoen maal vervloekt land. De Hollandse Brigade in Spanje, 1808-1813* (Amsterdam: Meulenhoff, 1991).

2 M.A. van Alphen et al., *Mars et Historia. Themanummer: 1799 – De Brits-Russische invasie in Noord-Holland* 33/4 (1999); J. Zuurbier, et al. (eds), *De lange herfst van 1799: De Russisch-Engelse invasie in polder en duin* (Castricum: Stichting Herdenking 1799, 1998); G. van Uythoven, *The Secret Expedition. The Anglo-Russian Invasion of Holland 1799* (Warwick: Helion, 2018); P. Ball, *A Waste of Blood and Treasure. The 1799 Anglo-Russian Invasion of the Netherlands* (Barnsley: Pen & Sword, 2017); G. Bond, *The Grand Expedition. The British Invasion of Holland in 1809* (Athens, GA: University of Georgia Press, 1979).

3 H.T. Colenbrander, *Inlijving en Opstand* (Amsterdam: J.M. Meulenhoff, 1941), pp.1–5; J.W. Sypesteijn, *Geschiedenis van het regiment Nederlandse rijdende artillerie* (Zaltbommel: Joh. Noman & Zoon, 1852), p.163.

considerable casualties. However, it was not until the retreat from Russia that the Dutch regiments were ostensibly destroyed.

The Dutch never fully accepted annexation to France and in November 1813, following Napoleon's defeats in Russia and Central Europe, the Dutch rose up and independence was declared by a provisional government.[4] The provisional government recognised that to succeed it needed a military force, and so without delay they set about reconstituting the Dutch army. The historiography of the Dutch army highlights the success of recruitment in the Netherlands.[5] Indeed, the recruitment efforts in the first weeks of the uprising were impressive. Within hours of declaring independence, Dutch officers were dispatched to take command of the military forces stationed in the Netherlands, both Dutch home defence units and the French units stationed in the Netherlands. The Dutch troops eagerly took service in the new Dutch army.[6]

As to the French troops, because Napoleon had stripped the Netherlands bare of troops to reinforce his armies after the defeat in Russia, there were actually few French troops in the Netherlands. Those troops that remained in the Netherlands were of poor quality. They included veteran battalions, deserters and foreign prisoners of war who had been taken into French service.[7] Some of these units melted away at first contact. Others, like the 4th Foreign Regiment, which consisted of Prussian prisoners of war, switched their allegiance and they were integrated into the new Dutch army.[8] To place recruitment on a more structural footing, two recruitment centres were set up in Amsterdam and Delft. These centres would see a steady inflow of recruits.[9] In addition to these government efforts, there were many grassroots initiatives. The Dutch archives are scattered with references to local

4 I. de Haan. 'Een Nieuwe Staat', in I. de Haan, P. den Hoed and H. te Velde (eds), *Een Nieuwe Staat: Het Begin van het Koninkrijk der Nederlanden* (Amsterdam: Prometheus-Bert Bakker, 2013), pp.12–17; W. Uitterhoeve, *1813–Haagse Bluf: De korte chaos van vrijwording* (Nijmegen: Vantilt, 2013); J. Koch, *Koning Willem I, 1772-1843* (Amsterdam: Boom, 2013), pp.224–226; P.J. Blok, 'Staatkundige geschiedenis van de omwenteling', in G.J.W. Koolemans Beijnen (ed.), *Historische gedenkboek der herstelling van Neêrlands onafhankelijkheid in 1813* (Haarlem: De Erven F. Bohn, 1912–1913), vol.I, pp.1–33; Colenbrander, *Inlijving en opstand*, pp.171–318; C.H.E. de Wit, *De strijd tussen aristocratie en democratie in Nederland, 1780-1848. Herwaardering van een periode* (Heerlen: Winants, 1965), pp.312–336.

5 W.E.A. Wüppermann, *De vorming van het Nederlandsche leger na de omwenteling van 1813 en het aandeel van dat leger aan den veldtocht van 1815* (Breda: Koninklijke Militaire Academie, 1900), pp.1–17; W.E. van Dam van Isselt, *De ontwikkeling van ons krijgswezen sedert November 1813* (Haarlem: Vincent Loosjes, 1902), pp.1–3; G.J.W. Koolemans Beijnen, 'De militaire geschiedenis van de omwenteling,' in *Historische gedenkboek*, pp.104–110.

6 'Kemper and Fannius Scholten to General Administration, 24 November 1813', Netherlands, Nationaal Archief (NL-NA): 2.02.01, 6084; 'Krayenhoff to Prince of Orange, 1 December 1813', NL-NA: 2.02.01, 6565. Cf. Koolemans Beijnen, 'De militaire geschiedenis van de omwenteling', pp.74–75.

7 Koolemans Beijnen, 'De militaire geschiedenis van de omwenteling', p.74.

8 G.C. Dempsey, *Napoleon's Mercenaries. Foreign Units in the French Army Under the Consulate and Empire, 1799 to 1814* (Barnsley: Frontline Books, 2016), pp.236–244; Koolemans Beijnen, 'De militaire geschiedenis van de omwenteling', pp.104–105; Colenbrander, *Inlijving en Opstand*, pp.293, 304.

9 'J. van den Bosch to Krayenhoff, 4 December 1813', NL-NA: 2.02.01, 6565.

Dutch notables organising voluntary units. For example, two former officers, W.F. Boreel and L.N. Hartingh, each raised a cavalry regiment.[10] Baron Frederick von Bouchenröder organised a unit of 300 volunteers in the early days of the uprising.[11] And in Friesland, two notables mustered 104 recruits by early December.[12] Not all initiatives were successful, but as the volunteers were fed into the cadre of regular units, they did strengthen the new Dutch army. The first official overview of Dutch troops of 7 February 1814 shows that 13 infantry regiments, two cavalry regiments, and four artillery batteries had been raised, totalling about 10,000 men.[13]

What is less well known is that, in addition to these domestic efforts to reconstitute the Dutch army, the exiled House of Orange undertook several initiatives to re-establish an independent Dutch army in 1812–1814. These efforts by the House of Orange were crucial to the Dutch success in navigating the challenging international climate to secure independence for an enlarged United Kingdom of the Netherlands. This chapter examines the House of Orange's efforts to reconstitute a Dutch armed force. The chapter first briefly discusses the Dutch army in 1810 and its incorporation into the Grande Armée. The chapter then concentrates on Orange's two most prominent efforts to organise a Dutch fighting force: their recruitment of Dutch survivors of the Russian Campaign and their efforts to retrieve Orange troops from the Peninsula. The conclusion reflects on the significance of Orange's efforts for the history of the Dutch armed forces and the history of the Netherlands more broadly.

The Dutch Army in 1810

In 1810, the Dutch army had a strength of about 28,000 men. However, not all troops were available for campaigning. About 6,000 troops were employed for internal defence, such as manning coastal batteries, garrisoning key fortresses, and internal policing. Additionally, as mentioned, a contingent had been dispatched to serve Napoleon in the Peninsula. Initially, this contingent was about 3,500 men strong, but by 1810 it had dwindled to about half that size. So, in 1810 the Dutch field army numbered about 20,000 men.[14]

After of the Netherlands was annexed to the empire, on 18 August 1810 the Dutch army was incorporated into the Grand Armée. The Dutch infantry was amalgamated and renumbered the 123rd–126th Line Infantry Regiments, and the 33rd Light Infantry Regiment. The cavalry became the 11th Hussars and the 14th Regiment of Cuirassiers. The artillery was merged into the 7th Regiment of Horse Artillery and the 9th Regiment of Foot Artillery. The five companies of support services were split

10 'Timmermans to Hartingh, 10 December 1813', NL-NA: 2.02.01, 6565.
11 'Bouchenröder to William I, 14 December 1813', NL-NA: 2.02.01, 6591.
12 'Krayenhoff to William I, 8 December 1813', NL-NA: 2.02.01, 6565.
13 'Staat der Sterkte der Verschillende Corpsen, uitmakende de Sterkte der Staande Armée, 7 February 1814', NL-NA: 2.02.01, 6620.
14 'Corps d'Observation de la Hollande, 15 July 1810', France, Service Historique de la Défense (FR-SHD): GR 2C 690.

up and attached to French parent units. One company became 6th Company of the 1st Battalion of Miners, one company was transformed into the 5th Company of Armourers, two companies were transformed into the 17th and 18th Companies of Artificers, and the Dutch bridging train became the 11th Company of the 1st Battalion of Pontoniers. Louis Bonaparte's Royal Guard – 'La gloire de la Hollande' according to Napoleon – became the 3rd Regiment of Foot Grenadiers and the 2nd Regiment of Lancers of Napoleon's Imperial Guard (the Red Lancers).[15] There were some other units of the French-Imperial army with links to the Netherlands, for example 131st Line Infantry Regiment. The unit was formerly known as the regiment of the Isle of Walcheren, after the eponymous island in the Dutch province of Zeeland. It was a penal regiment consisting of a hodgepodge of refractory conscripts from the northern imperial departments and prisoners of war of various nationality. Although some Dutch conscripts are found in the muster books, the regiment was not really a Dutch unit.[16] There were also the 146th-148th Line Infantry Regiments, which were raised in 1813, after Napoleon's defeat in Russia. The three regiments contained conscripts from the Dutch departments. However, the regiments had only a short existence and they saw little action.[17]

The Dutch Regiments in the Russian Campaign

There is some confusion about the strength of the Dutch contingent that participated in the Russian Campaign. Most Dutch historians, like Funekotter and Van der Spek, follow the French historian Fabry, who gives a detailed breakdown of the strength of the various units that made up the Grande Armée that invaded Russia. Adding up his numbers for the Dutch units gives a total of 14,842 men.[18] However, this figure can be contested on the basis of the memoires of well-placed Dutch officers who participated in the Russian Campaign. For example, as Van der Spek also notes, *Generaal* F.R. Pouget and *Kolonel* Jan Demoulin both give considerably higher

15 H. Ringoir, *De Nederlandse Infanterie* (Bussum: C.A.J. van Dishoeck, 1968), pp.51–53; F.H.A. Sabron, *Geschiedenis van het 124ste regiment infanterie van linie onder keizer Napoleon I* (Breda: Koninklijke Militaire Academie, 1910), pp.6–7; F.H.A. Sabron, *Geschiedenis van het 33ste regiment lichte infanterie (het oud-Hollandsche 3de regiment jagers) onder keizer Napoleon I* (Breda: Koninklijke Militaire Academie, 1910); C.D.H. Schneider, *Het 126ste regiment Hollandsche infanterie in Rusland in 1812* (Amsterdam: P.N. van Kampen, 1898), 6; J.W. Sypesteijn, *Geschiedenis van het regiment Hollandsche hussaren [...]* (The Hague: De Gebroeders Van Cleef, 1849); Sypesteijn, *Nederlandse rijdende artillerie*, p.163; G.A. Geerts, 'De veldtocht naar Rusland in 1812 onder keizer Napoleon 1', *Militaire Spectator* (1983), p.52; J.P.C.M. van Hooff, 'George Diederich Benthien: een bruggenbouwer pur sang', *Armamentaria*, (1998-1999), p.83; C. van der Spek, *Sous les Armes. Het Hollandse leger in de Franse tijd, 1806-1814* (Amsterdam: Boom, 2016), pp.140–152.

16 '131e Régiment d'infanterie de ligne', FR-SHD: GR21 YC 895-900.

17 D.G. Chandler, *The Campaigns of Napoleon* (New York: Macmillan, 1966), pp.866–867; Ringoir, *De Nederlandse Infanterie*, p.52.

18 G. Fabry, *Campagne de Russe (1812). Documents Annexes* (Paris: R. Chapelot & Cie, 1903), pp.262–397; B. Funnekotter, *De hel van 1812. Nederlanders met Napoleon op veldtocht naar Rusland* (Amsterdam: Prometheus, 2015), p.299; Van der Spek, *Sous les Armes*, pp.264–265.

figures than Fabry for the 124th and 126th Line Infantry respectively.[19] Presumably the difference is the result of Fabry only counting first line units, whilst the contemporaries also include rear units in the count. As the rear units do play a role in the reorganisation of the Dutch army, they must be included. Knowing that all the units that made up the Dutch field army of 1810 participated in the Russian Campaign, but lacking detailed listings for all Dutch units, a sensible approach would be to take the size of the Dutch field army when it was placed on its new footing in 1810 as a good indication of the number of Dutch troops that participated in the Russian Campaign of 1812, that is about 20,000 men. This number does not include the class of 1813, which were organised into the 146th-148th Line Infantry Regiments.

Dutch units were in the thick of all major engagements. In particular, two feats of arms are much quoted by Dutch military historians. The first is the Battle of Krasnoi, which was a series of skirmishes fought between 15 and 18 November 1812.[20] After Napoleon left Moscow on 19 October 1812, the Russian *Generalfeldmarschall* Mikhail Kutuzov had been trailing his army. By mid-November, Kutuzov engaged in the hope of splitting the Grande Armée into two. It was at this moment that Napoleon committed his Guard, including the Dutch Foot Grenadiers, and also the 33rd Light. To hold off the Russian attack both regiments formed up in squares. They resisted multiple charges by Russian cavalry, which was supported by artillery, but both units incurred heavy casualties. The Dutch Guard Regiment suffered 460 casualties out of 500 men. The 33rd Light Regiment was down to 80 men, of whom only 25 were uninjured.[21]

The second much quoted Dutch feat of arms is the bridging of the Berezina. During the retreat from Moscow, Napoleon called on his pontoniers to lay two bridges across the Berezina River so as to allow his army to escape the advancing Russians. Seven companies of the Bridging Train were available, but five companies had marched to Moscow and back, and they were down to a collective 200 men. Two other companies, the 7th Bridging Company and the 11th (Dutch) Bridging Company, had not participated in the march on Moscow. At 100 men apiece they were at good strength. Supported by 750 artificers, these 400 pontoniers laid two bridges across the Berezina near Studianka. This allowed a large part of the Grande Armée to retreat to relative safety, but it came at a high cost. Only 40 pontoniers survived the icy water, and of the 100 Dutch pontoniers, only eight managed to cross the Berezina.[22]

It is in part due to glorification and the mythification of such heroic feats that it is commonly accepted that the Dutch contingent of the Grande Armée all but

19 Van der Spek, *Sous les Armes*, pp.264–265; See also: Schneider, *Het 126ste*, pp.7, 9, 22.

20 D. Lieven, *Russia against Napoleon: the Battle for Europe, 1807 to 1814* (London: Allen Lane, 2009), pp.267–268.

21 Geerts, *De veldtocht naar Rusland*, p.60.

22 J. Eysten, *Geschiedenis der Nederlandsche pontonniers* (Breda: Koninklijke Militaire Academie, 1908), pp.110–126; J. Eysten, 'Doorloopend verhaal van de dienstverrichtingen der Nederlandsche pontonniers onder den majoor G.D. Benthien 1797-1825', *Bijdragen en Mededeelingen van het Historisch Genootschap* 32 (1911), pp.149–158; Van Hooff, '*George Diederich Benthien*', pp.83–84.

perished on the fields of Russia and Central Europe.[23] But to acknowledge that the Dutch contingent was destroyed in Russia does not mean to say that each and every single Dutch solider died. Nothing could be further from the truth.

The Destruction of the Dutch Contingent of the Grande Armée?

The regimental muster books of the post-1814 Dutch army remain safe and well in the Dutch national archives.[24] These books have a template for registering new recruits, which included entry lines for previous military experience, the unit in which one had served if any, and the campaigns and battles one had fought in if any. The muster books clearly reveal that many recruits had previously served in the Dutch regiments that participated in Napoleon's invasion of Russia. The author has not yet had the opportunity to study all muster books but extrapolating from a close examination of four of the 54 infantry battalion muster books,[25] and a more superficial reading of another 12 infantry battalion muster books,[26] the author would posit that about 8,000–10,000 Dutch soldiers survived the Russian Campaign. This amounts to about 40–50 percent of the Dutch contingent of the Grande Armée if one adheres to a strength of 20,000 men, and 53–67 percent if one adheres to the lower estimate of 15,000 men. Further study would need to quantify the survival rate of the Dutch contingent of the Grande Armée with more precision.

Accepting that the exact number of survivors is subject to further study, this research finding raises two questions. First, how did so many of the Dutch troops of the Grande Armée survive the Russian Campaign whilst the scholarly consensus is that most of the force perished in Russia? The key lies in the fact that many Dutch troops were taken captive. This happened in various ways. First, Dutch troops were taken captive during foraging. A good example is the 33rd Light. On the road to Minsk, they struggled to find sufficient provisions and so they scattered to forage. In fact, they had scattered to such an extent that when called for review by *Maréchal* Davout, the entire regiment could only muster 35 men.[27] Most of the troops later rejoined their regiment, but a significant number continued to roam and were taken captive. Second, during the many skirmishes and battles in Russia and the retreat through Central Europe, many Dutch soldiers became prisoners of war. For example, at the aforementioned Battle of Krasnoi, 78 men of the 33rd Light were taken captive.[28] The 125th and 126th Line were part of the French rearguard

23 For example: Van der Spek, *Sous les Armes*, pp.278–279; Colenbrander, *Inlijving en Opstand*, pp.151–152; Van der Hoeven, *Van de Weser tot de Weichsel*, pp.21, 80; Wüpperman, *De vorming van het Nederlandsche leger*, p.1; P. van Rooden, *In de achterhoede van Napoleon. Gezondheidsofficier J.S. Zembsch en het 125e regiment in 1812* (Dordrecht: P. van Rooden, 2016), pp.11–12.

24 NL-NA: 2.13.09, Inventaris van het archief van het Ministerie van Oorlog: Stamboeken van Onderofficieren en Minderen van de Landmacht, 1813-1924.

25 NL-NA: 2.13.09, 7, 10, 10A, 199, 227.

26 NL-NA: 2.13.09, 8-9, 13-17A, 68, 65.94, 120, 145, 356, 382.

27 Sabron, *Geschiedenis van het 33ste*, pp.44–45.

28 Ringoir, *De Nederlandse Infanterie*, pp.51–52.

that was tasked with holding off the Russian advance at Borisov on 21 November 1812 and Berezina on 26–29 November 1812. The historiography has it that both regiments were destroyed.[29] This is true, but not all men were killed. A good number were taken captive.[30] Jean Victor, Baron de Constant Rebecque, a Swiss officer and trusted military advisor of the Prince of Orange, further notes that large numbers of Dutch soldiers were taken captive by Allied armies when hostilities resumed after the Armistice of Pläswitz broke down. Scores of Dutch soldiers were taken at Großbeeren (23 August 1813), Katzbach (26 August), Dresden (27 August), Kulm (29–30 August), and Dennewitz (6 September).[31] Finally, many Dutch troops were taken captive as a result of how the Dutch regiments were deployed. With the exception of the Guard and the 33rd Light, all Dutch units dispatched only part of their regiment, several battalions or sometimes even only several companies, to participate in the invasion proper. The remainder of the unit remained in the rear to perform second line duties. And when the invasion of Russia turned into retreat, these rear units withdrew into strategically located towns and fortresses. These places were subsequently invested by the Allies, and when they fell, the garrisons were taken captive. For example, 1,000 Dutch soldiers were taken captive after the fall of Stettin on 5 December 1813, with a further 400 picked up as stragglers.[32] Another 1,200 Dutch troops were taken captive at Wittenberg on 14 January 1813.[33] The Hamburg-Harburg area in northern Germany had a strong Dutch presence too. By 25 January 1814, the allies had collected 2,000 Dutch soldiers from the region.[34]

The second question that this research finding (that many Dutch soldiers survived the Russian campaign) raises, is what happened to the Dutch survivors? As was common in the age, captive soldiers were given the choice of either taking service in the victor's army or becoming prisoners of war. From anecdotal evidence it is clear that many Dutch soldiers opted to join the Allied ranks. For example, there was a significant Dutch presence in the Hansa Legion, the Lutzow Freikorps, and the Saxon contingent of the Army of the North. The 2nd battalion of the Russo-German Legion was an all-Dutch unit.[35] From archival evidence, it is also clear that some Dutch troops preferred captivity over Allied service. These troops were transported

29 Van der Spek, *Sous les Armes*, pp.276–279
30 Ringoir, *De Nederlandse Infanterie*, pp.51–52; Schneider, *Het 126ste*, pp.37–49.
31 'Dagboeken, 4 October 1813', NL-NA: 2.21.008.01, 24.
32 'General Grandeau to the Prince of Neuchatel and Wagram [Berthier], 4 December 1813', FR-SHD, 2C 163; Colenbrander, *Inlijving en Opstand*, p.256; Sabron, *Geschiedenis van het 124ste*, pp.92–93.
33 'Dowager Princess to Constant Rebecque, 2 December 1813', NL-NA: 2.21.008.01, 34; Sabron, *Geschiedenis van het 124ste*, p.95.
34 'Boreel to William I, 25 January 1814', NL-NA: 2.02.01, 6566; 'Benningsen to William I, 30 January 1814', NL-NA: 2.02.01, 6566; J. Huck, *Das ende der Franzosenzeit in Hamburg. Quellen und Studien zur Belagerung und Befreiung von Hamburg 1813-1814* (Hamburg: Kabel, 1984), p.12.
35 'Princess Louis to Prince of Orange, 10 March 1813', in J.W.A. Naber (ed.), *Correspondentie van de Stadhouderlijke familie 1777-1820* (The Hague: Martinus Nijhoff, 1931-1933), vol.V: p.187; J.W.A. Naber, *Prinses Wilhelmina, Gemalin van Willem V, Prins van Oranje* (Amsterdam: Meulenhoff, 1908), pp.278–281; G. Venzky, *Die Russisch-Deutsche Legion in den Jahren 1811-1815* (Wiesbaden: Harrassowitz, 1966), p.86.

to camps in Russia.[36] Finally, at least occasionally, the Allies simply released non-French captives without any conditions on their future conduct. A good example is the capture of Danzig on 24 December 1813. After taking the city, the Allies ordered the non-French part of the garrison to gather at the Russian gate to be released unconditionally.[37] So rather than the Dutch contingent of the Grande Armée wholly perishing in Russia, we find Dutch troops in Allied ranks, Dutch troops in prisoner of war camps, and Dutch stragglers roaming Central Europe.

Orange in Exile

At this point the House of Orange enters onto the scene. The role of the House of Orange in reorganising the Dutch armed forces is often overlooked. In fact, it is key to understanding the history of the Dutch army in 1812–1814. The swift conquest of the Netherlands by Revolutionary France in 1794–1795 forced the House of Orange to flee the Netherlands for Britain. With reference to the treaty of 1788, which committed Britain to military intervention in case the House of Orange was ousted from the Netherlands, Orange lobbied the British government for support for a return to the Netherlands.[38] It was not until 1799 that Britain consented to land an expeditionary force in the north of Holland – the invasion of Den Helder. The failure of the invasion caused a rift in Anglo-Orange relations, but the definitive break did not come until 1 October 1801, when Britain and France signed the preliminary articles of peace in London. This prompted Stadtholder William V to leave Britain to settle in Dietz (currently Diez in the Rhineland-Palatinate, Germany) in November 1801.[39]

Accepting loss, the House of Orange decided to negotiate with Napoleon to salvage what was possible from their once considerable portfolio of titles, offices and lands in the Netherlands. Agreement was achieved quickly. In return for renouncing all claims to previously held titles, offices and lands in the Netherlands, the House of Orange's dynastic lands in Germany were enlarged.[40] However, this was not the end

36 '3 November 1813, London', NL-NA: 2.21.008.01, p.25; Sabron, *Geschiedenis van het 124ste*, pp.94–95; 'Boreel to William I, 25 January 1814', NL-NA: 2.02.01, 6566; 'Benningsen to Willim I, 30 January 1814', NL-NA: 2.02.01, 6566; Huck, *Das ende der Franzosenzeit in Hamburg*, p.12.

37 'Capitulation de la Place de Dantzig', FR-SHD, C2 162; P.-H. D'Artois, *Relation de la Défense de Danzig, en 1813, par le 10e. corps de l'armée française, contre l'armée combinée russe et prussienne* (Paris: Ladrange, 1820), p.452.

38 'Traité d'Alliance défensive entra le Roi de la Grand-Brétagne et L.H.P. les Etats-Généraux D.P.U., 23 April 1788', in G.F. de Martens, *Recueil de Traités d'Alliance [...]* (Gottingen, 1818), vol.IV, pp.372–377; 'Traité d'Alliance défensive entra le Roi de Prusse et L.H.P. les Etats-Généraux D.P.U., Berlin, 15 April 1788', Martens, *Recueil de Traités*, vol.IV, pp.377–382 and 'Traité provisionel d'alliance défesive entre le Roi de Prusse et le Roi de la Grenade-Brétagne. Loo, 13 Juin 1788', pp.382–385.

39 Koch, *Willem I*, pp.88–118; L.A. Struik, *Oranje in Ballingschap 1795-1813. Een Odyssee* (Amsterdam: De Bataafsche Leeuw, 2006), pp.164–166.

40 'Dossier Fulda', Netherlands, Koninklijk Huisarchief (NL-KHA): A35, XV2; Koch, *Willem I*, pp.119–139; Struik, *Oranje in Ballingschap*, pp.108–120, 138–213; J.A. Bornewasser, 'Koning

of the matter. After receiving compensation from Napoleon, the House of Orange opened negotiations for further compensation with the new Dutch government. When Napoleon caught word of this, he intervened to stop Orange acquiring additional recompense. This set relations between Napoleon and the House of Orange on the wrong path, from which they would not recover.

In September 1804 Napoleon held an audience for the lesser German princes in Mainz. As German rulers, both the former Stadtholder William V and his son the Hereditary Prince of Orange, were invited, but both refused to attend.[41] Napoleon was furious, and he responded by occupying part of Orange's German lands.[42] The remainder of the territory got caught up in Napoleon's reorganisation of Central Europe after the defeat of the Habsburgs in the War of the Third Coalition. During his reorganisation of Central Europe, Napoleon invited Orange to join the Confederation of the Rhine, but if they refused, he warned, their territories would be incorporated into other states. For the Orange, however, things had gone too far already. Rather than join the Confederation of the Rhine, the Prince of Orange, entered Prussian service to fight in the War of the Fourth Coalition. In hindsight, this was an unfortunate decision. The prince commanded a Prussian division, but he was captured at Erfurt on 16 October 1806.[43] Napoleon now seized the remaining Orange territory in Germany.[44] Affairs continued to go downhill thereafter. Initially the Prince of Orange hoped to receive compensation for the loss of Orange territory in Germany, and he made three desperate attempts to re-establish relations with Napoleon, but Napoleon held Orange responsible for their misfortune and dismissed the overtures. Defeated and resigned, Orange retired to the Niederländisches Palais in Berlin.[45] The outbreak of the War of the Fifth Coalition offered the Prince of Orange a new opportunity to regain his losses. He entered Habsburg service as a *Feldmarschallleutenant*, but he was wounded at Wagram and forced to retire from active service.[46] The prince now retreated to his private estates in Silesia.[47]

Willem I,' ' in H.P.H. Jansen and C.A. Tamse (eds), *Nassau en Oranje in de Nederlandse Geschiedenis* (Alphen aan de Rijn: Sijthoff, 1979), p.236; B. Woelderink, 'Oranje tussen Nassau en Nederland, 1795-1802,' *Oranje in Revolutie en Restauratie. Jaarboek Oranje-Nassau Museum* (1996), pp.98–108.

41 Struik, *Oranje in Ballingschap*, pp.208–210, 220–225.

42 French troop movements: 'De Heerdt d'Eversberg to William V, 10 March 1806', NL-KHA: A35, XIV14; 'Charles de Dalwijk to William v, 12 March 1806', NL-KHA: A35, XIV14; A. Hallema, *Oranjevorsten in Ballingschap: Van Dilleburg en Londen uit voor Vrijheid en Recht* (Maastricht: Leiter-Nijpels, 1947), p.148.

43 'Prince of Orange to Wilhelmina, 24 July 1806', Naber, *Correspondentie,* vol.IV, pp.244–245; B. Schoenmaker and C.M. Schulten (eds), *Oranje op de Bres: Vorstenhuis en Leger in de Nederlandse Geschiedenis* (Amsterdam: De Bataafsche Leeuw, 1989), p.40; Koch, *Willem I*, pp.167–172; Struik, *Oranje in Ballingschap*, pp.245–263.

44 Struik, *Oranje in Ballingschap*, pp.269–288.

45 H.T. Colenbrander (ed.), *Gedenkstukken der algemeene geschiedenis van Nederland van 1795 tot 1840* (The Hague: Nijhoff, 1905-1922), vol.V, pp.761–762, 764–767.

46 Schoenmaker and Schulten, *Oranje op de Bres*, p.40.

47 J.A. van Hamel, "s Erfprinsen Toevluchtsoord. De Latere Koning Willem I als Landheer op het Posensche Riddergoed Raçot, Gedrurende Zijne Verdrijving uit het Vaderland', *Bijdragen voor Vaderlandsche Geschiedenis en Oudheidkunde* (1932), pp.231–232.

It was at this low ebb in the fortunes of the House of Orange that their luck changed. On 15 March 1813, Czar Alexander I, in pursuit of the retreating Grande Armée, passed through the Prussian city of Breslau, close to Orange's estates. The prince seized the opportunity to offer his services in exchange for the Czar's assistance in retaking the Netherlands for the House of Orange. The Czar pledged his support, and he accepted Orange into the anti-Napoleonic coalition that would defeat Napoleon in 1814.[48] The Czar's acceptance of Orange into the alliance might seem puzzling, because, at first sight, the House of Orange had little to contribute to the anti-Napoleonic war effort. But the Prince of Orange had several things going for him. To start, he had luck. The prince caught the Czar at a time when, after a long and exhausting military campaign in Russia, he was in dire need of allies, both to continue the war and to assert his position as leader of the soon-to-be Sixth Coalition. And so, one may expect the Czar to have been receptive to offers of alliance, in particular if it came from a house that had opposed Napoleon uninterrupted since 1804. More importantly, since Napoleon's intervention had collapsed the compensation deal with the new Dutch regime, *de facto* the House of Orange retained an outstanding claim to the Netherlands. This could be utilised to reinforce the Allied legitimacy of challenging Napoleon. Of course, it was now up the House of Orange to live up to their commitment of assisting to defeat Napoleon.

The Dutch Legion of Orange

The House of Orange quickly made two contributions to the allied cause. First, the indomitable Dowager Princess Wilhelmina set about organising a military force consisting of Dutch soldiers of the Grande Armée. She was quick to set up two recruitment centres, one in Berlin and one in Stralsund, on the Baltic coast, which could receive Dutch stragglers and deserters. Later these two recruitment centres would be moved to the more conveniently located centre at Schwedt on the Oder, which was commonly referred to as the Rassemblement, or the rallying point.[49] The rallying point successfully attracted Dutch stragglers. The intake proceeded at a steady pace of about two to three men per day.[50] Additionally, Wilhelmina actively sought out Dutch prisoners of war to request their transport to the Dutch rallying point. It seems she was well aware where Dutch prisoners of war were located, because one finds many references to large contingents of Dutch troops being released to the rallying point.[51] For example, an Orange envoy had discussed the fate of the Dutch garrison of Wittenberg even before the city was stormed. An agreement was easily reached and after the city was taken, the Dutch troops were

48 'Prince of Orange to Hardenberg, 19 March 1813', Colenbrander, *Gedenkstukken*, vol.VI, p.1864; 'Prince of Orange to Wilhelmina, 19 March 1813', Naber, *Correspondentie*, vol.V, pp.198–199.
49 Naber, *Prinses Wilhelmina*, p.280.
50 Colenbrander, *Inlijving en Opstand*, p.256.
51 'Dowager Princess to Constant Rebecque, 26 November 1813', NL-NA: 2.21.008.01, 34.

transported to the rallying point.[52] Likewise, the Dutch troops in the Hamburg-Harburg area were transferred to Orange service.[53] Obtaining command over troops that had been pressed into Allied service proved more difficult. Few generals like to see their numbers diminished. For example, *Feldmarschallleutnant* Ludwig von Wallmoden-Gimborn, who commanded the Russo-German Legion, was reluctant to release his Dutch battalion.[54] Despite the occasional set back, the House of Orange gathered sufficient Dutch soldiers of the Grande Armée to organise the of the so-called Legion Hollandaise d'Orange, or the Dutch Legion of Orange, which consisted of three infantry battalions and a detachment of artillery. But many more Dutch troops remained at the rallying point to recuperate. They were to be fed into units which were being raised in the Netherlands.[55]

The Nassau Contingent in the Peninsula

Whilst the Dowager Princess set about organising Dutch prisoners of war of the Russian Campaign, her son attempted to regain command of Orange troops in the Peninsula. As mentioned, in 1808 the new Dutch regime had dispatched a contingent to Spain. The Prince of Orange did not attempt to regain command of these Dutch troops. Presumably, unlike in Russia, they did not have detailed intelligence on the whereabouts of the Dutch contingent. However, there was also a Nassau contingent serving Napoleon in the Peninsula, and the Prince of Orange developed a plan to retrieve these troops.[56] In order to understand how he could claim and gain command of Nassau troops, it is necessary to reflect briefly on the history of the House of Nassau.

On the eve of the French Revolution the House of Nassau was divided into two branches: the Walramian Nassaus and the Ottonian Nassaus. The Walramian Nassaus were subdivided into three branches: Nassau-Saarbrücken, Nassau-Weilburg and Nassau-Usingen. The Nassau-Saarbrücken branch died out in 1797, and its territory, on the left bank of the Rhine, was inherited by Nassau-Usingen, but fell to France after the Imperial Recess of 1803. Territorially, Nassau-Weilburg and Nassau-Usingen were within the Holy Roman Empire.[57] The territory of the Ottonian Nassaus is referred to as Nassau-Dietz, which was an amalgamation of four previously separate counties, Dietz, Hadamar, Dillenburg and Siegen. Nassau-Dietz also lay entirely within the Holy Roman Empire, but in addition to these lands,

52 'Dagboeken, 3 November 1813', NL-NA: 2.21.008.01, 25; Sabron, *Geschiedenis van het 124ste*, pp.94–95.
53 'Boreel to William I, 25 January 1814', NL-NA: 2.02.01, 6566.
54 Colenbrander, *Inlijving en Opstand*, p.256; Venzky, *Die Russisch-Deutsche Legion*, p.81.
55 For the mention of the artillery: 'Dagboeken, 5-6 December 1813,', NL-NA: 2.21.008.01, 25.
56 W. Schüler, *Das Herzogtum Nassau 1806-1866: Deutsche Geschichte im Kleinformat* (Wiesbaden: Historische Kommission für Nassau, 2006), pp.41–45.
57 B.C.D. Anderson, 'Ernst Marschall von Bieberstein and the Foundation of Modern Nassau (1770-1814)', (PhD. Diss, University of Virginia, 1987), pp.23, 28–30; Schüler, *Das Herzogtum Nassau*, p.3; B.C.D. Anderson, 'State-Building and Bureaucracy in Early-Nineteenth-Century Nassau', *Central European History*, 24/3 (1991), pp.223–225.

the Ottonian Nassaus possessed extensive territories in the Netherlands, and traditionally they were the principal contenders for the stadtholdership.[58] The Ottonian Nassaus, of course, are commonly known as the House of Orange-Nassau, or simply the House of Orange.

The relationship between the various branches of the House of Nassau was generally good. The Princes of Orange were always sent on a tour of Nassau and the surrounding states to meet local rulers and notables, and the Princesses of Orange frequently married into the other branches. But with the signing of the 'Nassauischer Erbverein', the Act of Inheritance of 1783, the intra-dynastic ties took on a new meaning. The act guaranteed that the Nassau lands remained an undivided entity and that alienation of Nassau lands was forbidden. Moreover, it established a clear line of succession within the dynasty.[59] The Prince of Orange-Nassau-Dietz, who was already *de facto primus inter pares*, became President of the House of Nassau. But the act was not merely aimed at pre-empting potential intra-dynastic disputes over succession and territory.[60] It was also a commitment to collaborate in international politics. In the multipolar international order of the 1780s, this dynastic alliance makes much sense. As small geopolitical actors, the Netherlands and the Nassaus risked being dominated by the larger international powers. By allying into a dynastic network there was a greater chance of cancelling out these risks. Moreover, for small geopolitical actors, it was challenging and expensive to maintain relations with all key international powers. Conducting international politics through dynastic networks allowed for one component part of the dynasty to focus on maintaining ties with one, or two actors, whilst the other actors remained accessible through its partners. Ideally, a dynastic network would have members with ties to all key actors. The House of Nassau, in which Orange had strong ties with Britain and Prussia and the Walramians had strong ties to the Habsburgs and the Holy Roman Empire, closely approached this ideal.

The ascendancy of France on the eve of the nineteenth century severely strained the dynastic ties of the House of Nassau. As mentioned, the House of Orange had opted for confrontation with Napoleon. Walramian Nassau, on the other hand, had taken the path of co-operation. The Walramian Nassaus were original signatories of the Confederation of the Rhine Act, and they were greatly rewarded for it.[61] Usingen and Weilburg were united into a single duchy, and Frederick William of Nassau-Weilburg was elevated to Prince of Nassau. His cousin, Prince Frederick

58 E. Treichel, *Der Primat der Bürokratie: Bürokratischer Staat und bürokratische Elite im Herzogtum Nassau 1806-1866* (Stuttgart: Steiner, 1991), pp.37–45; H.P.H. Jansen, 'De Bredase Nassaus', in Jansen and Tamse (ed.), *Nassau en Oranje*, pp.13–44; Woelderink, 'Oranje tussen Nassau en Nederland', p.93; Struik, *Oranje in Ballingschap*, p.77.

59 'Kirberger Conferenz Protocoll, pp.7–24 January 1783', NL-KHA: B6, 38i.

60 B. Woelderink, 'De erfprins in Nassau in 1789. Het bezoek van prins Willem Frederik aan de Nassause erflanden als onderdeel van zijn Duitse studietijd,' *Jaarboek Oranje-Nassau Museum* (1994), pp.7–24; Struik, *Oranje in Ballingschap*, pp.17, 77; Anderson, 'State-Building', pp.223–224; Anderson, 'Ernst Marschall von Bieberstein', pp.23–28.

61 'Convention relative à la Confédération du Rhin [...]', in *Collection des Actes, Reglemens, Ordonnances et Autres Pièces Officielles Relatives a la Confédération du Rhin* (Paris: Schoell, 1808), vol.I, pp.11–22.

Augustus of Nassau-Usingen, remained Duke of Nassau. In 1816, the Walramian branches were united, when both Frederick William and Frederick Augustus died in quick succession. Frederick William's son, William, became sole ruler of the Walramian Nassaus. Territorially, the Walramians also benefitted from joining the Confederation of the Rhine. The lands of three princes, three imperial counts and eight imperial knights were added to the united Duchy of Nassau.[62]

With elevation came new responsibilities. To start, Nassau was to reorganise its military and participate in Napoleon's campaigns. The Walramians complied by reorganising all home defence units and troops from annexed territories into four infantry battalions and one squadron of cavalry.[63] In 1807, a second squadron of cavalry was raised.[64] In 1808, the four infantry battalions were converted to two regiments, and, after seeing minor action in Central Europe, the entire Nassau contingent was sent to Spain.[65] It was these troops that the Prince of Orange hoped to retrieve.

In order to gain command of the Nassau troops, the Prince of Orange needed to reassert his position as President of the House of Nassau. This was easier than expected, as international dynamics were forcing Nassau to seek to revive the dynastic network. By September 1813, the Allied armies were pushing back Napoleon's armies and it would not be long before they reached Nassau territory. Thus, for Nassau the time for defection had come. Defection is a risky international manoeuvre. One must abandon old allies before requesting membership to the new alliance. It is at this friendless moment that the new alliance tends to put forward their conditions for acceptance. In the case of the Napoleonic allies in Central Europe, like Nassau, the Allies of the Sixth Coalition had clearly defined conditions for entry: new allies were to contribute and finance a contingent of twice the size of the contingent that they raised for Napoleon. This contingent was to be placed under

62 'Proklamation zur Errichtung des Herzogtums 1806', Schüler, *Herzogtum Nassau*, pp.306–307. Territorial mutations: Articles 15, 20, 24 of 'Convention relative à la Confédération du Rhin [...]', *Collection des Actes*; Anderson, 'Ernst Marschall von Bieberstein', pp.152–191; M. Bernath, 'Die auswärtige Politik Nassaus 1805-1812. Ein Beitrag zur Geschichte des Rheinbundes und der politischen Ideen am Mittelrhein zur Zeit Napoleons,' *Nassauische Annalen* (1952), pp.130–147; Anderson, 'State-Building', p.233.

63 The following: I 'Leib' battalion under Todenwarth, later Pöllnitz, formerly the garrison company of Biebrich; II battalion under August von Kruse, formerly two companies of Weilburger Jäger; III Light Jäger battalion under Major von Schaeffer, formerly a 'light Jäger Korps' from Kurmainz; IV 'Musketeer' battalion under von Holbach, formerly the garrison of Wiesbaden. The infantry was organised according to the Austrian system. Each battalion of the regiment contained one grenadier and three musketeer companies, ideally of 147 men each.

64 Schüler, *Das Herzogtum Nassau*, p.36; P. Wacker, 'Die Hzgl. Nassauischen Truppen im Feldzug gegen Preußen 1806/07,' *Depesche* 10 (1988), p.1; P. Wacker, 'Das nassauische Militärwesen,' in V. Eichler and C. Heinemann (eds), *Herzogtum Nassau 1806-1866. Politik, Wirtschaft, Kultur* (Wiesbaden: Historische Kommission für Kultur, 1981), pp.75–79.

65 The two regiments had one grenadier, one voltigeur, and four fusilier companies. The 1st Nassau Infantry Regiment consisted of the Usingen battalions (Nos I and IV), the 2nd Nassau Infantry Regiment was made up of the Weilburg battalions (Nos II and III); Schüler, *Das Herzogtum Nassau*, pp.41–42.

the command of one of the current members of the alliance.[66] For Nassau, whose troops were fighting in Spain, this would mean raising a new contingent entirely – a near impossible task both due to constraints of time and money. So, in order to meet conditions for acceptance into the Sixth Coalition, whilst not being overly burdened, the Walramians and Orange reconfirmed the Act of Inheritance of 1783, which reconfirmed the Prince of Orange as President of the dynasty.[67] And as President, the Prince of Orange, who was already a member of the alliance, gained command of all Nassau troops, including those in the Peninsula. All that now needed to be done was repatriate the contingent from the Peninsula.

The history of the defection of the Nassau troops in the Peninsula is well known. On the evening of 10 December 1813, during the Battle of the Nive, the 2nd Nassau Infantry Regiment, together with an attached battalion from Frankfurt, defected to British forces.[68] This defection prompted the French to disarm and imprison the remaining German regiments under their command, including the other Nassau troops.[69] What is less well known is that this was not a spontaneous act. It was orchestrated by the Prince of Orange and his Walramian cousins. The ploy was developed as follows. The Walramians would instruct their troops to defect to the British army under Wellington.[70] To avoid the risk of the troops being imprisoned or pressed into British service, the Prince of Orange would notify the British government that *his* troops were willing to defect to Wellington, and request for their transportation to the frontline in Germany.[71] London was keen to assist in the repatriating of the Dutch contingent of the French army in the Peninsula, and instructions were drawn up for Wellington to assist in the defection. The Prince of Orange was then presented with these instructions and signed off on them.[72] It was only a few days later that the prince felt the need to rectify a misunderstanding that hitherto had gone supposedly unnoticed to him: he had not requested for Dutch troops to be repatriated, but for Nassau troops, of which he had only recently

66 'Protokoll über die zur Regulierung des Verteidigungssystems von Deutschland abgehaltene Kommission, Frankfurt, 24 November 1813', in *K. vom und zum Stein,* E. Botzenhart and W. Hubatsch (eds), *Briefe und amtliche Schriften* (Stuttgart: W. Kohlhammer, 1957–1964), vol. IV, pp.338–340; A. von Janson, *Geschichte des Feldzuges 1814 in Frankreich* (Berlin: Mittler, 1903), vol.I, p.16, and vol.II, annex 13, 7*–8*.

67 '[One of the Walramian Nassaus] to Prince of Orange, 13 October 1813', NL-NA: 2.02.01, 6564; 'Letter from Baron de Gagern to the commanding officers of the Nassau troops on the frontline in Spain, October 1813', NL-NA: 2.02.01, 6564; 'Treaty of Frankfurt, 26 November 1813', NL-KHA: A35, XIV23.

68 'John Cameron to Campbell, 13 December 1813', National Army Museum (NAM): 9007-95-7; 'Hendrik Fagel [to William I], 30 December', NL-NA: 2.02.01, 6564; 'William I to the Prince of Nassau-Weilberg, 7 January 1814', NL-NA: 2.02.01, 6564; 'Several officers of the 2nd Nassau Infantry Battalion to William I, 12 February 1814' NL-NA: 2.02.01, 6564.

69 H.J. Davies, *Wellington's Wars. The Making of a Military Genius* (New Haven: Yale University Press, 2012), pp.199–202; C. Esdaile, *The Peninsular War* (London: Allen Lane, 2002), p.481; Wacker, 'Das nassauische Militärwesen', p.79.

70 '[Walramian Nassaus] to Prince of Orange, 13 October 1813', NL-NA: 2.02.01, 6564; 'Gagern to Nassau officers, October 1813', NL-NA: 2.02.01, 6564.

71 'Prince of Orange to Bathurst, 2 October 1813', NL-NA: 2.02.01, 6564.

72 'Prince of Orange to Bathurst, 3 October 1813', NL-NA: 2.02.01, 6564; 'Bathurst to [Prince of Orange], 6 October 1813', NL-NA: 2.02.01, 6564.

gained command.[73] By now, of course, the instructions to Wellington had already been sent off and the wheels for the transfer of the Nassau troops had been set in motion.[74]

Operational Deployment and Incorporation into the New Dutch Army

So, by late 1813, the House of Orange had rounded up Dutch prisoners of war and stragglers of the Russian Campaign and re-organised them into the Dutch Legion of Orange, and they had gained command of a Nassau contingent. However, the military contribution of these troops to the liberation of the Netherlands must not be overstated. The Dutch Legion of Orange was poorly armed and equipped and it arrived in the Netherlands at a relatively late date. Via Coesfeld, Vreden, Doesburg, the 1st Battalion of the Dutch Legion of Orange made its way to Arnhem, where it arrived on 11 January 1814.[75] The Dutch Legion of Orange artillery was ordered to Delft, where it would be resupplied from the central artillery depot in that city.[76] By the third week of January the 1st Battalion had been moved to the frontline at Breda, to participate in the Prussian *Generalleutnant* Friedrich Wilhelm von Bülow's imminent invasion of the southern Netherlands, but on 29 January, the battalion was redirected to join the Allied forces besieging the French held fortress of Gorinchem. The artillery from Delft, which had been formed into a battery of 6-pounders and two howitzers, was also transferred to the siege of Gorinchem.[77] After the fall of Gorinchem on 20 February 1814, the 1st Battalion was incorporated into the newly formed Dutch Brigade under Hendrik George de Perponcher, which was attached to the British forces under Lieutenant General Thomas Graham. Graham's troops would assist Bülow's Prussian forces in their advance south.[78]

The departure of the 2nd Battalion of the Dutch Legion of Orange was delayed due to many troops being hospitalised.[79] It is uncertain when exactly the 2nd Battalion commenced its march on the Netherlands. The first mention of the unit is 28 February 1814, when it is listed as arriving on the returns of the strength of the

73 'Prince of Orange to Bathurst, 8 October 1813', NL-NA: 2.02.01, 6564.

74 'Bathurst to Wellington, 6 October 1813', NL-NA: 2.02.01, 6564.

75 'Willhardt to William I, Coesfeld, 8 January 1814' NL-NA: 2.02.01, 6566; 'Dagboeken, 11 January 1814', NL-NA: 2.21.008.01, 25; Naber, *Prinses Wilhelmina*, pp.288–289; 'Nota', NL-NA: 2.21.008.66, 3.

76 'Constant Rebecque to Ritmeester Heskuzius [?],12 January 1814', NL-NA: 2.02.01, 6579, no. 8.

77 F.H.A. Sabron, *De vesting Gorinchem van november 1813 tot maart 1814.* (Breda: Koninklijke Militarie Academie, 1902), pp.98–99, 102

78 Fall of Gorinchem: Sabron, *De Vesting Gorinchem*, p.107; Battalion 'in the field': 'Weekelijksche Sterkte Lijsten der Verschillende Corpsen der Staande Armée en der reeds georganiseerde Battalions Landmilitie volgens ingekomene Rapporten der verscheidene Commandanten op den 28e February 1814', NL-NA: 2.02.01, 6620; 7th Infantry Battalion of the Line attached to Dutch Brigade under Perponcher, and placed under Graham: 'William I to Bentinck tot Buckhorst, 28 February 1814', NL-NA: 2.13.67, 1.

79 'Schwartz to William I, 2 January 1814', NL-NA: 2.02.01, 6566.

Dutch army.[80] After crossing the Dutch frontier, the battalion moved to Zwolle, from where it was ordered to join the forces besieging the city of Deventer.[81] A detachment would also assist in the securing of the fortress town of Coevorden, after the French surrendered on 4 May 1814.[82]

The 3rd Battalion of the Dutch Legion of Orange departed Berlin on 21 February 1814. It reached the Netherlands on 19 March, when it entered Enschede. From there it was forwarded to Utrecht to be armed. En route the battalion was sent to assist in the blockade of fortress Delfzijl. The battalion was eventually armed whilst besieging the fortress.[83]

The Nassau troops were set to arrive at Plymouth on 12 January 1814, but before their arrival, the Prince of Orange redirected their destination to the Netherlands to join his forces.[84] Unfortunately, after successfully performing the complicated manoeuvre of defecting, and surviving a lengthy sea voyage to Britain, disaster struck in the last leg of the voyage. The ships transporting the troops to the Netherlands were caught in a storm, and two ships carrying 230 men were lost.[85] To bolster the regiment it was complemented with the battalion of Frankfurter troops.[86] This contingent arrived in the Netherlands at least as early as the second week of February 1814. After being re-equipped, the troops were attached to the Dutch Army Corps in the southern Netherlands, and they participated in driving out remaining French forces in the Low Countries.[87]

But even if the Dutch Legion of Orange and the Nassau contingent played a limited role in the liberation of the Netherlands, it is important to emphasise that they took over important second-line duties from the Allied armies in the Netherlands. This

80 'Weekelijksche Sterkte Lijsten der Verschillende Corpsen der Staande Armée en der reeds georganiseerde Battalions Landmilitie volgens ingekomene Rapporten der verscheidene Commandanten op den 28e February 1814', NL-NA: 2.02.01, 6620.

81 L.W. van Hoek, 'Deventer,' in *Historische Gedenkboek*, vol.IV, p.36; 'Generale Staat Zijner Koninklijke Hoogheids Troupen in de Verenigde Nederlanden op den 29e April 1814', NL-NA: 2.02.01, 6620; F.K. van Ommen Kloeke, 'Overijssel en Zwolle,' in *Historische Gedenkboek*, vol.III, p.605.

82 F.H.A. Sabron, *In en Om Coevorden in 1813-14* (Breda: Koninklijke Militaire Academie, 1913), p.74.

83 F.H.A. Sabron, *De Blokkade van Delfzijl in 1813-14* (Breda: Koninklijke Militaire Academie, 1906), pp.101–102, note 3.

84 'Bathurst to Clancarty, 12 January 1814', The National Archives, UK, (TNA): FO 238/2; 'Bathurst to Clancarty, 18 January 1814', TNA: FO 238/2; 'Fagel to [William i], 30 December 1813', NL-NA: 2.02.01, 6564; 'William I to Fagel, 8 January 1814', NL-NA: 2.02.01, 6564.

85 Schüler, *Das Herzogtum Nassau*, pp.42–43; W.G. de Bas, 'De Blokkade der Stelling van Den Helder', in *Historisch gedenkboek*, vol.II, p.164.

86 'Untitled, anonymous, s.a.', NL-NA: 2.02.01, 6564; 'Bathurst to Clancarty, 15 March 1814', TNA: FO 238/2.

87 'William I to Bentinck tot Buckhorst, 24 January 1814', NL-NA: 2.13.67, 1; 'Several officers of the 2nd Nassau Infantry Battalion to William I, 12 February 1814', NL-NA: 2.02.01, 6564; Koolemans Beijnen, 'De militaire geschiedenis van de omwenteling', in *Historische Gedenkboek*, vol.I, pp.222–223; G.L. Breedtvelt, 'De bestorming van Bergen-op-Zoom 8-9 Maart 1814', in *Historische Gedenkboek*, vol.IV, p.560; H. Dyserinck, 'Maastricht, Vaals en Sittard', ibidem, p.606.

limited Allied strategic consumption and allowed the Allies to focus on the march to Paris.

In the broader context of re-establishing the Dutch army, the Dutch Legion of Orange and the Nassau contingent were important. As mentioned, in the aftermath of the uprising of November 1813, many volunteers came forward to fight for Dutch independence. However, few of these volunteers had any recent military experience. The House of Orange organised three battalions of infantry and one detachment of artillery from Dutch veterans of the Russian Campaign. The deployment of the legion to the Netherlands did not mean that recruitment stopped. Numerous Dutch troops were still recuperating at the rallying point. These soldiers were forwarded to the Netherlands only once they were back to full health. Additionally, hundreds of Dutch stragglers still trailed the Allied armies, were stranded in hospitals along marching routes, or remained in Allied prisoner of war camps. Orange continued to dispatch officers to locate and transport these troops to the Netherlands.[88] Finally, a considerable number of Dutchmen remained in foreign service. For example, by the end of January, the Dutch troops of the Russo-Germans Legion had not yet been released.[89] It is unclear when they were released, but when the Russo-German Legion was incorporated into the Prussian army in the middle of 1814, all non-Prussian nationals were released from service.[90] It seems likely that at this point the Dutch troops transferred to Dutch service. The three infantry battalions of the Dutch Legion of Orange were renumbered the 7th, 8th and 9th Infantry Battalions of the Line of the new Dutch Army.[91] The Dutch soldiers at the rallying point would be fed into the new Dutch army.

The 2nd Nassau Infantry Regiment was taken into Dutch service with a strength of 1,696 men.[92] The Nassau troops from the Peninsula and the Frankfurters formed the cadre of the regiment. Additional recruits from Nassau would bring the regiment up to strength.[93] On 16 July 1814, this contract was upgraded. The 2nd Nassau Infantry Regiment was expanded to three battalions and two depot companies, making a total of 3,032 men. Henceforth the regiment would be referred to as the 2nd Nassau Light Infantry Regiment. In addition, a second regiment was recruited. This would become known as the Regiment Orange-Nassau and consisted of two battalions and two depot companies, making a total of 2,000 men. The contracts were negotiated for a period of six years, which meant that the aforementioned Nassau troops were an integral part of the Dutch Army during the Waterloo campaign, and not, as is

88 'Koninklijk Besluit, 6 January 1814', NL-NA: 2.02.01, 6577; 'Bovié to William I, 20 January 1814', NL-NA: 2.02.01, 6566. POWs in Russia: 'Nota', NL-NA: 2.13.67, 1. POWs in Austria: 'Van Hogendorp to William I, 10 January 1814', NL-NA: 2.02.01, 6090; 'William of Orange to Bentinck tot Buckhorst, 22 January 1813', NL-NA: 2.13.67, 1.

89 'Prince of Orange to Alexander I, 31 January 1814', NL-NA: 2.02.01, 6206.

90 Venzky, *Die Russisch-Deutsche Legion*, pp.110–113.

91 Ringoir, *De Nederlandse Infanterie*, pp.96, 107, 110.

92 'William I to the Prince of Nassau-Weilberg, 7 January 1814', NL-NA: 2.02.01, 6564; 'Frederick of Nassau to William I, 14 January 1814', NL-NA: 2.02.01, 6564; 'Frederick of Nassau to William I, 21 January 1814', NL-NA: 2.02.01, 6564; 'Untitled, anonymous, s.a.', NL-NA: 2.02.01, 6564.

93 'Comments to 'untitled, anonymous, s.a.'', NL-NA: 2.02.01, 6564.

often assumed, part of the independent Nassau contingent that served under British command.[94]

Based on a select examination of the muster books of the new Dutch army, the author estimates that about 50 percent of the Dutch contingent of the Russian Campaign was rounded up and incorporated into the new Dutch army. Together with the Nassauers, they formed the backbone of the new Dutch army. They would prove of invaluable worth in the years to come, when the Dutch were forced to defend the integrity of their expanded United Kingdom of the Netherlands at Waterloo.

Conclusion

This chapter offers a new perspective on the re-establishment of the Dutch army in 1810–1814. The historiography of the Dutch army emphasises the success of domestic recruitment. Indeed, the aftermath of the Uprising of November 1813 was a rare moment in Dutch history when many Dutchmen stepped forward to fight for the independence of their country. However, this is not the whole story. Since its ousting from the Netherlands in 1795, the history of the House of Orange and the history of the Netherlands continued on separate, but parallel paths. The Netherlands came into French orbit and participated in Napoleon's campaigns, whilst Orange resisted Napoleon's domination of Europe. The year 1804 is a turning point in Dutch history. Napoleon intervened to prevent the House of Orange from gaining additional compensation for the loss of titles, offices and lands in the Netherlands. This soured relations between Orange and Napoleon beyond repair. It also meant that, at least from the perspective of the House of Orange, Orange had an outstanding claim on the Netherlands. Of course, to confront Napoleon often spelt disaster, and Orange's successive failures marginalised the dynasty from Dutch and European affairs. It was not until early 1813 that Orange's luck turned. The Czar, seeing use in a well-connected dynasty with a claim to the Netherlands, accepted Orange into the alliance that would become the Sixth Coalition. This offered the House of Orange the legitimacy it needed to present itself as a government in exile to rival French rule of the Netherlands. Orange used this position to organise military forces to participate in the campaigns to liberate the Netherlands and to defeat Napoleon. The immediate military contribution of the forces raised by House of Orange was limited. The new

94 'Convention, 34 articles, 16 July 1814', Germany, Hessisches Hauptstaatsarchiv (DE-HHA): 202, 1397; 'Convention, 27 articles, 16 July 1814', DE-HHA: 202, 1123, Band 1; 'Gagern [Minister of State (of the Netherlands)] to Mollerus [Commissioner General at the Dutch Department of War], 29 July 1814', DE-HHA: 202, 1123, Band 1; 'Janssens to Gagern, 12 August 1814', DE-HHA: 202, 1123, Band 1; 'Verzeichniss [sic] der [...] abgegebene Armatur, Montur und Rustsorten', DE-HHA: 202, 1123, Band 1; 'Conventie van 1814 betreffende Nassausche troepen in Nederlandsche dienst, 1814-1815', NL-KHA: A35, XIV30; 'Stukken betreffende de voor de Nederlanden in Nassau aan te werven Koloniale Troepen, 1814-1815', NL-KHA: A35, XIV28; 'Stukken betreffende het Nassausche regiment in Nederlandsche dienst, 1814-1817', NL-KHA: A35, XIV29; J. Rudersdorf, 'Prinz Wilhelm von Oranien, Wellington und die Nassauer bei Quatre-Bras und Waterloo,' *Nassauische Annalen* (2009), p.280; M. Mittelacher, 'Die Nassauer bei Waterloo,' *Nassauische Annalen* (1998), p.266.

Dutch army, with veterans of Russia and Spain at its core, had to wait until Waterloo to prove its worth. The real value of Orange's conduct lay in the realm of international politics. The participation of the Dutch Legion of Orange in the campaign to liberate the Netherlands and in the campaign to defeat Napoleon gave Orange a stake in the fight, which allowed them to portray themselves as liberators and victors, rather than as liberated or defeated. The benefits for the Netherlands were not to be gained until 6 December 1813, when the House of Orange was restored to the Netherlands. It was on this date that the two distinct Dutch experiences of the Napoleonic era converged, the experience of defeat by the French regime in the Netherlands and the experience of victory by the Orangist government in exile. Conveniently, the Orange experience, that of victory and defeat of Napoleon, emerged as the dominant interpretation of the Dutch experience of the Napoleonic era. And this was not only the case nationally, for purposes of coming to terms with the divisions of the past, but also internationally. Proof of this is to be found in the Congress of Vienna, where no 'Dutch Question' arose, because the Allies of the Sixth Coalition had embraced Orange in exile as the legitimate government of the Netherlands. Or in other words, when Dutch history bifurcated into a national path and a dynastic path, it was Dutch fortune that the House of Orange kept the embers of resistance burning until a European coalition came together to defeat Napoleon. The military forces organised by the House of Orange are the tangible reflection of Orange's successful manoeuvrings to ensure a restoration to a liberated and independent Netherlands. For this reason, the Dutch Legion of Orange, and to an extent the Nassau contingent, deserve more recognition in the historiography of the Dutch armed forces.

Bibliography

Archival Sources

Nationaal Archief (NL-NA)

- 2.02.01: Inventaris van de archieven van de Algemene Staatssecretarie en van het Kabinet des Konings, met de daarbij gedeponeerde archieven, 1813-1840
- 2.13.09: Inventaris van het archief van het Ministerie van Oorlog: Stamboeken van Onderofficieren en Minderen van de Landmacht, 1813-1924
- 2.13.67: Inventaris van het archief van het Ministerie van Oorlog: Geheim Verbaalarchief en Gedeponeerde archieven, 1813-1844, 1905-1945
- 2.21.008.01: Inventaris van het archief van de familie De Constant Rebecque
- 2.21.008.66: Inventaris van het archief van de familie van De Constant Rebecque

Koninklijk Huisarchief (NL-KHA)

- A35: Archief Willem I
- B6: Erbverein

The National Archives – UK (TNA)

- FO 238: Foreign Office: Consulate and Legation, Netherlands: General Correspondence

National Army Museum – UK (NAM)

- Accounts, Letters and Diaries of Maj John Campbell

Service Historique de la Défense (FR-SHD)
GR C: Premier Empire (1804-1815)
GR Y: Archives administratives collectives et individuelles
Hessisches Hauptstaatsarchiv (DE-HHA)
202: Herzoglich-Nassauische Militärverwaltung

Printed Primary Sources

Anon., *Collection des Actes, Reglemens, Ordonnances et Autres Pièces Officielles Relatives a la Confédération du Rhin* (Paris: Schoell, 1808)

Stein, K. vom und zum, E. Botzenhart and W. Hubatsch (eds), *Briefe und amtliche Schriften* (Stuttgart: W. Kohlhammer, 1957–1964)

Secondary Sources

Anderson, B.C.D., 'Ernst Marschall von Bieberstein and the Foundation of Modern Nassau (1770-1814)', (PhD. Diss, University of Virginia, 1987)

Anderson, B.C.D., 'State-Building and Bureaucracy in Early-Nineteenth-Century Nassau', *Central European History*, 24/3 (1991), pp.222–157

Ball, P., *A Waste of Blood and Treasure. The 1799 Anglo-Russian Invasion of the Netherlands* (Barnsley: Pen & Sword, 2017)

Bas, W.G. de, 'De Blokkade der Stelling van Den Helder', in G.J.W. Koolemans Beijnen (ed.), *Historische gedenkboek der herstelling van Neêrlands onafhankelijkheid in 1813* (Haarlem: De Erven F. Bohn, 1912–1913)

Bernath, M., 'Die auswärtige Politik Nassaus 1805-1812. Ein Beitrag zur Geschichte des Rheinbundes und der politischen Ideen am Mittelrhein zur Zeit Napoleons,' *Nassauische Annalen* (1952), pp.106–191

Blok, P.J., 'Staatkundige geschiedenis van de omwenteling', in G.J.W. Koolemans Beijnen (ed.), *Historische gedenkboek der herstelling van Neêrlands onafhankelijkheid in 1813* (Haarlem: De Erven F. Bohn, 1912–1913)

Bond, G., *The Grand Expedition. The British Invasion of Holland in 1809* (Athens, GA: University of Georgia Press, 1979)

Bornewasser, J.A., 'Koning Willem I,' in H.P.H. Jansen and C.A. Tamse (eds), *Nassau en Oranje in de Nederlandse Geschiedenis* (Alphen aan de Rijn: Sijthoff, 1979)

Breedtvelt, G.L., 'De bestorming van Bergen-op-Zoom 8-9 Maart 1814', in G.J.W. Koolemans Beijnen (ed.), *Historische gedenkboek der herstelling van Neêrlands onafhankelijkheid in 1813* (Haarlem: De Erven F. Bohn, 1912–1913)

Colenbrander, H.T. (ed.), *Gedenkstukken der algemeene geschiedenis van Nederland van 1795 tot 1840* (The Hague: Nijhoff, 1905-1922)

Colenbrander, H.T., *Inlijving en Opstand* (Amsterdam: J.M. Meulenhoff, 1941)

Chandler, D.G., *The Campaigns of Napoleon* (New York: Macmillan, 1966)

D'Artois, P.-H., *Relation de la Défense de Danzig, en 1813, par le 10e. corps de l'armée française, contre l'armée combinée russe et prussienne* (Paris: Ladrange, 1820)

Dam van Isselt, W.E. van, *De ontwikkeling van ons krijgswezen sedert November 1813* (Haarlem: Vincent Loosjes, 1902)

Davies, H.J., *Wellington's Wars. The Making of a Military Genius* (New Haven: Yale University Press, 2012)

Dempsey, G.C., *Napoleon's Mercenaries. Foreign Units in the French Army Under the Consulate and Empire, 1799 to 1814* (Barnsley: Frontline Books, 2016)

Dyserinck, H., 'Maastricht, Vaals en Sittard', in G.J.W. Koolemans Beijnen (ed.), *Historische gedenkboek der herstelling van Neêrlands onafhankelijkheid in 1813* (Haarlem: De Erven F. Bohn, 1912–1913)

Eichler, V., and C. Heinemann (eds), *Herzogtum Nassau 1806-1866. Politik, Wirtschaft, Kultur* (Wiesbaden: Historische Kommission für Kultur, 1981)

Esdaile, C., *The Peninsular War* (London: Allen Lane, 2002)

Eysten, J., 'Doorloopend verhaal van de dienstverrichtingen der Nederlandsche pontonniers onder den majoor G.D. Benthien 1797-1825', *Bijdragen en Mededeelingen van het Historisch Genootschap* 32 (1911), pp.100-177

Eysten, J., *Geschiedenis der Nederlandsche pontonniers* (Breda: Koninklijke Militaire Academie, 1908)

Fabry, G., *Campagne de Russe (1812). Documents Annexes* (Paris: R. Chapelot & Cie, 1903)

Funnekotter, B., *De hel van 1812. Nederlanders met Napoleon op veldtocht naar Rusland* (Amsterdam: Prometheus, 2015)

Geerts, G.A., 'De veldtocht naar Rusland in 1812 onder keizer Napoleon 1', *Militaire Spectator* (1983), pp.52–62

Haan, I. de, P. den Hoed and H. te Velde (eds), *Een Nieuwe Staat: Het Begin van het Koninkrijk der Nederlanden* (Amsterdam: Prometheus-Bert Bakker, 2013)

Hallema, A., *Oranjevorsten in Ballingschap: Van Dilleburg en Londen uit voor Vrijheid en Recht* (Maastricht: Leiter-Nijpels, 1947)

Hamel, J.A. van, "s Erfprinsen Toevluchtsoord. De Latere Koning Willem I als Landheer op het Posensche Riddergoed Raçot, Gedrurende Zijne Verdrijving uit het Vaderland', *Bijdragen voor Vaderlandsche Geschiedenis en Oudheidkunde* (1932), pp.219–242

Hoek, L.W. van, 'Deventer,' in G.J.W. Koolemans Beijnen (ed.), *Historische gedenkboek der herstelling van Neêrlands onafhankelijkheid in 1813* (Haarlem: De Erven F. Bohn, 1912–1913)

Hoeven, M. van der, *Van de Weser tot de Weichsel. Het leger van het Koninkrijk Holland en de Duitse veldtochten van Napoleon, 1806, 1807 en 1809* (Amsterdam: De Bataafsche Leeuw, 1994)

Hooff, J.P.C.M. van, 'George Diederich Benthien: een bruggenbouwer pur sang', *Armamentaria*, (1998–1999), pp.78–88

Huck, J., *Das ende der Franzosenzeit in Hamburg. Quellen und Studien zur Belagerung und Befreiung von Hamburg 1813-1814* (Hamburg: Kabel, 1984)

Jansen, H.P.H., 'De Bredase Nassaus', in H.P.H. Jansen and C.A. Tamse (eds), *Nassau en Oranje in de Nederlandse Geschiedenis* (Alphen aan de Rijn: Sijthoff, 1979)

Janson, A. von, *Geschichte des Feldzuges 1814 in Frankreich* (Berlin: Mittler, 1903)

Koch, J., *Koning Willem I, 1772-1843* (Amsterdam: Boom, 2013)

Koolemans Beijnen, G.J.W., 'De militaire geschiedenis van de omwenteling,' in G.J.W. Koolemans Beijnen (ed.), *Historische gedenkboek der herstelling van Neêrlands onafhankelijkheid in 1813* (Haarlem: De Erven F. Bohn, 1912–1913)

Koolemans Beijnen, G.J.W., (ed.), *Historische gedenkboek der herstelling van Neêrlands onafhankelijkheid in 1813* (Haarlem: De Erven F. Bohn, 1912–1913)

Lieven, D., *Russia against Napoleon: the Battle for Europe, 1807 to 1814* (London: Allen Lane, 2009)

Martens, G.F. de, *Recueil de Traités d'Alliance, de Paix, de Trève, de Neutralité, de commerce, de limites, d'échange etc et de plusieurs autres actes servant à la connaissance des relations étranères des Puissances et états de l'Europe* (Gottingen: Dieterich, 1818)

Mittelacher, M., 'Die Nassauer bei Waterloo,' *Nassauische Annalen* (1998)

Moor, J.A. de, and H.Ph. Vogel, *Duizend miljoen maal vervloekt land. De Hollandse Brigade in Spanje, 1808-1813* (Amsterdam: Meulenhoff, 1991)

Naber, J.W.A. (ed.), *Correspondentie van de Stadhouderlijke familie 1777-1820* (The Hague: Martinus Nijhoff, 1931–1933)

Naber, J.W.A., *Prinses Wilhelmina, Gemalin van Willem V, Prins van Oranje* (Amsterdam: Meulenhoff, 1908)

Ommen Kloeke, F.K. van, 'Overijssel en Zwolle,' in G.J.W. Koolemans Beijnen (ed.), *Historische gedenkboek der herstelling van Neêrlands onafhankelijkheid in 1813* (Haarlem: De Erven F. Bohn, 1912–1913)

Ringoir, H., *De Nederlandse Infanterie* (Bussum: C.A.J. van Dishoeck, 1968)

Rooden, P. van, *In de achterhoede van Napoleon. Gezondheidsofficier J.S. Zembsch en het 125e regiment in 1812* (Dordrecht: P. van Rooden, 2016)

Rudersdorf, J., 'Prinz Wilhelm von Oranien, Wellington und die Nassauer bei Quatre-Bras und Waterloo,' *Nassauische Annalen* (2009), pp.279–320

Sabron, F.H.A., *De Blokkade van Delfzijl in 1813-14* (Breda: Koninklijke Militaire Academie, 1906)

Sabron, F.H.A., *De vesting Gorinchem van november 1813 tot maart 1814.* (Breda: Kninklijke Militarie Academie, 1902)

Sabron, F.H.A., *Geschiedenis van het 124ste regiment infanterie van linie onder keizer Napoleon I* (Breda: Koninklijke Militaire Academie, 1910)

Sabron, F.H.A., *Geschiedenis van het 33ste regiment lichte infanterie (het oud-Hollandsche 3de regiment jagers) onder keizer Napoleon I* (Breda: Koninklijke Militaire Academie, 1910)

Sabron, F.H.A., *In en Om Coevorden in 1813-14* (Breda: Koninklijke Militaire Academie, 1913)

Schneider, C.D.H., *Het 126ste regiment Hollandsche infanterie in Rusland in 1812* (Amsterdam: P.N. van Kampen, 1898)

Schoenmaker, B., and C.M. Schulten (eds), *Oranje op de Bres: Vorstenhuis en Leger in de Nederlandse Geschiedenis* (Amsterdam: De Bataafsche Leeuw, 1989)

Schüler, W., *Das Herzogtum Nassau 1806-1866: Deutsche Geschichte im Kleinformat* (Wiesbaden: Historische Kommission für Nassau, 2006)

Spek, C. van der, *Sous les Armes. Het Hollandse leger in de Franse tijd, 1806-1814* (Amsterdam: Boom, 2016)

Struik, L.A., *Oranje in Ballingschap 1795-1813. Een Odyssee* (Amsterdam: De Bataafsche Leeuw, 2006)

Sypesteijn, J.W., *Geschiedenis van het Regiment Hollandsche hussaren [...]* (The Hague: De Gebroeders Van Cleef, 1849)

Sypesteijn, J.W., *Geschiedenis van het regiment Nederlandse rijdende artillerie* (Zaltbommel: Joh. Noman & Zoon, 1852)

Treichel, E., *Der Primat der Bürokratie: Bürokratischer Staat und bürokratische Elite im Herzogtum Nassau 1806-1866* (Stuttgart: Steiner, 1991)

Uitterhoeve, W., *1813–Haagse Bluf: De korte chaos van vrijwording* (Nijmegen: Vantilt, 2013)

Uythoven, G. van, *The Secret Expedition. The Anglo-Russian Invasion of Holland 1799* (Warwick: Helion, 2018)

Venzky, G., *Die Russisch-Deutsche Legion in den Jahren 1811-1815* (Wiesbaden: Harrassowitz, 1966)

Wacker, P., 'Das nassauische Militärwesen,' in V. Eichler and C. Heinemann (eds), *Herzogtum Nassau 1806-1866. Politik, Wirtschaft, Kultur* (Wiesbaden: Historische Kommission für Kultur, 1981)

Wacker, P., 'Die Hzgl. Nassauischen Truppen im Feldzug gegen Preußen 1806/07,' *Depesche* 10 (1988), pp.1–11

Wit, C.H.E. de, *De strijd tussen aristocratie en democratie in Nederland, 1780-1848. Herwaardering van een periode* (Heerlen: Winants, 1965)

Woelderink, B., 'De erfprins in Nassau in 1789. Het bezoek van prins Willem Frederik aan de Nassause erflanden als onderdeel van zijn Duitse studietijd,' *Jaarboek Oranje-Nassau Museum* (1994), pp.7–24

Woelderink, B., 'Oranje tussen Nassau en Nederland, 1795-1802,' *Oranje in Revolutie en Restauratie. Jaarboek Oranje-Nassau Museum* (1996), pp.91–111

Wüppermann, W.E.A., *De vorming van het Nederlandsche leger na de omwenteling van 1813 en het aandeel van dat leger aan den veldtocht van 1815* (Breda: Koninklijke Militaire Academie, 1900)

Zuurbier, J., et al. (eds), *De lange herfst van 1799: De Russisch-Engelse invasie in polder en duin* (Castricum: Stichting Herdenking 1799, 1998)

7

The French Method of Warfare in the Peninsula

Kenton White

The Peninsular War provides the historian with an abundant variety of the French methods of warfare, from small guerrilla actions involving only a few soldiers to large battles involving tens of thousands. There are sieges and amphibious operations in addition to the more run-of-the-mill campaigns of manoeuvre. What would now be called 'pacification' and 'stabilisation' operations in the Spanish and Portuguese countryside were undertaken throughout the war. During the campaigns in Spain and Portugal, the methods of warfare successfully employed in Italy and Central Europe were retained in the Peninsula by the French even when they were demonstrably failing. Why was that? This analysis will examine French strategy, operational planning and tactics. The general method of French operations will also be addressed.

To understand the Peninsular War, it is necessary to understand Napoleon's overall strategy. He saw the British as the arch enemy but could not reach them on their island as he could not compete with the Royal Navy at sea in open battle. The British, conversely, could not compete directly in battle on land to defeat the Imperial armies. This stalemate led to the Berlin Decrees of 1806 and subsequent sanctions, commonly known as the 'Continental System', which attempted to force Britain out of the war by economic and political, rather than direct military, means. The Continental System blocked the import of all British goods into Europe, and all the conquered and allied states were expected to conform with the decree. The goal of Napoleonic France was the complete imposition of this system but it faced the problem of Portuguese reluctance.

The concept of 'strategy' can cause confusion. The word is commonly used in business to describe a simple plan. However, its military meaning is somewhat different. War, as Clausewitz described it, is, '... not merely an act of policy but a true political instrument, a continuation of political intercourse, carried on with other means.'[1] He wrote, '... tactics teaches the use of armed forces in the engagement;

1 Carl von Clausewitz, *On War* (London: David Campbell, 1993), p.99.

strategy, the use of engagements for the objects of the war.'[2] Strategy is the tool of the military arm which makes everything else possible. In his 'Art of War' Jomini wrote, 'The art of war, as generally considered, consists of five purely military branches, – viz: Strategy, Grand Tactics, Logistics, Engineering, and Tactics.'[3] Clausewitz and Jomini were officers during the Napoleonic wars, and their opinions should be considered carefully.

Strategy, and its operational and tactical components, can be described under the headings of 'ends', 'ways' and 'means'. We must also add 'risks' and 'assumptions' to this list. In this work the 'ends' are described by the political objectives set by the respective governments. A crossover exists between 'ends' and 'ways' that includes the military goals. The 'ways' are how the ends were to be achieved and may not necessarily be purely military. The 'means' are the tools used to achieve victory, both on the battlefield and more broadly into what we now describe as the 'operational' aspect of war. 'Risk' in war is a constant, for the individual soldier as well as larger formations and nations, made worse by the friction of war described by Clausewitz in his seminal work *On War*. 'Assumptions' are those beliefs and ideas which serve to validate the strategy or doctrine employed. This last factor can make or break any campaign or strategy if the assumptions made are faulty.

Napoleon, in July 1807, had instructed Talleyrand to, '... inform the Portuguese ambassador that by the first of September the ports of Portugal must be closed to England; failing which, I will declare war on Portugal ...'[4] Spain and France would withdraw their ambassadors from Lisbon and declare a united war against Portugal. Britain was a significant trading partner and long-time ally of the Portuguese, who continued to trade. Following the failure of the Portuguese to comply quickly and thoroughly enough, the first invasion in 1807 left the French in control of Portugal and, more importantly, occupying Lisbon. Early success against the Spanish and the Portuguese gave hope to the French commanders that the war could be won quickly. The Portuguese army was disbanded, and the situation looked positive for France. But the enemy kept coming back. There was no complete, decisive victory, and the addition of British money, equipment, and manpower, to the Spanish and Portuguese resistance meant that Napoleon needed to commit more resources and troops to the Peninsula than he was prepared to do.

An expeditionary force from Britain under several successive commanders forced the French from Portugal. Through a series of operational misjudgements, the British field army was in its turn driven from the Peninsula, leaving only a small garrison in Lisbon under Lieutenant General Craddock. Despite forcing the British from Spain, and defeating the Spanish armies, Spanish resistance had not been destroyed. Several Spanish armies remained, but their operations were disjointed, and they were dealt with piecemeal. Some other Allied forces were still present. With the return of Wellesley to Portugal in 1809, repeated attempts were made to remove the British from the only nation not supporting the continental system.

---

2 Clausewitz, *On War*, p.146.

3 Antoine Henri Jomini, *The Art of War* (London: Greenhill Books, 2006), p.2.

4 12928, A M. de Talleyrand, Dresde, 19 July 1807, H. Plon and J. Dumaine (eds), *Correspondence de Napoléon I* (Paris: H. Plon & J. Dumaine, 1864), vol.15, p.541.

Some Spanish units, notably *Teniente General* Pedro, Marquis de la Romana's army, joined with the Anglo-Portuguese army under Wellesley. As time went on, more veteran troops were removed from the Peninsula to support Napoleon's campaigns in central Europe. The Allied army was growing in size and confidence as the French army was denuded of experienced troops and commanders

Strategy is always subject to chance and friction, but Napoleon increased the abrasion of the 'normal' friction of war by his actions, or sometimes his inaction. Clausewitz wrote that a general can best demonstrate his strategic capability, '… by managing a campaign exactly to suit his objectives and his resources, doing neither too much nor too little.'[5] Napoleon wrote, 'In war, men are nothing, it is a man who is everything.'[6] Although he is referring to the defeat of *Général de division* Pierre Dupont at Bailen, his words resonate throughout the Peninsular War. The focus of the Napoleonic Wars was, understandably, always wherever Napoleon was. What is apparent from most of the actions in Spain and Portugal is this absence of direct control in theatre: Napoleon's absence left the *maréchaux* and Princes in an almost impossible position of uncertain authority. In Spain there never was a truly unified command under a *maréchal* capable of performing with anything approaching the genius of Bonaparte. No true independent command was set up which consolidated overall control in one commander, although attempts were made, and generally ignored by those commanders already in the Peninsula. Joseph, Napoleon's brother, was nominal commander, but did not have the same charisma or competence as his brother. Perhaps no single commander was trusted because that person could then challenge Napoleon's authority.

No longer under the control of Napoleon, but subject to his instructions, we can gauge the command capabilities of the commanders who served in Spain. We also see the weaknesses in character which were normally held in check by the presence of Napoleon, but once remote from his influence were left to run rampant. Some *maréchaux* (most notably Soult) unashamedly chose to ignore instructions from Napoleon. Soult's avarice and stubbornness precluded any real cooperation with other commanders without the strong hand of the Emperor nearby. Wellington faced his most challenging opponent in the final campaign of the war. *Maréchal* Soult's defence of the Pyrenees and south-western France was one of the most difficult offensive campaigns undertaken by the Allied army. Soult was one of the most able of Napoleon's *maréchaux*, but with limited resources and small numbers of troops compared to the Allies, he was unable to avoid being manoeuvred out of several positions before his capitulation after the Battle of Toulouse in 1814.

Others followed Napoleon's orders and instructions as closely as possible, as did Masséna in 1810. Masséna when he was at his peak may have been closest in capabilities to Napoleon. However, by the time he was appointed to the command of the Army of Portugal in 1810 he was a shadow of his former self. He had been an extremely capable commander, demonstrating great ability in his early campaigns,

5 Clausewitz, *On War*, p.208.

6 14283, Saint-Cloud, 30 August 1808, Plon and Dumaine (eds), *Correspondence de Napoléon I*, vol.17, p.558.

but by then he was suffering from serious health problems. He was not the resolute soldier of the Revolutionary Wars, or even the same man who had fought so determinedly at the Battle of Aspern-Essling in 1809.

Ney, as Masséna's subordinate, had shown the difficulties of leading commanders of equal rank. Notoriously quick tempered but brave, Ney would have operated differently to Masséna in the 1810 campaign, but was prone to flights of fancy, or downright dangerous plans, such as the idea of a thrust into Portugal while masking Almeida, counter to Napoleon's orders. However, his approach at Buçaco might have changed the outcome of the battle, but not necessarily the campaign. Ney was keen to attack at Buçaco, arguing strongly for a full-scale attack on 26 September. It is an indication, perhaps of Masséna's lethargy, or his overconfidence, possibly of his disdain for the Allied forces, that he did no more than a cursory reconnaissance before ordering an attack to take place on the morning of the 27th. Masséna, hamstrung somewhat because his duty was to represent the Emperor, and to carry out his instructions, seemed reluctant to deviate in any way from those orders, despite the terrible consequences for his army.

Maréchal Ney was ignominiously sent back to France for insubordination by Masséna. Other *maréchaux* commanded forces in the Peninsula without long-term success for their efforts. Marmont, one of the third promotion of *maréchaux*, began his career in the Peninsula confidently. However, wounded at Salamanca he had no chance to prove his abilities against the Allies.

More broadly, the French were working under a permanent disadvantage imposed by the local conditions, which included the ever-present threat from guerrillas in both Spain and Portugal. Their armies lacked everything in terms of easy access to food and water from the local area, something the Imperial armies were used to having available in abundance when campaigning in Central Europe. The French certainly had the experience, manoeuvrability, and élan to win battles, and to function operationally with speed. *Maréchal* Ney wrote: 'In offensive warfare, the French soldier has inexhaustible resources; his active genius, and his bravery in storming, double his energy, and a French commander ought never to hesitate in marching against the enemy with the bayonet if the ground is at all adapted to a charge in line with one or more battalions at a time.'[7] What the French commanders lacked, among other things, was military intelligence and topographical information.

Operationally the French fought an unsustainable war when faced with an active and reliable foe. There was never quite enough force concentrated to overwhelm and defeat the enemy. As Henri IV of France said, in Spain small armies are beaten, and large armies starve. The French official figures for 1811 show just under 300,000 men under arms, with 350,000 troops in total in the Peninsula. Most of the time the troops needed to be dispersed in garrisons and foraging parties. Dispersal was the only means the French had of maintaining their forces. But this very act demonstrated the limitations of French power, which reached only as far as a musket or cannon shot from where French soldiers were stationed. Collecting and maintaining

7 M. Bulos, *Memoirs of Marshal Ney* (London: Bull and Churton, 1833), vol.2, p.370.

sufficient troops to overwhelm the enemy was particularly difficult, even without the antagonism between the commanders.

An indication of just how difficult even straightforward operations could be is demonstrated in Ney's attempt to take Ciudad Rodrigo in early 1810. Soult wrote to Ney inviting him, by the orders of King Joseph, to invest the fortress.[8] The suggestion in Soult's message was that the town would rapidly surrender. Ney quickly concentrated his corps and attempted to take the fortress by coup-de-main. Ney summoned the governor, *Teniente General* Perez de Herrasti, to surrender but was refused. Ney's artillery briefly cannonaded the town and received a vigorous reply from the defenders' guns. Clearly the town would not capitulate as easily as expected. Ney gave the order for his army to retire on 13 February, and by the 16th he was back in Salamanca, with his corps dispersed in the region. The attempt had been a failure and had used almost all of the resources VI Corps had managed to accumulate over the previous months. The only achievement was a drop in morale of VI Corps, a veteran formation which had served under Ney since it was formed in Boulogne in 1805.

Actions such as those undertaken by Ney might work in fertile country with a generally passive population, but the guerrilla war made French operations far more difficult than they were accustomed to. Although never a direct threat to the Imperial armies, they provided the worst sort of friction to all operations undertaken by the French, intercepting messages and denying control of the food supply. In contrast, the guerrillas provided the Allies with those intercepted dispatches, denying the French any sort of operational surprise.

Logistics, the least sexy of all the military disciplines, is probably the most vital. Strategy naturally has a logistical as well as an economic component.[9] The disposition of troops, their supplies and general fitness, should all have been overseen before a campaign began. Jomini defined logistics as the practical art of moving armies. Within this broad description he includes such things as the, 'Preparation of all the material necessary for setting the army in motion … Providing for the successive arrival of convoys of supplies. Collecting all the means of transportation of the country and of the army, and regulating their use … looking out also for preserving suitable means of communication of the army with its base.'[10] If these are ignored, or paid scant attention, any attempted strategy will fail at the operational and tactical levels. The commanders of the armies should have done much of their work before battle commenced.

The problem of supplying even a small army was made clear by *Maréchal* Marmont. In 1812 he wrote to Napoleon, complaining:

> The Emperor, it seems to me, reckons as nothing the difficulties of surviving. These difficulties are everything: and, if they had ceased by the formation

8 Henri Bonnal, *La Vie Militaire Du Marechal Ney, Duc d'Elchingen, Prince de La Moskowa* (Paris: Chapelot, 1914), vol.3, pp.290–291.
9 Kenton White, *The Key to Lisbon: The Third French Invasion of Portugal, 1810-11* (Warwick: Helion & Company, 2019), pp.79–83.
10 Jomini, *The Art of War*, pp.252–255.

> of stores, all that the Emperor could order would be carried out with punctuality and ease ... We could only get food for daily consumption in our cantonments by using armed force: there is a long distance between this state of affairs and the formation of magazines which would allow us to move the army freely ... we have not four days' food in any of our magazines, we have no transport, we cannot draw requisitions from the most wretched village without sending thither a foraging party two hundred strong: to live from day to day we have to scatter detachments to vast distances, and always to be on the move ...[11]

Marmont went on to say that if the Emperor disagreed with his evaluation of the situation, he would be happy to let another commander have a go.

Many of the problems associated with this part of strategy is often obliquely referred to as 'wastage', or 'supply problems' rather than death and famine. Perhaps that is why it is an under-studied part of any military operation. Wastage applies equally to the logistic support for an army as it does to the loss of soldiers. This is demonstrated in the number of horses Masséna lost in the invasion of Portugal. According to Fririon, Masséna's chief of staff, a lack of fodder during the siege of Almeida had resulted in the deaths of 1,500 horses from the artillery train alone. Of the more than 14,000 horses listed in the Army of Portugal in September 1810, only around 11,000 were present on 31 December 1810. In the first two weeks of March 1811 the army lost a further 700 horses. This wastage of horses – the main transport animal – was enormous. Much of the French cavalry became useless as the state of the horses deteriorated, leaving them incapable of carrying a fully laden cavalryman. But food was not just a problem for the horses. The task of feeding an army is immense, and never-ending

During Reynier's Corps' march across Biscay in February 1810, nearly 3,000,000 rations of biscuit were ordered to be provided by the bakeries of Vittoria, San Sebastian, Burgos and Madrid. *Général de division* Dorsenne was ordered to make 500,000 rations of biscuit and '... several millions of rations of food ...' over and above those needed by his own troops, to provide for the forces passing through to Masséna's army.

However, logistics do not only apply to food. The wagons themselves broke down quickly on the rough roads of Spain and Portugal. Although the French system used standardised wheels, the roads broke so many that supply could never keep up with demand. Commander in chief of the artillery in 1810, *Général de division* Jean Éblé, reported to Masséna that in the caissons belonging to the various army corps, there were nearly three million rounds of musket ammunition, and in the park reserve just over a million cartridges. With those carried by the soldiers, he estimated a total of just over six million rounds with the army. But Éblé, with obvious frustration, reported that for want of transport he had been forced to leave nearly a million rounds of ammunition at Almeida. He also related that there would be only two

11 Auguste Frédéric Louis Viesse de Marmont, *Mémoires Du Maréchal Marmont, Duc de Raguse* (Paris: Perrotin, 1857), vol.4, pp.346–347.

forges, a caisson of tools, and six caissons of gunpowder with the army.[12] Thus the lack of transport translated into a reduction in the supply of ammunition available to the army.

This lack of equipment caused friction between commanders. After the siege of Almeida in 1810 a magazine of tools, including shovels and pickaxes, had been commandeered by the engineers, despite them, ostensibly, belonging to the artillery. An officer of engineers had told the artillery commander that tools would only be handed over by order of the Masséna. Confrontations like this, over limited resources, were repeated throughout the army during the Peninsular War. When items were not available the troops resorted to other methods to obtain them. As tools were always in short supply, axes and saws were made from iron obtained from local sources, usually by requisitioning any metal available such as door hinges. Beams, planks and ropes were made locally by felling trees when they were on hand, or by demolishing houses when they were not. Thus, the local population was stripped not only of its food, but of its metal, wood and even stocks of sulphur and saltpetre to make gunpowder.

Logistical problems extended to even knowing where a unit was, or where it was meant to go. *Chef de bataillon* Jean-Jacques Pelet, Masséna's ADC, complained continually about the poor quality of the maps available to him during the 1810 campaign. The French had ample opportunities to map Spain and Portugal in 1801, and again in 1807 and 1808. Indeed, a survey of Portugal had been undertaken by French topographical engineers during Junot's occupation. When Junot's army was returned to France by the British Navy in 1808, these documents had been deposited at the Dépôt de Guerre in Paris. Some excellent maps and documents which covered Central and Southern Portugal were available in Paris when Masséna was appointed to command the Army of Portugal in 1810 but were never sent into theatre.

If enough transport for the army was obtained, it now had to move to the right place at the right time, and in a condition good enough to fight the enemy if necessary. Marching through an inhospitable country whose inhabitants have been raised in armed resistance meant any movements would require detailed plans for routes of supply and creation of magazines. A lack of reconnaissance left the French with little current information. *Capitaine* Jean-Nicolas-Auguste Noël of the artillery mentions that he had trouble identifying where he was, even though he had copies of Lopez and Mentelle's maps to guide him.[13] If the villages were empty it could be very difficult to fix one's location accurately, as Jean-Baptiste Barrès wrote, '… it was more often than not impossible for me to discover the names of the town or villages we passed through, for we did not meet in them a single inhabitant.'[14]

A key part in any military operation is intelligence – the sort of information about the topography and your enemy, not the cerebral type (although this is useful!). This

12 Maurice Girod de l'Ain, *Le Général Eblé (1758-1812)* (Paris: Berger-Levrault, 1893), pp.185–187. Pièces Justificatives, général Eblé au maréchal Masséna, Almeida, 11 September 1810.

13 Jean-Nicolas-Auguste Noël, *With Napoleon's Guns: The Military Memoirs of an Officer of the First Empire* (London: Greenhill, 2005), p.96.

14 Jean-Baptiste Barrès, *Memoirs of a French Napoleonic Officer* (London: Greenhill, 1988), p.142.

is a core part in planning, and then adjusting the plan following contact with the enemy. Clausewitz acknowledged the need for intelligence, but warned of over-reliance on uncertain information, and the increased chance of friction of action and reaction. Dispatches and messages took more than six weeks to travel from Portugal to Paris, and the same time to return, if they made it to their destination at all. This became slower during the war as larger forces were needed to protect the messages from interception by growing guerrilla bands. If intelligence was sent to Napoleon, he was then reading information six weeks old, at least. Instructions ordering the commanders to cooperate were effectively out-of-date as soon as they were written. In an order dated 30 March 1811 Napoleon directed Masséna to stay in Coimbra and occupy Oporto, and Soult to coordinate movements with Masséna to put pressure on the Allies. As the instructions were being written, Masséna's army had retreated over the river Coa, and crossed the border back into Spain. The army was not fit for any active operations, and Napoleon's instructions were irrelevant.

To understand why Napoleonic battles were fought in the style they were, the capabilities of the weapons used need to be understood. The way weapons are employed, and their limitations, dictate the tactics that are demanded from the armies. The majority of infantry of both armies were equipped with the smoothbore musket. Inaccurate even at close range, this weapon needed to be use en-masse to obtain significant results. Hence, the infantry stood shoulder-to-shoulder and were trained to fire in volleys. To maximise the number of muskets able to fire, both sides employed infantry in lines. The commonly understood routine to a firefight would involve units from both armies standing in line some tens of metres away from each other firing into the enemy ranks until one side broke and fled. The British, however, adapted this and would normally fire one or two volleys, then charge with the bayonet. Fifteen or 16 inches long, this was a fearsome weapon that could penetrate all the way through a soldier's body.

Orders issued at the beginning of the battle relied on the sub-commanders understanding the prevailing doctrine. In the case of the French infantry, this was generally understood by all commanders to be an advance to range in column, protected by a cloud of skirmishers. In his 'Instructions for the Troops Comprising the Left Corps' *Maréchal* Ney wrote,

> Marches and evolutions executed in column form the essential parts of military tactics ... In such cases , commanders of battalions and of platoons cannot pay too much attention to all that relates to the direction of the march ... resuming the line of battle either to the front , or on one of the divisions or subdivisions of the centre , or on one of the two flanks.[15]

The columns would then deploy into line, fire volleys and advance. Deploying into line maximised the number of muskets available to fire, and did the same for the number of bayonets available for a charge at the enemy. Wellington's tactic of hiding his main battle line behind a ridge crest or other natural obstacle often led

15 Bulos, *Memoirs of Marshal Ney*, vol.2, p.294.

the French manoeuvre columns to be caught before they could deploy into line. The commander of the advancing column did not have a clear idea of where the Allied line was, and thus could not correctly predict the best time to form line. Several accounts of battles against the Allies talk of attempts to deploy into line. At Albuera, Lieutenant Colonel Sir Edward Blakeney of the 7th Regiment says of a French column, 'During the closest part of the action I saw their officers endeavouring to deploy their columns, but all to no purpose. For as soon as the third of a company got out, they would immediately run back, to be covered by the front of their column.'[16] In his account of the attack of the 31e Légère at Buçaco, Lemonnier-Delafosse indicates that his battalion attempted to deploy into line after advancing in column: '… some regiments succeeded in forming themselves into line, but, in mine, only part of the first battalion could carry out the command.'[17] His description is very much like Blakeney's, in that the infantry would begin their deployment into line, but then break and seek cover behind the column. The overall effect of Allied musket fire prevented the French from deploying, and once halted, the officers found it was impossible to regain the column's momentum. Officer casualties mounted in greater proportion to other ranks' as they urged their men forward. Second Lieutenant George Simmons of the 95th recalled the fighting at Almeida in 1810; 'French officers like mountebanks running forward and placing their hats upon their swords, and capering about like madmen …' to encourage their soldiers.[18]

There was, and still is, a belief mistakenly held by some historians that the French infantry would always attack in column to punch a hole through the enemy line. This seems to be a misunderstanding of the formation called 'colonne d'attaque'. This, and the formation called 'colonne de division' were used extensively for manoeuvre on the battlefield. The infantry would move in column and attempt to deploy into line at the last moment, in order to move quickly into action and then fire volleys from line at the enemy. The misunderstanding originates from interpretations of Charles Oman's work, but even he revised his view on French tactics when he was presented with new information about the Battle of Maida.[19] However, Oman's previous work has been so influential that the idea of 'attack columns' in the Peninsula still holds sway. A description of Waterloo describes French tactics in the following terms; 'French success was based on the impact of columns of infantry, preceded by swarms of skirmishers.'[20]

16 Thomas Wade, 'General Correspondence: Sir Lowry Cole and Colonel Wade on the Movement of the Fourth Division at the Battle of Albuera', *The United Service Magazine*, vol.35, no. 1 (1841), pp.536–539.

17 Marie Jean Baptiste Lemonnier-Delafosse, *Campagnes de 1810 à 1815. Souvenirs militaires.* (Havre: Alph. Lemale, 1850), p.70.

18 Willoughby Verner (ed.), *A British Rifle Man* (London: A & C Black, 1899), p.77.

19 James R. Arnold, 'A Reappraisal of Column versus Line in the Peninsular War', *The Journal of Military History*, vol.68, no. 2 (2004), pp.535–552.

20 'Battle of Waterloo: Armies, Battle Tactics and Orders', *FutureLearn*, <https://www.futurelearn.com/courses/wellington-and-waterloo/0/steps/24850>, accessed January 2022. See also Andrew Field, *Talavera: Wellington's First Victory in Spain* (Barnsley: Pen & Sword Military, 2006), chap. 4.

In 1808 Napoleon issued a decree reorganising the establishment of infantry regiments and battalions, changing the battalion from nine companies to six. The selection of formation, according to the decree, was dependent on whether all the companies were present.

> In battle, the company of grenadiers will hold the right of the battalion, that of the voltigeurs the left. When the six companies are present in the battalion … it will always act by divisions. When the grenadiers and voltigeurs are absent from the battalion, it will manoeuvre and will always parade by platoon [peloton] … Two companies will form a division; each company will form a platoon …[21]

If either the grenadiers or voltigeurs were detached, then the battalion would deploy in 'colonne d'attaque'. This was one company wide, and five deep (the voltigeur company presumably skirmishing). The 'colonne de division' was two companies wide, and three deep.

An established part of French doctrine was the use of skirmishers to pave the way for their attacks. There are many allied accounts of swarms of skirmishers heralding their advance.[22] Often a French regiment would detach all the voltigeur companies from its battalions to act as skirmishers ahead of the attacking column. This screen of skirmishers may also include battalions from the light, or Légère, regiments of the division. Regiments such as the 26e de Ligne at Buçaco, 1,532 men comprising the 4th, 5th and 6th battalions of the regiment, could throw more than 240 skirmishers ahead of any attack. This presented a not inconsiderable force to be countered by the Allies, sometimes with more success than others. Additionally, French infantry not designated as light were capable of being used in the skirmishing role. At Jena in 1806, individual battalions of infantry from line regiments were deployed in skirmish order.[23] In 1810, at the Battle of Buçaco, almost an entire division, Marchand's of Ney's VI Corps, would fight in 'dispersed' formation.[24] The role of the French skirmishers would be the same as that of those of the Allied army: to push the enemy skirmishers back and stop them harassing the main battle line.

The continental armies were slow to adopt these tactics at the beginning of the wars, but Britain already had light troops capable of countering the French skirmishers. Each British regiment contained one company, or approximately one tenth, which was designated the light company. The Portuguese had Caçadores and Atiradores, and the Spanish Cazadores and Tiradores. These would combine to form the skirmish screen in front of the main Allied battle line and to a large degree neutralise the French advantage. Additionally, Britain had rifle armed troops

21 Plon and Dumaine (eds), *Correspondence de Napoléon I*, vol.16, pp.338–341.

22 Charles Oman (ed.), *Adventures with the Connaught Rangers, 1809-1814* (London: E Arnold, 1902), p.31; Sir Andrew Leith Hay, *A Narrative of the Peninsular War* (London: John Hearne, 1850), p.163.

23 Jean-Lambert-Alphonse Colin (ed.), *La Tactique et La Discipline Dans Les Armées de La Révolution: Correspondance Du Général Schauenbourg Du 4 Avril Au 2 Août 1793* (Paris: Librairie militaire R. Chapelot, 1902), p.LXXXVI.

24 White, *The Key to Lisbon*, pp.167–169.

in small numbers distributed throughout the army. Although initially fewer than their musket-armed French opponents, these rifle armed troops would quickly grow in number as their utility was recognised. They included the Brunswick Oel Jäger, the 5th battalion of the 60th regiment, Portuguese Atiradores and King's German Legion light battalions. With a greater range and accuracy than a conventional musket, these specialist troops could target individuals, such as officers and NCOs, disrupting the enemy's discipline and order.

A French tactic which had promise was 'ordre mixte' (mixed order). Originating in the Revolutionary Wars, it comprised a mixture of columns and lines in one formation. The combination of different unit structures allowed the benefits of both line and column, whilst reducing their vulnerabilities. In his introduction to Schauenburg's *Correspondance*, Jean-Lambert-Alphonse Colin wrote:

> It was Guibert who was the first to advocate the mixed order of battle, after having explained the advantages of compact columns and line. 'Deployed battalions are suitable for being combined in a general arrangement with columns, either for marching with the same front, and in concert with them, either to support them, or to be supported by them. There is such an attack where it is about mingling deployed battalions with columns, to march together and in concert ...'[25]

Several times this formation is mentioned in the same introduction. What is interesting is that the assumed formation for *deployed* battalions is line. The better trained troops could be used in the line part of the formation as they were more capable of retaining discipline and organisation. Those more poorly trained would be used in the columns, as these required less control. The formation had been part of French tactical doctrine for more than a decade but was infrequently used in the Peninsula. As the quality of troops deteriorated from their peak soon after the invasion of Spain the French found it more difficult to employ complex tactics against the Allies. Soult is supposed to have used a mixed order in his attacks at Albuera as he had some veteran units available, but this is convincingly questioned by Guy Dempsey.[26] This formation could have provided the flexibility which might have been adapted to overcome the successful Allied tactics.

Perhaps an attack in column worked against other armies, such as the Spanish at the beginning of the war. But once the French realised the Allied discipline and firepower were too great, why was there no change in tactics, no adoption of more flexible battlefield deployments such as ordre mixte? The answer may be the capability of the troops. Even though some of the formations had been in the field for several years, many of the soldiers were replacements or recently conscripted. One memoir records that a soldier, who said of himself that he had a '... weak constitution ...' was conscripted on 11 June 1808, but only issued with cartridges after he had reached the border with Spain in December. He had received little instruction

25 Colin (ed.), *La Tactique et La Discipline*, pp.LXXIV–LXXV.
26 Guy C. Dempsey, *Albuera, 1811: The Bloodiest Battle of the Peninsular War* (London: Frontline, 2008), pp.110–111.

in battlefield manoeuvres.[27] The French did not have the time, or opportunity as in 1805, to train together in large formations, with a single coherent command structure directing their operations. Many veteran infantry units were taken from the Peninsula to reinforce Napoleon's armies in Central Europe, most notably for the campaign of 1812 in Russia. As the war progressed the French units were made up of many conscripts, and filled out with other foreign troops, many from occupied nations conscripted into the French army. These units also contained prisoners of war and deserters. Some divisions were made up almost entirely of new or foreign regiments, such as Loison's division in 1810. The complicated evolutions employed by well-trained troops, such as deployment from column into line under fire and on uneven terrain, takes confidence and repeated exercise. As the ranks of the army were filled out with more conscripts so the task of developing new tactics, or even implementing those existing, became more difficult.

French cavalry and artillery tactics were similar in form to the Allies. A vital role undertaken by cavalry was that of intelligence gathering. The situation in the Peninsula was much more troublesome for the French. Unlike British exploring officers, the French could not roam the countryside individually or even in small groups. The French constantly reported the sighting of small groups of Allied cavalry, maintaining visual contact whilst avoiding a fight. Conversely, the French relied on large numbers of cavalry, perhaps of squadron strength, for reconnaissance. This proved to be a clumsy method, as any approaching cavalry would be visible at a distance, and measures to avoid them quickly taken. French allied cavalry proved to be another weakness, with a willingness to desert shown when an opportunity arose. A party of chasseurs from the Légion Hanovrienne, composed mainly of German troops, was captured while on reconnaissance who were, '... very glad at being taken'.[28] Thus, little useful information could be gathered, and the French army was effectively blind to any enemy movement outside of its immediate vicinity.

French cavalry was supposed to be, individually and collectively, better than that of the Allies. Wellington wrote:

> I considered our cavalry so inferior to the French from the want of order, that although I considered one squadron a match for two French, I didn't like to see four British opposed to four French: and as the numbers increased and order, of course, became more necessary I was the more unwilling to risk our men without having a superiority in numbers.[29]

Wellington reckoned as late as 1812 that their unreliability was, '... occasioned entirely by a trick our officers have acquired of galloping at everything, and then

27 Philippe Gille (ed.), *Mémoires d'un Conscrit de 1808: Les Prisonniers de Cabrera* (Paris: V. Havard, 1892), p.34.

28 John H. Leslie (ed.), *The Dickson Manuscripts: Being Diaries, Letters, Maps, Account Books, with Various Other Papers, for the Year 1810* (Cambridge: Trotman, 1987), p.261, Letter to Major General MacLeod, Sarzedas, 27 August 1810.

29 Charles Oman, *A History of the Peninsular War: 1807-1809: From the Treaty of Fontainebleau to the Battle of Corunna* (London: Greenhill Books, 2004), vol.1, p.119.

galloping back as fast as they gallop at the enemy. They never consider their situation, never think of manoeuvring before the enemy …'[30] *Général de division* Maximilien Foy agreed with Wellington's assessment of the superiority of the French cavalry, and added that the dragoons, '… supplied exclusively almost the whole service of the cavalry in the war in Portugal and Spain.'[31] However, there were few opportunities to make them a battle winning force. Probably the closest they came to turning a battle was at Fuentes de Oñoro in 1811. The French cavalry were to take part in a flanking movement by the French left, and Montbrun's cavalry, the reserve dragoons, Fournier's and Wathier's brigades were to deploy to the left of VI Corps. This was, effectively, the entire cavalry strength of the Armée de Portugal, with only a small, detached force of cavalry being retained by the individual corps for reconnaissance. In addition, there was a force of 800 cavalry of the Imperial Guard, comprising squadrons of the élite Grenadiers à Cheval, Chevau-Légers-Lanciers, Chasseurs-à-Cheval and Mamelukes, under the command of *Maréchal* Jean-Baptiste Bessières. This force of more than 3,000 cavalry attacked in an uncoordinated fashion with several divisions of infantry. This lack of coordination, combined with difficult terrain, meant that they could not be the battle winning force hoped for.

French doctrine made extensive use of artillery to batter the enemy lines before an attack. The continental habit of deploying troops visible to the French made these bombardments quite effective, reducing the capacity to resist any subsequent assault. Wellington's habit of concealing his main body behind topographical features tended to neutralise this approach. Where he was unable to do this effectively, such as the British centre at Talavera, the troops suffered correspondingly heavily. Ensign John Aitchison describes how, at that battle, 'Till about two o'clock … our men from daybreak were for the greater part exposed to a tremendous cannonade – shot and shells were falling in every direction …'[32]

The artillery comprised companies of foot and horse artillery distributed throughout the divisions of the army. The horse artillery used smaller, more mobile, guns. They were typically 4-pounder cannon and 6-inch howitzers, and usually had six guns per company. Foot artillery used either 8-pounder or 12-pounder guns and had eight guns per company. The artillery allocated to infantry divisions would tend to be the 8 pounder companies, with the 12-pounders in the reserve park. A foot artillery company consisted of approximately 30 vehicles with a minimum of 140 horses. Moving in single file along the narrow paths and roads of Spain and Portugal a company would have taken up a large amount of space. The roads were not built to carry their weight, with an 8-pounder cannon weighing almost 1,300lbs (half a ton, or 580kg), the unmade roads and paths would have quickly broken up. The uneven state of the roads caused extensive damage to the wheels and carriages of the guns.

30 To Lieutenant General Sir R. Hill, Salamanca, 18th June 1812, John Gurwood (ed.), *The Dispatches of the Field Marshal The Duke of Wellington. An Enlarged Edition in Eight Volumes* (Cambridge: Cambridge University Press, 2010), vol.5, p.712.

31 Élisabeth Augustine Foy (ed.), *History of the War in the Peninsula, under Napoleon; to Which Is Prefixed a View of the Political and Military State of the Four Belligerent Powers* (London: Treuttel and Würtz, 1827), vol.1, pp.76–77.

32 W. F. K. Thompson (ed.), *An Ensign in the Peninsular War: The Letters of John Aitchison* (London: Joseph, 1981), p.57, Belem, 14th September 1809.

The standardisation of French artillery made the replacement of broken wheels and other components simpler, but the supply of new and repaired parts could not keep up with demand. In addition, the wastage of horses made bringing guns to the battlefield more difficult. The same can be said of supplying ammunition. Because of the loss of horses during the campaign of 1810 in Portugal the French army was outgunned by the Allied army for the first time at Fuentes de Oñoro in 1811.

More fundamental even than the doctrine and tactics of the troops was the supply of necessities such as gunpowder. Without this, all of the projectile weapons carried by the army were useless. During a battle several million rounds of musket, plus several thousand rounds of artillery, ammunition might be used. The supply of gunpowder could quickly be exhausted. Without regular supply, or even secure lines of communication, sometimes gunpowder needed to be manufactured on campaign. As the French army clung on to their position at Santarem in Portugal at the end of 1810, *Général de division* Jean Éblé, commander of Masséna's artillery, was instructed to make more gunpowder for the army but had to report, 'I am sorry to announce that the country is entirely destitute of the raw materials which go into the composition of the powder. I sent for sulphur; I could have hardly collected a pound; it was the same with saltpetre …'[33] With such basic material in short supply, we should perhaps be surprised that the French armies were capable of staying in the Peninsula as long as they did.

Conclusion

A strategy need be only marginally better than one's opponent's for it to succeed. A good strategy can succeed even if the forces available are only 'adequate.' Conversely a poor strategy will not be saved even by the most effective of forces.

Given the overall numerical advantage, the initial tactical and operational superiority over the Spanish and Portuguese, and the land-based lines of communication back to France, why was the Peninsular War a such disaster for the French? The French defeats in the Peninsula cannot be ascribed to any one factor discussed here, but rather the compound effects of several elements. This discussion has attempted to cover several different problems encountered by the French armies during their occupation of Spain and Portugal. Historians have sometimes attributed Napoleon's failure in the Peninsula to one or two of these problems. This author's opinion is that they all conspired, along with others not mentioned here, to make French success in the Peninsula almost impossible.

The most damaging act by Napoleon was to leave the Peninsula to his subordinates without successfully concluding the campaign in 1808–1809. It was his duty to achieve lasting victory there in 1808 when he had the Spanish and British armies at his mercy. Speed and flexibility achieved under Napoleon's direct command was replaced by delay, disagreement or an overly methodical approach, such as with Masséna in 1810. Once he had left, Napoleon, through remote oversight, carried out

33 Girod de l'Ain, *Le Général Eblé*, pp.187–188, Pièces Justificatives, général Eblé au maréchal Masséna, Santarem, 17 October 1810.

a strategy formulated with out-of-date instructions, and executed through truculent or downright unresponsive army commanders. Some commanders, although impetuous, were more adapted to the Napoleonic way of war than others.

The most telling difficulties for the French occurred at the operational level. These beset the French during the whole of the Peninsular War. Had they been able to coordinate sufficiently large forces to overwhelm the smaller allied armies, any problems with tactics would effectively have been removed. But they continued to face the problem of the failure to collect up-to-date intelligence. There was a dearth of resources vital for an army to operate – food, water, ammunition, maps and guides. It was impossible for the French commanders to order a concentration of forces without the risk of running out of supplies once the campaign had begun. The successes in war which Napoleon achieved in central Europe, and initially in Spain and Portugal, by utterly defeating his opponents by his capability, flexibility and speed, were not obtainable in the Iberian Peninsula.

Tactically the French made no concerted effort during the war to alter their approach to counter effective enemy tactics. Doctrine continued without modification, despite repeated failures in battle. Any changes would have demanded a modification in training for all conscripts; a potentially disruptive and time consuming process. The French persisted in fighting in two or three deep lines, and attempting to deploy from column into line and exchange fire with the enemy before closing to bayonet range. Alterations were not made for the circumstances and environment in which the campaigns were being fought. The answer to this fundamental question rests on the experience and reliability of the troops employed at the time. As the experienced soldiers were killed, wounded or redeployed, so the quality of the army deteriorated. As this decline continued, so the ability of the troops to adopt new techniques and more flexible tactics diminished. From the soldiers' point of view there was little understanding of the overall strategy, and their experience changed little throughout the campaigns. However, their training lessened as heavier demands were placed on them. The consequence of this reduction in the quality of infantry was that officer casualties increased as they repeatedly moved to the front of the unit to encourage soldiers to manoeuvre and fire. These officers became targets, especially for the rifle armed soldiers in the allied skirmish lines. The consequent loss of experienced men added to the problem of maintaining discipline, and contributed to the inability, or unwillingness, to change formation under fire. As more of the experienced men were lost as casualties, or reinforcements to other theatres, so the problem was compounded. A failure to adapt tactics and doctrine meant that as the allied armies in the Peninsula increased in numbers, reliability and capability, those of the French deteriorated. As the occupation continued, a lessening of French control provoked greater resistance, both in the Peninsula and further afield. Britain's resolve against Napoleon became firmer following the success of the campaign of 1810–1811. Napoleon's invasion of Russia in 1812 served to further weaken his position.

The failure of all aspects of strategy – ends, ways and means – for the Imperial armies conspired to make the Peninsular War unwinnable. The overall conclusion must be that the French lost the Peninsular War by what was *not* done, rather than what was. By not having a unified, unquestionable authority; by failing to equip and supply their armies efficiently; by failing to win over, or at least suppress, the population; by continuing to use tactics against an enemy despite their lack of success.

Bibliography

Arnold, James R., 'A Reappraisal of Column versus Line in the Peninsular War', *The Journal of Military History*, vol.68, no. 2 (2004), pp.535–552

Barrès, Jean-Baptiste, *Memoirs of a French Napoleonic Officer* (London: Greenhill, 1988)

Bonnal, Henri, *La Vie Militaire Du Marechal Ney, Duc d'Elchingen, Prince de La Moskowa* (Paris: Chapelot, 1914)

Bulos, M. (ed.), *Memoirs of Marshal Ney* (London: Bull and Churton, 1833)

Clausewitz, Carl von, *On War* (London: David Campbell, 1993)

Colin, Jean-Lambert-Alphonse (ed.), *La Tactique et La Discipline Dans Les Armées de La Révolution : Correspondance Du Général Schauenbourg Du 4 Avril Au 2 Août 1793* (Paris: Librairie militaire R. Chapelot, 1902)

Dempsey, Guy C., *Albuera, 1811: The Bloodiest Battle of the Peninsular War* (London: Frontline, 2008)

Field, Andrew, *Talavera: Wellington's First Victory in Spain* (Barnsley: Pen & Sword Military, 2006)

Foy, Élisabeth Augustine (ed.), *History of the War in the Peninsula, under Napoleon; to Which Is Prefixed a View of the Political and Military State of the Four Belligerent Powers* (London: Treuttel and Würtz, 1827)

Gille, Philippe (ed.), *Mémoires d'un Conscrit de 1808: Les Prisonniers de Cabrera* (Paris: V. Havard, 1892)

Girod de l'Ain, Maurice, *Le Général Eblé (1758-1812)* (Paris: Berger-Levrault, 1893)

Gurwood, John (ed.), *The Dispatches of the Field Marshal the Duke of Wellington. An Enlarged Edition in Eight Volumes* (Cambridge: Cambridge University Press, 2010)

Jomini, Antoine Henri, *The Art of War* (London: Greenhill Books, 2006)

Leith Hay, Sir Andrew, *A Narrative of the Peninsular War* (London: John Hearne, 1850)

Lemonnier-Delafosse, Marie Jean Baptiste, *Campagnes de 1810 à 1815. Souvenirs militaires* (Havre: Alph. Lemale, 1850).

Leslie, John H., *The Dickson Manuscripts: Being Diaries, Letters, Maps, Account Books, with Various Other Papers, for the Year 1810* (Cambridge: Trotman, 1987)

Marmont, Auguste Frédéric Louis Viesse de, *Mémoires Du Maréchal Marmont, Duc de Raguse* (Paris: Perrotin, 1857)

Noël, Jean-Nicolas-Auguste, *With Napoleon's Guns: The Military Memoirs of an Officer of the First Empire* (London: Greenhill, 2005)

Oman, Charles (ed.), *Adventures with the Connaught Rangers, 1809-1814* (London: E Arnold, 1902)

Oman, Charles, *A History of the Peninsular War: 1807-1809: From the Treaty of Fontainebleau to the Battle of Corunna* (London: Greenhill Books, 2004)

Plon, Henri, and J. Dumaine (eds), *Correspondence de Napoléon I* (Paris: Plon and Dumaine, 1864–1866)

Wade, Thomas, 'General Correspondence: Sir Lowry Cole and Colonel Wade on the Movement of the Fourth Division at the Battle of Albuera', *The United Service Magazine*, vol.35, no. 1 (1841), pp.536–539

Thompson, W. F. K. (ed.), *An Ensign in the Peninsular War: The Letters of John Aitchison* (London: Joseph, 1981)

Verner, Willoughby (ed.), *A British Rifle Man* (London: A & C Black, 1899)

White, Kenton, *The Key to Lisbon: The Third French Invasion of Portugal, 1810-11* (Warwick: Helion & Company, 2019)

8

Light Bobs and Jäger Battalions of Light Companies in the Peninsular War

Robert Griffith

On 3 August 1808, shortly after landing in Portugal, Lieutenant General Sir Arthur Wellesley issued a general order outlining how the army would march and deploy in battle. One paragraph read:

> The Lieutenant-General requests the General officers commanding brigades will, on all occasions of march and formation of the line of their respective brigades, place the light infantry companies belonging to the several regiments under their command in a separate corps under the command of a field-officer. In the ordinary formation on parade, and in route marches, these corps of light infantry will be on the left of the brigade. In formation in front of the enemy they will be in front or in rear, according to circumstances; and in the marches of columns to take up a position, they will be on the reverse flank of the column. The light infantry companies will, however, encamp, and do all duties with the regiments.[1]

In May 1809, shortly after resuming command of the British and Portuguese forces in Portugal, Wellesley repeated these instructions in another general order.[2]

This tactical separation of the light companies from their parent battalions, and their grouping together with detached companies of riflemen and other troops, continued for the duration of the Peninsular War. Most discussions of allied light infantry in the Peninsula tend to concentrate on the Light Division, which was composed entirely of specialist light infantry and rifle units. Wellington frequently

1 General Order, 3 August 1808, quoted in, Duke of Wellington, 2nd (ed.), *Supplementary Despatches, Correspondence and Memoranda of Field Marshal Arthur Duke of Wellington, K.G.* (London: Murray, 1860), vol.VI., pp.96–97.

2 General Order, 4 May 1809, quoted in, Wellington (ed.), *Supplementary Despatches*, vol.VI., p.251.

used the Light Division as a vanguard for his army and to maintain chains of outposts, but in several of the battles in the Peninsula the Light Division was positioned on a flank or held in reserve while the brunt of the fighting was borne by other divisions. For these other divisions it fell to the men of light companies of the line battalions, the riflemen of the 5/60th, the Portuguese Caçadores, and the Brunswick and other light infantry units to counter the numerous and skilled French light infantry. The combined light companies of the brigades became a vital element of Wellington's defensive and offensive tactics.

The duties of light troops during the Napoleonic Wars encompassed reconnaissance, forming advanced and rear guards, outpost duty, and patrolling. However, this chapter will concentrate on the use of the composite battalions of light infantry from the British brigades in battle.

As Rory Muir writes in *Tactics and the Experience of Battle in the Age of Napoleon*:

> In battle light infantry, fighting in open order and relying on the initiative of individual soldiers, would occupy rough terrain, woods, even villages; they would harass enemy formations, sniping at officers, distracting and unsettling the men by their fire. Ideally they acted like a cloud of midges, giving way in the face of any determined enemy advance but quickly returning if the enemy halted, and constantly biting.[3]

Flank Battalions

Forming flank battalions comprised of the light or grenadier companies of line regiments was an established part of British military doctrine throughout the eighteenth century. It gave commanders extra units of picked men without weakening their parent regiments too much. The British generals commanding in North America during the War of Independence formed the flank companies under their commands into light and grenadier battalions, some of which remained embodied for much of the conflict.[4] Lieutenant General Sir Charles Grey formed three battalions each of light troops and grenadiers for his campaign in the West Indies in 1794.[5] There are many other examples from the Revolutionary and Napoleonic Wars of flank battalions being formed, including by Lieutenant General Sir Thomas Graham in his campaign in eastern Spain that led up to the Battle of Barossa.

However, in most of these cases the flank battalions were usually completely operationally separated from their parent battalions for the duration of a short campaign. Prolonged detachments could lead to problems of logistics, and even discipline, as the companies felt the lack of leadership and resources from their battalion headquarters. The flank battalions would also have had to develop their own esprit de corps and unit cohesion. Wellington did not form any battalions of

3 R. Muir, *Tactics and the Experience of Battle in the Age of Napoleon* (New Haven: Yale University Press, 1998), p.52.
4 See D. Hagist, *These Distinguished Corps* (Warwick: Helion: 2021).
5 S. Brown, *By Fire and Bayonet* (Solihull: Helion, 2017), p.62.

grenadier companies during the Peninsular War. The grenadiers were typically the tallest and steadiest men in a battalion, but they did not have any specialist roles or training when compared to the centre companies of the battalions.

The way that Wellesley split the light companies from their parent battalions when their brigade was on the march or in battle enabled them to maintain their logistical and administrative links, and still benefit from regimental, and in time brigade, esprit de corps. It also enabled the light companies to support their own parent regiments directly in combat, something that would not have been possible had they been completely separated. The composition of many of the brigades within the army remained relatively stable over time, enabling their constituent units to form good working relationships, and there is every reason to suppose that this would have extended to the light companies becoming used to drilling, training, and fighting together.

It was not just the British that formed flank battalions, the practice was also common in continental armies. Johann von Ewald, an officer who had served in the Hessian and Danish armies, advocated it in his influential *A Treatise on Upon the Duties of Light Troops*.[6] He also emphasises the importance of training the companies together and instructing their officers and NCOs in all the duties and skills required, and says: 'How advantageous it would be for an army to have a body of light troops formed in this manner! 200 of them, under an able commander would perform what in general requires a thousand ...'[7]

The Theory

General David Dundas formulated the British Army's 1792 drill manual, *Rules and Regulations for the Formations, Field-Exercise and Movements of His Majesty's Forces*, but outlined only the most basic of light infantry movements and duties. When a battalion was formed in line its light company was to be split into two divisions and positioned 30 paces behind the line, near both flanks. If ordered to the front to cover the battalion, the divisions would march around the flanks and then extend their files so that they covered the frontage of the battalion. If called in, they would return to their position at the rear of the battalion.[8]

The manual also covered forming the light companies into battalions: 'When two or more companies are together, they are to consider themselves as a battalion, the senior officer is to take command, leaving the immediate command of his own company to the next officer belonging to it.'[9]

All movements were to be in quick time, but the battalion could also be ordered to run in certain circumstances, such as when hurrying to occupy a position before

6 J. von Ewald, *A Treatise on Upon the Duties of Light Troops*, in *Rifle & Riflemen* (Driffield: Leonaur, 2011), p.16.
7 Von Ewald, *Treatise*, pp.16–17.
8 D. Dundas, *Rules and Regulations for the Formations, Field-Exercise and Movements of His Majesty's Forces* (London: War Office, 1798), pp.276–277.
9 Dundas, *Rules and Regulations*, p.278.

the enemy. The manual then covers how a column of light infantry should form line to the front or flanks, how to clear a wood, and emphasises that when firing and advancing the pace must be slow and the fire deliberate and well-directed. The section also mentions the need for an intelligent commander and the importance of maintaining a portion of the force as a reserve.[10]

In December 1797 the Adjutant General, General Sir William Fawcett, sent a circular to all the generals commanding districts, referencing a letter from March of the same year where, at the Duke of York's request, he had sent them all printed copies of the section of Dundas's regulations dealing with light infantry for distribution to the regiments under their command:

> His Royal Highness thinking it highly expedient, at the present juncture, that the Light Infantry Companies, in general throughout the whole Army, should be diligently exercised and perfected, as much as possible, in those Movements and Manoeuvres, which are more particularly adapted to them than to the Heavy Infantry, is therefore pleased to direct, that you should give immediate orders for all the Light Companies, attached to the several Battalions, in the District under your command to be frequently taken out in separate Bodies, and practiced at firing Ball at a Mark, and is such other different Exercises, as they are principally formed and intended for, when opposed to an Enemy, so that in case circumstances should, at any time, render it necessary to assemble and form them into distinct Battalions, they may be thoroughly prepared to do their duty in the Field, with the Precision, Skill and Uniformity which will be expected from them.[11]

However, it soon became clear that the few pages in the standard drill manual were insufficient and the Duke of York arranged for a specific light infantry manual to be produced, based upon the instructions that Lieutenant Colonel Baron Francis de Rottenburg had originally written for Hompesch's Light Infantry, one of the many foreign corps that were in British pay. *Regulations for the Exercise of Riflemen and Light Infantry and Instructions for their Conduct in the Field* prescribed the training, drill and movements of light infantry in far more detail. One of the core principles was that half of any body deployed as skirmishers should be held to the rear in reserve, but if the skirmishers were covering a larger body, then that body could be taken as the reserve.

The greater part of the manual covered outpost duty, patrolling and forming advance and rear guards, as well as setting out the drill and formations light infantry were to use. It did also briefly describe how a light or rifle company was to screen and support a battalion during a battle. However, the army was often slow to adopt new methods and tactics.

Harry Ross-Lewin of the 32nd Foot recalled that as a young lieutenant his light company joined a composite light battalion during the Irish Rebellion of 1803

10 Dundas, *Rules and Regulations*, p.280.

11 Fawcett to District Commanders, The National Archives (TNA): WO 3/31: 25 Dec 1797, pp.106–107.

and formed up in Phoenix Park to demonstrate their abilities to Lord Cathcart, Commander-in-Chief in Ireland:

> General Rotenberg's treatise on light infantry tactics had been put into our hands only a few days before, and our commanding officer was totally uninformed on the subject; he therefore determined to divide the battalion into small parties, to serve out to the men a great quantity of ammunition, and to let them fire away from behind the bushes as long as it lasted. The morning came, and so did Lord Cathcart. The light battalion was soon hid among the bushes; our fire was most furious; and the park seemed all in a blaze; but it would have been difficult for his lordship to discover any plan in this military spectacle.[12]

In the same year General François Jarry, commandant of the senior department of the Royal Military College and a veteran of both the Prussian and the French armies, wrote *Instructions Concerning the Duties of Light Infantry in the Field* and this too became required reading for rifle and light infantry officers. As with de Rottenburg's manual, Jarry's concentrated on pickets, outposts and patrols. This *Petit Guerre* would always be light infantry's primary purpose, but he did also outline their role in battle. If a force was preparing to attack: '...it is the business of the light infantry to cover the deployment of the columns, by occupying the houses, hedges, hollow ways, and thickets, in front, to the distance of about six or seven hundred paces, according to the proximity of the first batteries of the enemy, and the situation of his out-posts.'[13] Then, when the battle commenced, they should cover the flanks or attempt to turn the enemies flank and attack them in the rear. When defending light infantry were to occupy the same type of key posts and hold them at all costs to allow the main force time to deploy.[14] If the battle was won, then the light infantry could be used to pursue the enemy. Should it be lost then the light infantry would form the rear guard, slowing and harassing the enemy to let the main army withdraw.

In 1813 and 1814 a series of articles entitled 'The Field Day' in the *Royal Military Panorama or Officer's Companion* by Captain Ernst Olferman of the 97th Foot set out 10 movements and scenarios for an infantry brigade to practice on a field day, and included sections on the battalion of light companies and where they should be relative to their brigade in various situations. They are worth quoting at length as such details are almost never included in the accounts of individual actions. Olferman had been a brigade major in the Peninsula and his manoeuvres were formulated whilst he was serving there. The first section deals with a brigade, of three battalions, marching in column to the field:

12 H. Ross-Lewin, *With the Thirty-Second* (Dublin: Hodges, Figgis & Co., 1904), p.63.
13 F. Jarry, *Instructions Concerning the Duties of Light Infantry in the Field* (London: Dulau & Co. 1803), pp.197–198.
14 Jarry, *Instructions*, pp.203–204.

Light Company detached.—The light companies are detached under the command of an experienced Field-Officer, who must be well acquainted with light-infantry movements, to form the advanced-guard, to cover the column during its march, and to mask the several evolutions of the brigade.

Attention of the officer commanding the light companies.—The chief attention of the officer commanding these companies, must be directed to the several cautions which the General may give, previous to the intended movements of the brigade, and his own judgment must guide him in giving the necessary orders to the officers and men under his immediate command for their timely advancing or retreating, extending or closing, inclining to the right or left, &c.. &c.. so that the operations of the brigade may never be impeded by them.

Disposition of the light companies during the route march of the column.—During the march of the brigade to the ground of exercise, one company will form the advanced-guard in the usual manner; another will move in open file along, and at some distance from the pivot-flank of the column; and the third company in the same manner and distance on the reverse flank, detaching a Serjeant and a few men to form the rear-guard, so that the whole column is covered.[15]

As the brigade begins to deploy into line:

> *Light companies.*—The light companies cover the left flank of the column during its entry of and march on the alignment; they move through the intervals of the column, when line is formed, and are posted by subdivisions or sections in the rear of their own battalions, ready to file round the flanks of the line, and through the intervals between battalions, as circumstances may require.[16]

When the brigade was forming column again from being deployed in line:

LIGHT COMPANIES.

They advance.—When the caution is given for the formation of close column, the signal will sound for those companies to advance to such ground as may be best adapted for them to cover the front of the brigade in *extended order.*

They close.—During the formation of the close column they will *incline* and gradually *close* towards the right, observing to cover that part of the brigade which is moving in files.

They cover the column en mass.—When the column en mass is formed, they mask the same in the following manner—the *right company* covers

15 J. Phillipart (ed.), *The Royal Military Panorama or Officer's Companion* (London: Martin & Co., 1813), vol.III, October 1813, p.49.

16 Phillipart (ed.), *Royal Military Panorama*, vol.III, October 1813, p.50.

obliquely the right flank, the *centre company* the head, and the left company obliquely the left flank of the column.

They march parallel with their own columns, &c. They extend, &c.—When contiguous columns are formed and marched to the right flank, the light companies move parallel with their respective battalions; and when the columns deploy into line they extend successively to the right, covering the front of their own battalions.

They close and retire, &c.—If the battalions are to fire, the light companies close by sub-divisions and retire; but if not to fire, and another change of front is to be made, they remain in extended order in front of the line.

If the forming of close columns is interrupted by the enemy, &c.—If the formation of close columns or deployment is threatened to be interrupted by the enemy, they will cover the movement by their fire, and when pressed, retire behind such part of the line which is formed, or in the centre of the column which may have prepared against cavalry.[17]

If the brigade was forming close columns of battalions to move to the right and rear in the face of a determined enemy attack:

> Each [light] company having detached a section at some distance in its front, from which advanced files arc to be thrown out, the rest will remain as reserve.
>
> They will occupy their old ground as long as consistent with safety to themselves, in order that the enemy may not immediately perceive the change of position.
>
> When the enemy approaches in force, they must concentrate themselves as much as possible, and not remain in loose files; and when obliged to fall back upon the columns, they will do so by moving towards one of the flanks, which ever may appear the safest; thereby not obstructing the immediatc action of such columns as may be ready to afford them assistance, and clearing the front. During the attack, they may fire from between the intervals of columns, or be disposed of in such manner as may be most advantageous.
>
> When the columns are to resume the march, they are previously thrown out again, and secure the movements of the columns, conforming to the change of direction which the columns have taken.
>
> During the deployment of the columns on the new position, they will take possession of such ground in front as may secure them from a surprise, and insure the safety of the line.[18]

In the event of a threat to the rear of the line the light companies were to deploy as a rear guard while the brigade changed its frontage:

17 Phillipart (ed.), *Royal Military Panorama*, vol.III, November 1813, p.148.
18 Phillipart (ed.), *Royal Military Panorama*, vol.III, February 1814, p.463.

When the enemy makes approaches upon them with infantry, they will gradually fall back in their present order; but if with cavalry, they will concentrate themselves by companies, and more in checquered squares of companies upon the line which may hare reached their new ground by that time, and if not, they must take possession of such strong ground between the old and new position, as to enable them to protect the formation of the troops: should they, however, be too weak, some companies from the rear of the flank columns may be sent to their support.—

Should a few houses or ruins present themselves during their retiring, they must be taken possession of, and not be abandoned until forced so to do by superior force.—

If the whole must pass a defile, one company mutt defend the mouth of the defile whilst the others form beyond it, after which, that company will retire under the fire of the others: should there, however, be no ground beyond the defile to allow them to take an elevated position, they must form in sections in the defile; the section nearest to the enemy firing, then facing outwards, and retiring by the flanks to the rear of the whole; in this manner they will successively fire and retire, until they may receive succour from their main body, or the enemy is foiled in his advance, by obstacles being thrown in his way, by which they will gain time to effect a safe junction with the troops in the new position: this, however, must greatly depend on the length of the defile which they have to pass, and on the nature of the terrain to their right and left, as no fixed plan for defensive movements can be laid down; and the Commander of such troops must in a great measure, nay almost ever, be guided by the enemy's disposition for attack,—and to his own judgment he will frequently be left to extricate his men from threatening danger, when no essential assistance can be given him as to additional force.

The final movement of the field day was to be an attack by the brigade, with the centre battalion in line and the flanking battalions in echelon of companies, so that the brigade formed a flat arrow formation. The centre battalion would advance to engage the enemy and when they halted the battalions on the flank would come up into line.

LIGHT COMPANIES.

They form in front of the centre battalion.— When the General has determined upon the advance of the brigade, these companies will be collected in front of the centre battalion, and pushed forward to secure the uninterrupted advance of the centre battalion in line, and so soon as this battalion is debouching from the narrow ground, and arrives where it is to commence the attack, they clear its front by inclining rapidly, but without confusion, to the right and left, clearing the front of the flank battalions as the companies come up into line ; after which they will form in rear during the firing, and when the line advances in echelon of battalions, such battalion is covered by a company which leads the attack; the left and the others move in extended order in a line with the first advancing battalion.

The leading company commences the attack.—The skirmishers fall to the ground. — So soon as the light company in front of the leading battalion arrives near enough to the enemy to bring its fire effectually upon him, it halts and opens a brisk fire, whilst the battalion advances close to the company in its front, when on a signal being sounded, the skirmishers fall flat to the ground, to admit the instantaneous fire of the battalion.

The other companies keep up a brisk fire with the battalion which led the attack, and fall to the ground as the battalions from the rear arrive in line, thereby allowing the battalions to fire as they come up, without making them wait until their front is cleared by closing and filing to the rear.

When the brigade has passed them in charging the enemy, they jump up, and form in rear of such part of the line from whence the further pursuit of the enemy may be likely to be followed up.—Should the success of the charge, be doubtful at any one point, they will hasten to the support of such part of the line which may require their assistance.[19]

The two official manuals were far from the only ones available to officers wishing to improve their knowledge of light infantry tactics. In 1806 Captain Thomas Cooper of the 56th Foot published *A Practical Guide for the Light Infantry Officer*. In his foreword address to the Secretary of State for War, Cooper wrote: 'the great importance of a well-disciplined Light Infantry is no longer disputed, though it has, till lately, been either too little attended to, or too little valued.'[20] Early in the text he also claims that:

> At present there are no fixed words of command for the discipline of these troops: Every one uses his own language; consequently, very few companies can act together upon an uniform plan. The instructions of General Dundas have been made a standard for the battalion. It is equally desirable that there should be a proper standard for the Light Infantry, in order to facilitate their operations in brigade.[21]

This implies that despite Dundas's and de Rottenburg's efforts there was still little uniformity in the movements and commands of light troops.

A more influential book perhaps, and one that perfectly reflects the evolutionary nature of light infantry practice in the British Army at the time, was Major Neil Campbell's *Instructions for Light Infantry and Riflemen*. Campbell had served in the 43rd and 95th Foot before exchanging into the 54th Foot. The book was based on a course of instruction for light infantry duties drawn up in Jamaica in 1807.[22]

19 Phillipart (ed.), *Royal Military Panorama*, vol.III, March 1814, p.628.
20 T.H. Cooper, *A Practical Guide for the Light Infantry Officer* (London: Wilks, 1806), p.v.
21 Cooper, *Practical Guide*, pp.ix-x.
22 N. Campbell, *Instructions for Light Infantry and Riflemen* (London: Egerton, 1813), p.vii.

Lieutenant General Sir Eyre Coote was commander-in-chief in Jamaica and Campbell was on Coote's staff.[23] Campbell makes it clear that his work is based on Dundas and de Rottenburg, but also influenced by his time in the 43rd and 95th. It would also, in all probability, have reflected Coote's experience commanding both a light company during the American War of Independence and one of Grey's light infantry battalions, plus the particular needs of light infantry operating in the rugged and heavily forested interiors of the islands of the West Indies. The work adds manoeuvres and formations for light infantry operating in the confines of rough or wooded country, increases the speed with which manoeuvres are performed, introduces some alternative methods for firing while advancing or retreating, and simplifies or clarifies parts of Dundas and de Rottenburg, but does not replace them. When *Marechal* Beresford required a light infantry manual for the Portuguese army it was Campbell's work that was selected and translated by one of his staff.[24]

Campbell also comments on the problems of light companies working together to a common system:

> The want of a book of *reference* in the *minute* parts of these instructions is universally felt by the officers of light infantry *companies,* though in some degree *lessened* by the publication already mentioned upon the exercise of riflemen and light infantry. It has been greatly felt, upon assembling a number of them together as a flank *battalion*, where the *total want* of light infantry instruction in some of them, and *various systems,* of so many captains of different regiments, rendered it a work of considerable time to prepare them for acting *together* in the field.[25]

There is little reason to believe that the regiments embarked for Portugal had any more consistent levels of light infantry skills or systems in 1808 than those on Jamaica in 1807.

Wellington and Light Infantry

In *Inside Wellington's Peninsular Army* Rory Muir writes: 'Wellington was not a great tactical innovator: rather he combined and improved existing methods and created circumstances in which their full potential could be seen.'[26] His orders of 1808 and 1809 regarding the light companies can certainly be seen in this light. It was not innovative to detach light companies but the way it was usually done, with the companies entirely detached, was not one Wellington agreed with. In March 1810 he wrote 'I disapprove of detaching flank companies from the battalion to

23 Anon., *Records of the 54th (West Norfolk) Regiment* (Rorkee: Thomason Civil Engineering College Press, 1881), p.35.
24 W. Warre, *Letters from the Peninsula* (London: Murray, 1909), p.97.
25 Campbell, *Instructions*, pp.x–xi.
26 R. Muir, et al, *Inside Wellington's Peninsular Army* (Barnsley: Pen & Sword, 2014), p.28.

which they belong, and I have not allowed such detachments in this army.'[27] His method of only tactically detaching the light companies enabled them to retain the support of their battalions, with the exception of the 5/60th and Brunswick companies which did spend long periods completely detached.

Wellington was an inexperienced battalion commander during the early campaigns of the French Revolutionary War when the lack of British light infantry became evident, and was away in India during the years that the Duke of York sought to address this shortcoming with a number of reforms, including the creation of specialist light infantry and rifle units. The nature of both the terrain and the troops in India limited the use of light infantry there. In 1805, in a memorandum responding to a proposal from the government to employ troops from the West Indies in India and Indian troops in the West Indies, Wellington provides some insight into his thinking about the qualities required in light infantry. When discussing whether Indian troops could make good light infantry he noted, 'the services of light troops naturally depend upon individual talents and exertion, and are carried on out of the sight of the officer.'[28] He continued to say that Indian troops could not be trusted to act out of sight of their officers. Writing in 1807 about the military establishment and defences of Ireland Wellington noted that the concentration on close order discipline had drawbacks for yeomanry and volunteer units, which would often be called upon to act as light troops.[29]

Wellington got first-hand experience of commanding light infantry later that year in Denmark. He commanded a brigade that included 1/43rd, 2/52nd, 1/92nd and companies from two battalions of the 95th. All but the 92nd, the only line battalion, were later to make up the Light Division. At Kioge he led his brigade in an attack on a Danish force, with the 95th providing the skirmishing screen. The attack was successful and afterwards he commented on the poor quality of the Danish troops.[30] In the Peninsula his troops would often be facing veteran French infantry who had fought and defeated the armies of all the other major European armies many times.

The Enemy

The French light infantry that Wellington's army faced in the Peninsula was comprised mainly of the voltigeur companies of the line infantry regiments. The French did have designated light infantry regiments, rising from 14 in 1790 to 35 in 1814. Whilst they often did have more elan and were often to be found in advanced and rear guards, they did not differ greatly from the line regiments.[31] *Général de division* Maximilien Sébastien Foy wrote:

27 Wellington to Stewart, 27 March 1810, quoted in J. Gurwood (ed.), *The Dispatches of Field Marshall the Duke of Wellington* (London: John Murray, 1835), vol.V, p.398.

28 Wellington (ed.), *Supplementary Despatches*, vol.IV, pp.528–529.

29 Wellesley to Hawksbury, 7 May 1807, in Wellington (ed.), *Supplementary Despatches*, vol.V, p.34.

30 R. Muir, *Wellington: The Path to Victory 1769-1814* (New Haven: Yale University Press, 2015), p.214.

31 T. Crowdy, *French Light Infantry 1784-1815* (Warwick: Helion, 2021), p.61.

> It was a happy idea to raise in the public esteem men of small stature, who are in general the most intelligent and most active. The voltigeurs constituted the real light infantry of France, inasmuch as they were made to perform habitually the service of railleurs [sic]. The regiments of light infantry, as they were called, were only so in name, for they were composed, armed, and exercised like the rest of the infantry.[32]

A reorganisation in 1808 saw all French infantry regiments, line and light, being made up of five battalions, up to four of which often served together in the field as a tactical unit with one serving at home as a depot and training unit. A French battalion was made up of six companies with one designated as grenadiers and one as voltigeurs. The term voltigeur originated historically from the word for vaulting, as skirmishers sometimes rode into battle riding pillion on the back of cavalry. The grenadiers and voltigeurs were both considered elite companies with their ranks filled with specially selected men who were paid more than those in the centre companies. The voltigeurs were fit, agile and good shots, but usually shorter than the grenadiers. Each company had a nominal strength of 121 voltigeurs and they were armed with a shorter dragoon-pattern musket. The officers and sergeants could carry the Versailles rifled-carbine, which was shorter, and of a smaller calibre, than the British infantry rifle.[33]

Unlike the British, the French army did not have a specific manual for light infantry and the way they deployed seems to have been largely at the discretion of the commander, with more emphasis placed on the initiative of the individual voltigeurs, but it is likely they deployed in a similar extended order, working in files, to the British system. *Maréchal* Louis-Nicolas Davout, who did not serve in the Peninsula, wrote a set of instructions for the voltigeurs of his corps in 1811 which may provide some insight into how the troops in Spain and Portugal operated. He also ordered that all companies practice light infantry tactics and manoeuvres. A captain commanding a skirmishing company would march his men 200 paces ahead of the rest of the battalion and divide it into three sections. He would remain with centre section as a reserve. The lieutenants would each take a flanking section off 100 paces to the left and right. They would then turn inwards, and the front two ranks would march across the centre section with 15 paces between each file. The third rank would remain as reserve on the flanks. The line of skirmishers would then advance 100 paces ahead of their reserves.[34]

The voltigeurs had a vital role to play in the French tactical system, as David Gates writes in *The British Light Infantry Arm*: 'The reconnaissance and the psychological and material weakening of the defending lines prior to the launching of what were intended as decisive assaults by the heavy infantry were the vital functions of the voltigeurs and artillery...'[35] Famously Wellington commented, just prior to sailing for Portugal, that he thought the French system 'a false one against steady troops.'

32 M.S. Foy, *History of the War in the Peninsula under Napoleon* (London: Treutell, 1827), vol.I, p.66.
33 T.E. Crowdy, *Napoleon's Infantry Handbook* (Barnsley: Pen & Sword, 2015), pp.5–36, 98–99.
34 Crowdy, *Handbook*, p.202.
35 D. Gates, T*he British Light Infantry Arm c. 1790–1815* (London: Batsford, 1987) p.168.

His tactics to defeat the French in the Peninsula, when fighting defensively, would be to place his men in cover, often behind high ground, so they could not be hit by the French artillery. He would then make sure his flanks were secure, and also deploy his own screen of skirmishers to stop the voltigeurs inflicting casualties and finding out where his main line was deployed.[36]

The voltigeurs nominally comprised one sixth of any French infantry formation, but with light infantry skills more widely practised even grenadier companies were often deployed as skirmishers. So, any French commander had a core of specialist light infantry he could deploy, plus many more men that could be sent forward to skirmish if the need arose. In the early years of the Peninsular War a British commander had more finite light infantry forces available to him as most of his formation would have been untrained in skirmishing. Major Baron Albert Gross, of the short-lived Dutch Brigade in British service, was clear what was needed to counter the voltigeurs: 'nothing can be effected against this disposition, but by opposing light troops to light troops.'[37] However, with few specialist light infantry or rifle regiments, the British Army's primary response to the voltigeurs would have to be the light companies of the line battalions.

The Battalions of Light Companies

A British line infantry battalion was made up of eight centre companies, plus the grenadier and light companies. When the battalion was in line the grenadiers would be on the right of the line and the light company on the left. Both flank companies were distinguished by cloth wings on their shoulders. The light company wore green tufts in their regimental caps, and their sergeants carried a fusil, a lighter and smaller calibre version of the Brown Bess musket, rather than a sergeant's nine-foot long spontoon.

The duties of the light company required men who were nimble and physically fit. Lieutenant General Sir John Moore was firmly of the opinion that the duties of light infantry: 'does not so much require men of stature as it requires them to be intelligent, handy, and active, and they should in the first instance be young, or they will neither take to the service nor be easily instructed in it.'[38] However, the reality of a long campaign may well have led to places being filled in light companies by whichever men were available. In *Wellington's Redjackets*, a history of the 45th Foot, Steve Brown notes that the light company had a higher turnover of NCOs and attributes this to the high standards that one of the light company's commanders, Captain Leonard Greenwell, set,[39] but evidence of any other process or criteria for selection to a light company is scant.

36 C. Oman, *Wellington's Army 1809–1814* (London: Arnold, 1913) p.79.

37 A. Gross, *Duties of an Officer in the Field and Principally of Light Troops* (London: Egerton, 1801), p.vii.

38 Moore to Brownrigg, 17 January 1803, quoted in J. F. Maurice (ed.), *The Diary of Sir John Moore* (London: Arnold, 1904), vol.II, p.69.

39 S. Brown, *Wellington's Redjackets* (Barnsley: Frontline 2015), p.109.

Few accounts from the rank and file of the light companies have survived. One of the best is *Rough Notes of Seven Campaigns in Portugal, Spain, France and America* by John Spencer Cooper of the 7th Fusiliers. Cooper was in the 7th's light company for much of the Peninsular War before being transferred to another company when he was promoted to sergeant. His memoir includes accounts of many skirmishes. At Aldea de Ponte his company:

> ... dashed forward indeed, and the enemy were driven in confusion into the valley whence they had issued. Our men pursued them more than a mile, but about sunset, a body of them dressed in their great grey coats were perceived among the trees and bushes stealing upon us. There being not more than fifty of us together, we fell back until a wing of our regiment came up, and then a smart fire was thrown into their ranks, and kept up in a wood till after dark. In this action I was nearly made prisoner by three Frenchmen. In this rough skirmish a cannon ball struck a heap of stones, one of which gave me a blow on the right shoulder; however, it did no injury, as I wore what are called wings on my jacket.[40]

James Hale of the 9th Foot, another light company man, outlined the difference between the grenadier company, which his brother joined, and the light company:

> Why, the grenadier company consists of all the tallest and stoutest men in the regiment, and always stands on the right; but the light company is generally young men, straight and slender, (who stand from about five feet seven to five feet mine inches high), and when in settled quarters, stands on the left of the regiment; but on the line of march, they are placed several hundred yards in front, as a sort of advance guard; that if the enemy should make an attack, they may be immediately extended at such a distance from each file, as would about cover the regiment when in line.[41]

Cooper often mentions the respect and affection the light company felt for their commander Captain Henry Percy: 'As a man, he was handsome as an officer, kind; and as a soldier, brave and adventurous.'[42] Ewald in his *Treatise* was clear what constituted an ideal officer for light troops: 'These corps require the cleanest, best behaved, trustiest, most active, capable and brave officers, who joyfully embrace this kind of warfare, despising danger, renouncing ease and comfort, and submitting with pleasure to the fatigues and hardships of war.'[43]

For an ambitious young officer, a position in the light company offered the chance for more independence and responsibility than the centre companies. Lieutenant Robert Blakeney of the 28th Foot was appointed to his battalion's light company in

40 J.S. Cooper, *Rough Notes of Seven Campaigns in Portugal, Spain, France and America* (London: John Russel Smith, 1869), p.68.
41 J. Hale, *Journal of James Hale* (Cirencester: Watkins, 1826), pp.39–40.
42 Copper, *Rough Notes*, p.10.
43 Ewald, *Treatise*, p.17.

October 1809, and his memoir gives an excellent account of the fighting through the Corunna campaign and on to Barossa. Recommended for the command of a company after Barossa he was disappointed to be given temporary command of a centre company.[44] He campaigned hard to get back to the light bobs and did join them in action at the Battle of Arroyomolinos.[45] Blakeney also mentions that in the 28th it was the practice to promote from within the light company if possible, presumably to retain experience and skills in the company.[46]

George L'Estrange was very proud of his appointment to the light company of the 31st in 1813, especially since he was still an ensign. Light companies were allocated an extra lieutenant instead of an ensign because their detached duties required officers of more experience. By June he had been promoted to lieutenant and at the Battle of Vittoria, Captain James Girdlestone, commander of light company was wounded. In his memoir L'Estrange writes:

> By the wound of Girdlestone I found myself placed in command of the light company of the 31st, who had been through the greater part of the Peninsular War, and, though reduced in numbers, were as gallant a lot of men as ever existed. I began to feel that, at the age of sixteen, I was placed in a very responsible position, and determined to keep myself as cool and steady as was possible.[47]

He led the company for the rest of the battle, and again when Girdlestone was wounded in the Pyrenees later that year. However, deemed too junior for such an important command, another captain was appointed early in 1814 but when he too was wounded L'Estrange again led the light company until the end of the campaign.

Ensign John Aitchison joined the light company of the 1st Battalion 3rd Foot Guards in the autumn of 1809, and even that early in the campaign he noted the high turnover of officers:

> Colonel Stopford has sent to request I would enter the Light company and I think it right to comply – I shall get a jacket made up in Lisbon and when equipped I shall set off. The Light company has been unfortunate in its officers in not one out of six now doing duty – two were wounded and taken prisoner, one is knocked up and not likely to join while here – one was put on the staff and two went home on promotion.[48]

He was later put into another company, but in May 1812 when a second light company was ordered to be formed he was appointed to its command.[49] It is not

44 J. Sturgis (ed.), *A Boy in the Peninsular War* (London: Murray, 1899), p.214.
45 Sturgis (ed.), *Boy*, p.222.
46 Sturgis (ed.), *Boy*, p.205.
47 G. B L'Estrange, *Recollections of Sir George B. L'Estrange* (London: Sampson Low, Marston & Searle, 1874), p.89.
48 Journal entry 21 October 1809, in W.F.K. Thompson (ed.), *An Ensign in the Peninsular War* (London: Michael Joseph, 1994), p.67.
49 Aitchison to father 27 May 1812, in Thompson (ed.), *Ensign*, p.157

clear where the order to form another light company originated. The 1st Foot Guards always had two light and two grenadier companies per battalion. Decisions to train other companies as light infantry may have been made by brigade or divisional commanders rather than by Wellington. Lieutenant Thomas Valentine Blomfield of the 48th Foot wrote to his brother-in-law in August 1810 regarding a change of command of the 2nd Division:

> We have lately had a new General join us. He is a terrible fellow. His name is the Hon. W. Stewart, who was once Colonel of the 95th Regt., and as the country here is very much adapted for light troops he has formed another light company from each battalion, so that now each battalion has two light companies. I am appointed to the one in our regiment, but we do not wear the light bob's dress, but merely distinguished by a piece of lace round the right arm above the elbow. I have now plenty of work – four hours drill every day, running up and down of immense hills.[50]

One can often detect a hint of admiration from centre company officers when they mention the light company. Ensign Robert Bakewell of the 27th Foot recalled seeing his brigade's light companies during the pursuit of the French out of Portugal in 1811:

> ... when we had marched about three miles, [the battalion of light companies] passed us at a jog trot with their arms trailed, and within three minutes had caught up with the enemy rearguard, when skirmishing immediately commenced, for pop-pop was the order of the day; and the rest of us followed them towards Redinha, where the French had chosen to make a stand.[51]

The officers of Wellington's army faced continual attrition from three sources: sickness; death or wounding in battle; and promotion. It was the convention that the senior of each rank in a regiment should be in the first battalion and the junior in the second. So, as an officer's seniority varied, they could be ordered from the battalion in the Peninsula to one at home or on another foreign station. This could mean that an experienced officer could be ordered home whilst one less experienced came out. Of course, those too badly wounded to serve again, or those who were killed or who died, could also be replaced by men with far less experience. Amongst centre companies this could be less important as they would be under the watchful eye of the battalion commander, but it could be a more serious problem for the light company. In the late summer of 1813 Captain Thomas Hilton arrived in Spain, joined the first battalion of the 45th Foot from the second and took over the light company, even though until 1810 he had been a cavalry officer with the 6th Dragoons before

50 Blomfield to Edwards 17 August 1810, in J. Blomfield, *Observations of Peninsula War Sieges and Battles: Letters of Lieutenant Thomas Valentine Blomfield* (Ocean View: Privately published, 2017), pp.1–2

51 I. Robertson, *The Exploits of Ensign Bakewell* (Barnsley: Frontline, 2012), p.56.

joining the 2/45th on home service. He had probably seen no active duty.[52] Such inexperience could extend to those commanding battalions. Thomas Blomfield wrote in March 1813: 'We have now a most ignorant, troublesome commanding officer as ever was at the head of a regiment. I want to see a French column, if it is only to send him away. Our regiment has been in this country for four years, and that fellow has never seen a shot fired.'[53]

Riflemen

The 5th battalion of the 60th Foot was the first all rifle-armed battalion of the British Army. Formed at the end of 1797 from émigré units in British pay, the rank and file were all foreign, mostly German, as were the majority of the officers at the beginning of the Peninsular War. Towards the end of the campaign the proportion of British officers increased. Francis de Rottenburg, the author of the manual for rifle and light infantry, was the battalion's commander for nearly 10 years. Prior to 1808 the riflemen had seen very little action with only four companies serving during the Irish rebellion of 1798. However, many of the officers and men had considerable service behind them in many European armies, including the French. The battalion had recruited direct from the German states but by 1808 its primary source of recruits came from Germans and other northern Europeans who had served with the French army and had either deserted or been taken prisoner and then held by the British. In common with all the foreign regiments in Wellington's the army the battalion did suffer from high rates of desertions as the men either tried to get back to their former colleagues, or simply one step closer to their homes.

On landing in Portugal, the 10 companies of the 5/60th were brigaded with four from the 2/95th to form a light brigade and operated as the vanguard of the army as it advanced inland. However, immediately after the Battle of Roliça five companies were detached from the battalion and posted to the other five brigades of the army.[54] Given that the Battle of Roliça involved an advance over rough ground and long skirmishes, it may be that Wellesley thought that the battalions of light companies required strengthening. When additional brigades arrived in Portugal another two companies of the 5/60th were detached to them.[55] In May 1809, in a general order reorganising the brigades and repeating the assignment of rifle companies to the brigades, Wellesley wrote the brigade commanders 'will find them to be most useful, active, and brave troops in the field, and that they will add essentially to the strength of their brigades.'[56] The 5/60th, apart from one brief period when they were in cantonments during the winter of 1809 to 1810, would remain divided for the rest of the campaign. Two companies served with two brigades of the 1st Division, three companies with the brigades of the 2nd, three companies and the battalion

52 Brown, *Redjackets*, p.235.
53 Blomfield to Edwards 9 March 1813, in Blomfield, *Observations*, p.29.
54 General Order 18 August 1808 in Wellington, *Supplementary Despatches*, vol.XIII, p.294.
55 General Order 21 August 1808 in Wellington, *Supplementary Despatches*, vol.VI, p.121.
56 General Order, 5 May 1809 in, Wellington, *Supplementary Despatches*, vol.VI., p.253.

headquarters in one brigade of the 3rd, one company in a brigade of the 4th, and one in a brigade of the 6th.[57]

The rifle companies enhanced the battalions of light companies in three important ways. Firstly, they simply increased the number of skirmishers in the brigades from a nominal maximum of 300 (for a three-battalion brigade) to 400, although, of course, once the campaign started no company fielded its established strength of 85 to 100 for very long. Secondly, as riflemen they could engage the French skirmishers at much longer range and to more deadly effect. The Brown Bess musket that the light companies were armed with had an accurate range of around 100-150 yards. The riflemen were trained to shoot at targets up to 300 yards, and specifically targeted French officers and NCOs. This disrupted the enemy command and control, but also presented the riflemen with richer pickings in post-battle plunder. In 1813, after the heavy fighting in the Pyrenees *Maréchal* Jean-de-Dieu Soult conducted an enquiry as to why the level of French officer casualties was so disproportionate and concluded the 5/60th were to blame.[58] Thirdly, and perhaps most importantly, the rifle companies gave the brigades a cadre of troops that were specialists in light infantry tactics and had trained and drilled as such for many years. Many of the British memoirs of the campaign mention that the riflemen of the 5/60th, and other German troops, were better light troops than the British and so served as a good example to improve, for example, their use of cover when skirmishing.[59]

With a few minor exceptions the same companies of the battalion remained with the same brigades for the duration of the campaign and were much valued by the brigade and divisional commanders. At the end of the 1809 campaign one brigade commander wrote to the 5/60th's commanding officer that the company that had been attached to his brigade consisted of 'the best behaved men I ever had attached to me in any military situation.'[60] In reply to praise for the battalion from another brigadier Wellington referred to the 5/60th as 'that excellent corps'.[61]

The Brunswickers

In November 1810 Wellington issued an order that further strengthened battalions of light companies by adding a company of the Duke of Brunswick's Light Infantry to a brigade of the 4th Division, and two companies to two brigades in the 5th.[62]

The Duke of Brunswick had raised a corps of volunteers to fight with Austria against the French during the summer of 1809. Following the allies' defeat at the

57 For more detail on the 5/60th see R. Griffith, *Riflemen: The History of the 5th Battalion, 60th (Royal American) Regiment – 1797–1818* (Warwick: Helion, 2019).

58 J. B. Dumas, *Neuf Mois de Campagnes à la suite du Maréchal Soult* (Paris: Henri Charles-La Vauzelle, 1907), pp.42–43.

59 J. Wardell (ed.), *With the Thirty-Second* (Dublin: Hodges, Figgis & Co., 1904), pp. 305–306.

60 Cameron to Davy 4 December 1809, quoted in G. Rigaud, *Celer et Audax* (Oxford: Hall & Stacy, 1879), p.108.

61 Wellesley to Donkin, 23 June 1809, quoted in Gurwood (ed.), *Wellington's Dispatches*, vol.IV, p.459.

62 G.O. 12 November 1810 in Wellington (ed.), *Supplementary Despatches*, vol.VI, p.640

Battle of Wagram the Duke refused to surrender and led his men across Germany until they were evacuated by the Royal Navy. The corps was organised into a light infantry regiment and a regiment of hussars, and entered British service. The infantry regiment comprised of one rifle company and 11 musket-armed light infantry companies. They arrived in Portugal in September 1810, and the bulk of the unit spent a brief period in the Light Division before moving to the 7th Division.

As stated previously the detached companies of the 5/60th added three benefits to the battalions of light companies: numbers; rifles; and specialist troops. However, only the company of the Brunswickers that went to the 4th Division was armed with rifles. In April 1811 Major General Lowry Cole praised 'the Rifle companies of the 60th and Brunswick Regiments' for their suppressing fire during the assault on Olivenza.[63] The companies that went to the 5th Division used muskets.[64] The companies attached to the 5th certainly helped bolster the light companies numbers, as a return for April 1812 shows that the three detached Brunswick companies mustered 86, 87 and 93 effective rank and file when the companies of the 5/60th varied between 27 and 59.[65] An inspection report from April 1810, prior to them sailing for the Peninsula, praised the regiment's 'extremely soldierlike' appearance and concluded with 'there appears throughout an Esprit de Corps which promises to render the Battalion highly Serviceable,'[66] so they may also have contributed skilled and experienced light infantry.

However, the regiment did suffer from a severe level of desertion which was far from ideal in a regiment often placed in advanced positions. Over time the regiment also had to increasingly rely upon deserters and prisoners from the French armies for recruits, although correspondence between the Duke of Brunswick and the commandant of the foreign depot at Lymington makes it clear that efforts were made to maintain both the national character and quality of the regiment.[67] They did suffer from one disadvantage though with an inspection report from 1812 noting that:

> The men's caps are of the same shape and form as those worn by the French, thereby subjecting the Regiment when at a distance to be taken for the Enemy. The Regiment being light infantry, consequently subject to be in front of the line, the similarity of the cap has in several instances occasioned a doubt and nearly attracted the fire from the Allied troops.[68]

By the start of 1812, of the 14 British infantry brigades outside of the Light and 7th Divisions, both of which were made up exclusively or largely of light infantry, only three did not have a company of the 5/60th or Brunswickers. One of the those was

63 Cole to Beresford 16 April 1811, in Wellington (ed.), *Supplementary Despatches*, vol.XIII, p.615.
64 TNA: WO 27/108: Field return Brunswick Light Infantry, May 1812. Regimental returns (WO 17/803) refer to 'the' rifle company.
65 TNA: WO17/2469: Army by Brigades & Divisions April 1812.
66 TNA: WO27/99: Confidential report, Brunswick Light Infantry, April 1810.
67 TNA: WO 7/82: Mosheim to Brunswick, 2 December 1810, pp.435–436; WO 7/84: Mosheim to Brunswick, 20 June 1811, p.148.
68 TNA: WO 27/108: Confidential report, Brunswick Light Infantry, May 1812.

the KGL Brigade, whose line battalions had their own rifle-armed sharpshooters, and another was the second brigade of the 3rd Division, which had three companies of the 5/60th in the first brigade. This left only the second brigade of the 6th Division without any additional light infantry support.[69]

Other Corps

The riflemen of the 95th mostly served in the Light Division and did not make a significant contribution to the battalions of light companies. One ad-hoc company of the regiment made up of men left behind in Portugal when their battalions marched into Spain with Sir John Moore was part of the composite 1st Battalion of Detachments until just after the battle of Talavera when they re-joined their regiment. The same battalion included companies made up of men from the 43rd and 52nd Light Infantry as well, who also added to the light troops available for the Oporto and Talavera campaigns. One company of the 95th also served briefly in the 1st Division from late 1810 to the summer of 1811. The arrival of a detachment of the 95th at Cadiz in 1810 led to the disbanding of the recently-formed battalion of light companies there, presumably because the riflemen could perform the same tasks.[70]

The light troops of the 1st Division were significantly strengthened by the presence of battalions from the King's German Legion. Formed from a core of the Hanoverian army in 1803 there were initially four and then three line infantry battalions in the division. The KGL brigade formed a battalion of light companies in the same manner as all the other brigades, but at times the line battalions were brigaded with specialist KGL light infantry detached companies, and then later the 1st and 2nd KGL Light Battalions. The light battalions mostly stayed with the 1st Division but spent some time in the 7th. They were skilled skirmishers and around two thirds of the men were armed with rifles.[71]

The other vital component of the light troops available to Wellington were the Portuguese Caçadore battalions. Formed as part of Beresford's reforms to the Portuguese army, the Caçadores were specialist light infantry, mostly recruited from the rugged mountainous regions of Portugal. Most of the men were armed with muskets but at least 200 of each battalion were armed with rifles.[72] Many of the British officers serving with the Caçadores had previous light infantry experience, including several from the 95th and 5/60th.[73] Major Thomas Bunbury, who took command of the Batalhão de Caçadores n.º 6 early in 1814, noted that: 'The Caçadore Battalion was a great favourite with Sir William Stewart who commanded

69 Oman, *Wellington's Army*, pp.358–359.

70 TNA: WO 28/339: Spain. Journal of the proceedings of the British Army serving at Cadiz and the I. of Leon, 5 March and 3 April entries.

71 TNA: WO 27/118 & WO 27/108: Field returns for the 1st and 2nd KGL Light Infantry.

72 M. Gaudêncio, 'Were the Portuguese Caçadores Armed with Baker Rifles?', The Napoleon Series, <https://www.napoleon-series.org/military-information/battles-and-campaigns/were-the-portuguese-cacadores-armed-with-baker-rifles/>, accessed 14 February 2021.

73 L. S. Challis, 'British Officers Serving in the Portuguese Army, 1809-1814', *Journal of the Society for Army Historical Research*, vol.27, No. 110 (Summer,1949), pp.50–60.

the division. He sometimes called them his Body Guard, at other times his Harriers. They were short muscular fellows, and made capital riflemen.'[74]

There were other light infantry regiments spread amongst the brigades. The 71st Highland Light Infantry served in the 2nd Division and could bolster the light companies of their brigade with more than one company when required, and on occasion the whole battalion would go forward to skirmish. The 7th Division included a high concentration of light infantry units, including at various times the 51st, 68th, and 85th Foot, the Brunswickers, the KGL light battalions, the Chasseurs Britanniques (whose commander had them adopt many of the elements of a light infantry regiment during the campaign),[75] and Caçadores.

Battalion Commanders

The command of his battalion of light companies was a key appointment for a brigadier, but one that he might have to make from a narrow pool of potential talent. Wellington's 1808 order stipulated they should be commanded by a field officer – a major or lieutenant colonel. His 1809 order lowers this bar to include captains, widening the potential pool. In theory each of Wellington's infantry battalions should have had one lieutenant colonel, commanding, and two majors. In practice illness, combat casualties, and leaves of absence meant that few battalions had their full establishment of field officers. Taking January 1812 as a random sample the 58 British infantry battalions in the Peninsula had 41 lieutenant colonels and 70 majors between them, or an average of just under two field officers each.[76] This would mean a brigadier realistically having probably only a couple of field officers to choose from. Opening the pool to captains vastly increased the number of officers, but many battalions were as short of company commanders as they were of field officers, and if one of the light company commanders was selected then he would need a reliable lieutenant to take over command of the company whilst he handled the composite battalion. Factoring in physical fitness and experience of light infantry duties, many brigadiers would have had a very short list of candidates.

Rod MacArthur's research into officers who commanded battalions of light companies, both at brigade and divisional level, establishes that such appointments were often relatively long term, lasting for one or two campaigning seasons.[77] Identifying who commanded the battalions of light companies from mentions in dispatches, memoirs, and other sources such as the list of Gold Medal recipients for a particular action is one thing, making any kind of assessment as to their experience and skills for the role is much harder.

74 T. Bunbury, *Reminiscences of a Veteran* (Uckfield: The Naval & Military Press Ltd. 2009), p.242.

75 A. Nichols, *Wellington's Mongrel Regiment* (Staplehurst: Spellmount, 2005), pp.100–101.

76 TNA: WO 17/2469: Army return, 25 January 1812.

77 R. MacArthur, 'British Converged Light Battalions', *Rod's Wargaming*, <https://rodwargaming.wordpress.com/miltary-historical-research/organisation/british-converged-light-battalions/>, accessed February 2020.

In the 3rd Division command of the light companies of the brigade containing the companies of the 5/60th was usually given to that battalion's commanding officer. If all the light companies in the division were deployed together, which often occurred, that officer was also usually given overall command, due to his seniority. For example, Lieutenant Colonel William Williams took command of the 5/60th in the spring of 1810 and led them until July of 1812 when, having been wounded in action six times, he decided to exchange into another regiment. Prior to joining the 60th Williams had seen action in many campaigns, including the Corunna campaign. A description of him in the memoirs of one of the brigade's commanders reads:

> He was of that small, slight, but well-proportioned figure, in which strength is usually combined with activity, and his disposition, wary and collected, yet ready, resolute, and decisive, admirably qualified him for a light infantry officer. He had served in this war from its commencement with distinguished reputation. The three great generals of those days, Abercromby, Moore, and Wellington, had each in their turn borne public and private testimony to his merit.[78]

Williams commanded the light companies in all the major actions during his time in command. Steve Brown, in his history of the 45th Foot, writes that in 1810 Thomas Picton, commander of the 3rd Division, began to deploy all his light troops as one unit and they 'were trained to fight together as an ad-hoc single formation under the overall command of Lieutenant-Colonel William Williams of the 60th.'[79]

The 1/45th Foot was brigaded with the 5/60th companies in the 3rd Division for much of the war. The aptly named Captain Thomas Lightfoot took command of their light company in the autumn of 1810. He was an experienced officer having been with the 45th since the start of the campaign but only got his chance to command the brigade's light companies at Vittoria in 1813 when the 5/60th's commander, Colonel John Keane, was leading the combined light companies of the division. It is interesting to note that even when grouped together at divisional level the brigade's battalions of light companies retained their own commanders rather than being subsumed into one unit and Lightfoot received his Gold Medal, which was only awarded to commanders of units larger than a company.[80]

Another recipient of the Gold Medal for Vittoria was Major Daniel Dodgin of the 2/66th Foot who led his brigade's light companies under another 5/60th officer, Lieutenant Colonel John Forster Fitzgerald who commanded the combined light troops of the 2nd Division. Dodgin's entry in the *Royal Military Calendar* states that

78 D. Le Marchant, *Memoirs of the Late Major General Le Marchant* (London: Bentley, 1841), pp.260–261.

79 Brown, *Redcoats*, p.110.

80 Brown, *Redcoats*, pp.125, 221. R. Burnham & R. McGuigan, *The British Army against Napoleon, Facts, Lists, and Trivia 1805–1815* (Barnsley: Frontline Books, 2010), p.287.

he led the light companies of the brigade 18 times from 1811 though to 1814, and he was wounded in his final action at Aire in France.[81]

Major Samuel Hext of the 83rd received a Gold Medal and two clasps for leading the light companies of his brigade in the 3rd Division. He was described by Captain John Patterson of the 50th: 'His success in life and war, corresponded with the high consideration he was held in by his superiors; constantly employed in military duty, he was sure to lead, when any thing in the way of enterprize was going forward.'[82] However, memoirs seldom contain descriptions of officers that are not complimentary and so perhaps the best way to evaluate the performance of the battalions of light companies and the men that led them is to look at their performance in battle.

Buçaco

The Battle of Buçaco in September 1810 is a good example of the use of the battalions of light companies in a defensive action. The allied position was along the top of a steep ridge and the night before the battle the light companies, and elements of the Light Division in front of their part of the allied line, were deployed near the base of the slope in a thick line of picquets, some of whom skirmished with the French during the night and then again more widely at dawn. Both the French main attacks were preceded by skirmishers, one was met by the Light Division but the other, composed of two columns, was directed at the 3rd Division's position. Lieutenant Colonel Williams of the 5/60th commanded his own three companies of rifles, plus the light companies of MacKinnon's brigade (the 1/45th, 74th, and 1/88th Foot). They were split in two positions near one of the tracks that the French were advancing up.

Severely outnumbered by their French opponents Williams and the light companies performed a fighting withdrawal up the ridge, as they were meant to do. At some point they were reinforced by another company of the 45th. Their role was not to stop the French but to delay and harass them. As they neared the top, Williams wheeled the 60th and 45th so that they were positioned along the flank of one of the columns and continued to fire on them as they were met and then repulsed by the main allied line. Picton had to rally the light companies of the 74th and 88th after they were driven from some rocks and then Major Smith of the 45th led them in successful a counterattack during which he was killed. Captain Thomas Lightfoot of the 45th later wrote that his company was deployed on the flank of one of the advancing columns:

> I opened a fire upon it, the men kneeling and concealing themselves among the bushes. Meantime the column appeared to be too much occupied in pushing the light troops before them to take much notice of us. Presently I saw the light troops driven over the ridge, and the next moment the ridge crowned by the tirailleurs, firing vigorously from it; when suddenly,

81 J. Phillipart (ed.), *The Royal Military Calendar* (London: Egerton, 1820), vol.IV, pp.469–470.
82 J. Patterson, *Camp and Quarters* (London: Saunders & Otley, 1840), vol.II, pp.222–223.

> without any reason apparent to me, the tirailleurs abandoning the ridge, poured down on the column; the column went to the right about, and both urged their course precipitately down the hill.[83]

The Light Division also defeated the attack that they faced. After the assaults had failed the French sent forward their voltigeurs and sporadic skirmishing continued for the rest of the morning. The light companies of some divisions were the only troops in those formations to be engaged on the day, for example the light companies and 5/60th company of the Guards Brigade were involved in a prolonged duel with French skirmishers, firing from the shelter of rocky outcrops.

Fuentes d'Oñoro

Light infantry were also often used during the Peninsular War for combat in urban areas. Street fighting often entails small groups fighting independently from house to house and so was more suited to troops trained to think for themselves. At the Battle of Fuentes de Oñoro in May 1811 the village was held initially by the light companies of three brigades of the 1st Division, including elements of the KGL, a company of the 3/95th and one of the 5/60th, and the light companies of three brigades of the 3rd Division, including another three companies of the 5/60th, with the 2/83rd in support, all under the command of Lieutenant Colonel Williams.

On the first day of the battle the French made a frontal assault across a small stream and up into the village streets. The light companies blockaded the narrow streets and fired from behind windows, doorways, and garden walls. The fighting became close quarters, and each house and street corner was fought over. The French took heavy casualties, but weight of numbers overwhelmed the defenders who were driven back to the church at the top of the hill, but Williams rallied his men and retook most of the village before French reinforcements arrived and took the village for a second time. Williams was severely wounded. Wellington sent the 2/24th, 1/71st and 1/79th to help retake the village again, which they did.

There are two accounts of the 79th Cameron Highlanders during the battle which shed some light onto why light troops were often used in urban environments. The first comes from a KGL officer:

> … a Scottish Line Battalion was deployed in order in the gardens of the village when the enemy cavalry advanced. The Scots, scorning every cover, stood upright as in line. One of the wiser ones had moved behind a wall to get a better shot. No sooner did his comrades notice this than when they said: 'Cannot you damned fellow show your enemies that you can face them!' They rushed at him, berated him, and applied to him a sound thrashing on a sensitive part of his body. The battalion was replaced by a battalion of Jägers of the 60th Regiment, who better understood light duties

83 T. Lightfoot, letter to the Editor, *United Services Journal*, 1837, Part III, p.390.

> and the appropriate use of cover; they also rapidly thinned the saddles of the French, who had ventured too boldly, without suffering any loss.[84]

Edward Costello, a rifleman of the 95th, who was posted on the banks of the stream near the village wrote: 'The 79th Highlanders had suffered very severely here, as the place was strewn about with their bodies. Poor fellows! they had not been used to skirmishing, and instead of occupying the houses in the neighbourhood, and firing from the windows, they had, as, I heard, exposed themselves, by firing in sections.'[85]

The third day of the battle also provides an example of the dangers of fighting forward of the main line. The light companies of the Guards Brigade, commanded by Lieutenant Colonel George Hill, were in extended order as French cavalry approached. They closed and formed square but as the French withdrew Hill ordered them to extend again, not realising more cavalry were close by. The French charged and killed or wounded 68 men and captured 21, including Hill.

Salamanca

The battalions of light companies from various divisions played key roles during the Battle of Salamanca. The fighting on 22 July 1812 started as French voltigeurs probed towards the Calvarrasa de Arriba ridge and encountered the pickets of the Brunswick Light Infantry from the 7th Division. Sporadic skirmishes continued for the rest of the day and drew in reinforcements from both sides. The rifle company of the Brunswickers, the light companies of the Fusilier Brigade from the 4th Division, the light companies of the Guards Brigade from the 1st Division and their company of the 5/60th, were also soon defending the village of Los Arapiles from French light infantry.

Both these prolonged skirmishes were part of an attempt by the French to probe the allied forces but were not a prelude to an attack. The French commander, *Maréchal* Marmont, wanted to manoeuvre Wellington into withdrawing rather than provoke a general action. Instead, when a gap opened between two French divisions it was Wellington who saw an opportunity. He ordered the 3rd Division to attack, and as they marched towards the enemy they were screened on their flanks by their light companies, the 5/60th, and the Batalhão de Caçadores n.º 12, all once again led by Lieutenant Colonel Williams. The light troops screened the leading British brigade as they advanced up a hill towards the French, engaging the voltigeurs on the slope before the rest of the division charged.[86]

As the 3rd Division launched their attack the 5th Division began their assault further along the French position, with the light companies, the Batalhão de Caçadores n.º 9, and two companies of Brunswickers extended to the front. The

84 H. Dehnel, *Erinnerungen Deutscher Officiere in Britischen Diensten aus den Kriegsjahren 1805 bis 1816* (Hannover: Rümpler, 1864) p.345.
85 E. Costello, *The Adventures of a Soldier* (London: Colburn, 1841) p.124.
86 J. Campbell, *A British Army As It Was, – Is, – and Ought to Be* (London: T & W Boone, 1840), p.225.

skirmishers drove their French counterparts back as the division marched across a valley and up the far slope. As the lines of redcoats neared the French, the light troops cleared to the flanks mixing with the 3rd Division light troops as they continued to press forward before the line troops fired a volley and charged, forcing the French to retreat. Captain Andrew Lieth Hay on the staff of the 5th Division recalled:

> … the ground between the advancing force and that to be assailed was also crowded with light troops in extended order, carrying on a very incessant tiraillade. The General desired me to ride forward, make the light infantry press up the heights to clear his line of march, and, if practicable, make a rush at the enemy's cannon … the light troops soon drove back those opposed; the French cannon were removed to the rear; every obstruction to the regular advance of the line had vanished.[87]

The 4th and 6th Division's light troops also screened their less successful attack, operating forward and on the flanks as the situation demanded. The presence of Caçadore battalions in each of the attacking divisions approximately doubled the number of light troops deployed and would have been a major factor in overwhelming their French opponents.

Orthez

At Orthez in February 1814 the French were in position along a ridge and when a flank attack by the 4th Division failed, Wellington ordered a frontal assault up the slope. The 3rd Division attacked in two brigade columns, both preceded by their light troops. There were four companies of the 5/60th, seven light companies, and a battalion of Caçadores. They advanced up the slope but the French resistance was fierce. French cavalry was spotted and voltigeurs occupied a ravine on the flank of the advance. Line companies from the battalions of both the 3rd and 6th Divisions, which was coming up behind in support, had to be detached to help the light troops deal with the French in the ravine. The attack of Brisbane's Brigade stalled as he dithered. Major General Edward Pakenham arrived and ordered Brisbane forward, telling him to detach the whole of the 45th Foot as skirmishers. Private William Brown was with the 45th:

> Two companies being left with the colours, the remaining eight ascended the hill, but were received in such a manners I had seldom before experienced. We were but a handful of men, a skirmishing party, opposed to a dense column of infantry, supported by artillery and cavalry; the bullets flew thick as hail, and literally tore up the ground from under our feet.[88]

87 A. Leith Hay, *A Narrative of the Peninsular War* (London: Hearne, 1839), p.258.
88 W. Brown, *The Autobiography, or Narrative of a Soldier – The Peninsular War Memoirs of William Brown of the 45th Foot* (Solihull: Helion & Company, 2017), p.152.

They drove the French from one ditch and then covered the brigade as the deployed into line. Brown continues: 'Our party having been reinforced by several light companies from the division, now advanced at double quick, and giving three cheers, charged the enemy's light troops, and drove them from a ditch, in a parallel with the one we had just left.'[89]

Conclusion

Thomas Bunbury, who fought his first action with the 3rd Foot's light company defending the Seminary during the Battle of Oporto, recalled his initial impression of the relative prowess of British and French skirmishers in his memoir: 'I observed that our men generally were better shots than the French, possibly the powder was superior. I think also that they showed more intelligence, although this opinion may be disputed.'[90]

Conversely, Major John Patterson, who served with the 50th Foot for most of the Peninsular War was critical of the level of expertise exhibited by the light companies who landed in Portugal in 1808:

> When our troops embarked for service, the regiments had, it is true, light companies attached to them that were previously drilled in all field-movements, but by no means to that extent they ought to have been; the most active, muscular, and even the most intelligent men, were chosen for those companies – but were they trained in the strictest sense to act as riflemen? On the contrary, beyond the mere platoon, they knew no more than other soldiers; they were scarcely initiated at the target, and seemed in general to have no superiority above their comrades... as marksmen, ill-taught and inexperienced, they were soon thrown back on their battalions by an active foe, whose skirmishers ... were wheeling round and round them, sending their rifle-balls about our ears in first-rate style.[91]

Patterson is using the term 'riflemen' in the wider sense of a skirmisher rather than that of being armed with a rifle. However, Charles Stevens of the 20th Foot remembered the light bobs doing much better at Vimeiro:

> I was detached during the action and was with two companies of the 95th (Rifles); we were engaged in driving some French riflemen out of a wood that was in front of the centre of our army; my company (the light company) behaved nobly on the occasion; I had only one man wounded; we knocked

89 Brown, *Autobiography*, p.152.
90 T. Bunbury, *Reminiscences of a Veteran* (Uckfield: The Naval & Military Press Ltd. 2009), p.35.
91 J. Patterson, 'On the Utility and Importance of Light Troops and Cavalry in the Field, Exemplified by Several Instances During the War in Spain', *United Service Journal*, Part III, 1844, p.276.

> over several of the enemy, and took many prisoners; the French hid themselves behind the trees and kept up a very heavy fire, but we advanced on them very rapidly, and drove them away in all directions, pouring in volley after volley of musketry.[92]

Moyle Sherer of the 34th Foot, commenting on the much later Battle of Vittoria, also criticises the performance of British light infantry: 'The English do not skirmish so well as the Germans or the French; and it really is hard work to make them preserve their proper extended order, cover themselves, and not throw away their fire; and in the performance of this duty, an officer is, I think, far more exposed than in line-fighting.'[93]

David Gates in *The British Light Infantry Arm*, the most comprehensive study of British light infantry of the period, does repeatedly characterise the allied skirmisher screen has 'heavy' or 'thick' which he contrasts with the lighter French screen. He states that a typical French division of eight battalions could deploy 800 voltigeurs, and then goes on to say, 'This was a far smaller proportion than that found in one of Wellington's divisions where battalion light companies were reinforced by whole battalions of riflemen and light infantry.'[94] However, if he is referring to the riflemen and light infantry of the Light Division then they did not reinforce the skirmishers of other divisions but operated on their own frontage.

If we look at the 3rd Division, for example, that took a major part in many of the actions of the Peninsular War, it typically consisted of six or seven British line battalions, plus three companies of the 5/60th. This meant it could nominally field a total of up to 1,000 skirmishers, without including the light companies and Caçadores of the Portuguese brigade that was often attached to the division, but that total was from a stronger formation as British battalions had larger establishments than their French counterparts. However, any discussion of relative numbers actually deployed in a particular action would have to account for the actual effective strengths of the units involved, how many were held in reserve, and of course, how concentrated the defending and attacking forces were at any point on the field. Gates mentions several occasions, such as Salamanca, where the allied skirmish lines outnumbered the French but the examples he gives are occasions where light infantry regiments were used rather than the battalions of light companies, and he also goes on to cite occasions where French commanders deployed additional companies to support the voltigeurs and overwhelmed the allied light troops.[95] Patterson maintains that the allied pickets and skirmishers were 'always driven in upon the first onset by the French (who were in five times out of six the assailing party,) and thrown back precipitately on the main body…'[96] However, in a reply to Patterson's article in the *United Service Journal* an officer of the 43rd Foot correctly points out that:

92 N. Steevens (ed.), *Reminiscences of My Military Life* (Winchester: Warren, 1877), pp.52–53.
93 M. Sherer, *Recollections of the Peninsula* (London: Longman, Rees, Orme, Brown, & Green, 1827), p.325.
94 Gates, *Light Infantry*, p.171.
95 Gates, *Light Infantry*, pp.171–172.
96 Patterson, 'On the Utility and Importance of Light Troops' p.280.

> … with respect to the light troops, skirmishers, &c, being borne in upon the position, by the advance of the main body of the enemy, I may venture to remark that I have always conceived such to be invariably the case at the commencement of an action, especially where an army in position awaits the advance and receives the attack of the enemy; and that neither out-line pickets nor skirmishers are intended or expected to hold their ground against the main body, or any very strong body of the enemy; but that having given notice of his approach, and having worried and caused him as much loss as they well could, in the course of it, their part was then to fall back and take their place with their regiments and brigades.[97]

As the Peninsular War progressed there were times when other companies of the line battalions had to be used as light troops to reinforce the battalions of light companies. James Campbell, who had been a brigade major in the 3rd Division, when discussing Picton's habit of always encouraging his men forward and describing the Battle of Vic-en-Bigorre in 1814, wrote:

> Besides the 5th battalion 60th, a battalion of Portuguese caçadores and our light infantry companies, whole regiments, (and here we felt the want of knowledge of light infantry movements in all corps) only retaining some companies in reserve and for support, were engaged as sharpshooters. They were, however, constantly pushed forward upon the French, and recommended not to throw away their fire in long shots, but rather, as much as possible, to endeavour to close with them; and if a halt was any where perceived in any part of the advancing skirmishers a staff officer was invariably sent to the point to ascertain the cause. The French, therefore, invariably gave way, and in their confused retreat they became exposed, in running from one enclosure to another, to the fire of our troops.[98]

The only significant changes to the brigade and divisional light infantry during the Peninsular War do seem to be the designation of second light companies in the battalions of some formations, although how widespread this was is not clear, and of the use of entire line battalions as skirmishers when the need arose. Both may imply that on occasion the light companies did not provide enough skirmishers to counter the weight of French voltigeurs, but it could also be a factor of the greater levels of experience in Wellington's army meaning that more officers and men had the skills and fitness required to be deployed as light infantry. Deploying them as such might have increased an advantage the allied army already had over the French, rather than compensating for a disadvantage in light infantry numbers.

Any generalisations about the relative numbers of skirmishers in the allied and French armies are problematic. Unfortunately, any discussion of the relative proficiency of the contending light infantry can only rely on anecdotal evidence and the opinions of individual officers.

97 Letter to the editor, *United Service Journal*, 1845, Part I, p.444.
98 Campbell, *A British Army As It Was, – Is, – and Ought to Be*, pp.252–253.

However, the most telling evidence that the system of forming battalions of light companies generally worked was that Wellington did not change it during the campaign, and, indeed, repeated it for the Waterloo Campaign.[99] Wellington in 1815 did not create a Light Division again, but did have a brigade made up of elements of the 95th, with the 52nd and 71st Light Infantry. In the Peninsula the Light Division gave him a specialist formation of light infantry but given the tactics of the day in battle it was frequently the 95th that was sent forward to skirmish while the red-coated 52nd and 43rd were frequently used as conventional line infantry. Long after the war, in 1831, one Light Division officer, using the pseudonym Vanguard, wrote in the *United Service Journal*, after commenting on the recent distribution of French light infantry regiments in their divisions:

> Every division of our army in the Peninsula had one or more regiments of Portuguese light infantry, (Caçadores,) who soon became very respectable troops; so that they, together with the British light companies of each brigade, furnished a force of light infantry sufficiently numerous and efficient in most cases for the operations of their respective divisions. But it should not be forgotten, that if the British army is again called into the field … it must … necessarily rely on its own resources for a due proportion of light troops; which, the practical soldier will not deny, are of the first importance in every situation in which an army can possibly find itself placed.
>
> … I trust that our light infantry battalions will, in future campaigns, be equally distributed amongst the different brigades and divisions. Should this appear a strange doctrine to emanate from the pen of a light-division-man, let it be borne in mind, that during the six latter campaigns in the Peninsula, no less than six British battalions of light infantry and riflemen—viz. 43rd, 52nd, (at one period the 52nd had two battalions in Spain,) and the three battalions of the 95th rifle corps – were together; and, although particularly calculated, from their composition and organization, for the arduous duties of the out-posts, advance, and rear-guards, &c. &c. … it may be questioned, whether to have given each of the eight divisions an equal proportion of British light troops would not have been desirable.[100]

Wellington did have enough light infantry regiments in the Peninsula to form a small brigade in each of his divisions but chose to persist with relying on the battalions of light companies. As Rory Muir puts it his online commentary for his biography of Wellington:

> Thus from the very outset of the war in the Peninsula Wellesley showed himself keenly aware of the importance of light infantry and devised a system which would provide both for a concentrated force of specialist

99 Wellington (ed.), *Supplementary Despatches*, vol.X, pp.262–263.
100 'Vanguard', 'Distribution of Light Cavalry and Light Infantry in the Field', *United Service Journal*, 1831, part II, pp.207–208.

skirmishers, and still protect the rest of the army. With some adaption to allow for the creation of divisions and the presence of Portuguese caçadores, this system would be employed, most successfully, in all his campaigns.[101]

Bibliography

Archival Sources

The National Archives (TNA)

WO 3 Office of the Commander-in-Chief: Out-letters
WO 7 Various Departmental Out-Letters
WO 17 Monthly Returns to the Adjutant General
WO 27 Inspection Returns

Online Sources

Gaudêncio, M., 'Were the Portuguese Caçadores Armed with Baker Rifles?', The Napoleon Series, <https://www.napoleon-series.org/military-information/battles-and-campaigns/were-the-portuguese-cacadores-armed-with-baker-rifles/>, accessed 14 February 2022

MacArthur, R., 'British Converged Light Battalions', Rod's Wargaming, <https://rodwargaming.wordpress.com/miltary-historical-research/organisation/british-converged-light-battalions/>, accessed February 2020

Muir, R., 'Commentary for Volume 1, Chapter 15: Vimeiro and Cintra (July–September 1808)', Wellington, <https://www.lifeofwellington.co.uk/commentary/chapter-fifteen-vimeiro-and-cintra-july-september-1808>, accessed May 2021

Published Sources

Anon., *Vicissitudes in the Life of a Scottish Soldier* (London: Colburn, 1827)

Anon. *Records of the 54th (West Norfolk) Regiment* (Rorkee: Thomason Civil Engineering College Press, 1881)

Anton, J., *Retrospect of a Military Life* (Edinburgh: Lizars, 1841)

Blakiston, J., *Twelve Years' Military Adventure in Three Quarters of the Globe* (London: Colburn, 1829)

Blomfield, J., *Observations of Peninsula War Sieges and Battles: Letters of Lieutenant Thomas Valentine Blomfield* (Ocean View: Privately published, 2017)

Brown, S., *Wellington's Redjackets* (Barnsley: Frontline 2015)

Brown, W., *The Autobiography, or Narrative of a Soldier – The Peninsular War Memoirs of William Brown of the 45th Foot* (Solihull: Helion & Company, 2017)

Bunbury, T., *Reminiscences of a Veteran* (Uckfield; The Naval & Military Press Ltd. 2009)

101 R. Muir, 'Commentary for Volume 1, Chapter 15: Vimeiro and Cintra (July–September 1808)', Wellington <https://www.lifeofwellington.co.uk/commentary/chapter-fifteen-vimeiro-and-cintra-july-september-1808>, accessed May 2021.

Burnham, R. & McGuigan, R., *The British Army against Napoleon, Facts, Lists, and Trivia 1805–1815* (Barnsley: Frontline Books, 2010)

Campbell, J., *A British Army As It Was, – Is, – and Ought to Be* (London: T & W Boone, 1840)

Costello, E. *The Adventures of a Soldier* (London: Colburn, 1841)

Cooper, J.S., *Rough Notes of Seven Campaigns in Portugal, Spain, France and America* (London: John Russel Smith, 1869)

Cooper, T.H., *A Practical Guide for the Light Infantry Officer* (London: Wilks, 1806)

Crowdy, T., *Napoleon's Infantry Handbook* (Barnsley: Pen & Sworde, 2015)

Crowdy, T., *French Light Infantry 1784-1815* (Warwick: Helion, 2021)

Dehnel, H., *Erinnerungen Deutscher Officiere in Britischen Diensten aus den Kriegsjahren 1805 bis 1816* (Hannover: Rümpler, 1864)

de Rottenburg, F., *Regulations for the Exercise of Riflemen and Light Infantry and Instructions for their Conduct in the Field* (London: Egerton, 1803)

Dumas, J.B., *Neuf Mois de Campagnes à la suite du Maréchal Soult* (Paris: Henri Charles-La Vauzelle, 1907)

Dundas, D., *Rules and Regulations for the Formations, Field-Exercise and Movements of His Majesty's Forces* (London: War Office, 1798)

Ewald, J., 'A Treatise on Upon the Duties of Light Troops', in *Rifle & Riflemen* (Driffield: Leonaur, 2011)

Fletcher, I.(ed), *In the Service of the King. The Letters of William Thornton Keep at Home, Walcheren, and in the Peninsula, 1808-1814* (Staplehurst: Spellmount, 1997)

Foy, M.S., *History of the War in the Peninsula under Napoleon* (London: Treutell, 1827)

Gates, D., *The British Light Infantry Arm c. 1790–1815* (London: Batsford, 1987)

Glover, R., *Peninsular Preparation: The Reform of the British Army 1795–1809* (Cambridge: Cambridge University Press, 2008)

Greentree, D., *British Rifleman versus French Skirmisher* (Oxford: Osprey, 2020)

Griffith, P. (ed.), *Modern Studies of the War in Spain and Portugal, 1808–1814* (London: Greenhill, 1999)

Gross, Baron, *Duties of an Officer in the Field and Principally of Light Troops* (London: Egerton, 1801)

Gurwood, J. (ed.), *The General Orders of Field Marshal The Duke of Wellington K. G. in Spain, Portugal & France* (London: Egerton, 1837)

Gurwood, J. (ed.), *The Dispatches of Field Marshall the Duke of Wellington* (London: John Murray, 1835)

Hale, J., *Journal of James Hale* (Cirencester: Watkins, 1826)

Hagist, D., *These Distinguished Corps* (Warwick: Helion: 2021)

Haythornthwaite, P.J., *British Light Infantry & Rifle Tactics of the Napoleonic Wars* (Oxford: Osprey, 2016)

Henry, W., *Events of a Military Life* (London: Pickering, 1843)

Jackson, R., *A Systematic View of the Formation, Discipline, and Economy of Armies* (London: Stockdale, 1804)

Jarry, F., *Instructions Concerning the Duties of Light Infantry in the Field* (London: Dulau & Co. 1803)

L'Estrange, G.B., *Recollections of Sir George B. L'Estrange* (London: Samson Low, 1874)
Le Marchant, D., *Memoirs of the Late Major General Le Marchant* (London: Bentley, 1841)
Maurice, J.F. (ed.), *The Diary of Sir John Moore* (London: Arnold, 1904)
Muir, R., et al, *Inside Wellington's Peninsular Army* (Barnsley: Pen & Sword, 2014)
Muir, R., *Wellington: The Path to Victory 1769-1814* (New Haven: Yale University Press, 2015)
Muir, R., *Tactics and the Experience of Battle in the Age of Napoleon* (New Haven: Yale University Press, 1998)
Nichols, A., *Wellington's Mongrel Regiment* (Staplehurst: Spellmount, 2005)
Oman, C., *A History of the Peninsular War* (Oxford: Clarendon Press, 1902)
Oman, C., *Wellington's Army 1809-1814* (London: Arnold, 1913)
Patterson, J., *Camp and Quarters* (London: Saunders & Otley, 1840)
Phillipart J. (ed.), *The Royal Military Calendar* (London: Egerton, 1820)
Phillipart J. (ed.), *The Royal Military Panorama or Officer's Companion* (London: Martin & Co., 1813 and 1814)
Phillips, R., *Essays on the Theory and Practice of the Art of War* (London: Gillet, 1809)
Rigaud, G., *Celer et Audax* (Oxford: Hall & Stacy, 1879)
Sherer, M., *Recollections of the Peninsula* (London: Longman, Rees, Orme, Brown, & Green, 1827)
Steevens, N., *Reminiscences of My Military Life* (Winchester: Warren, 1877)
Sturgis, J. (ed.), *A Boy in the Peninsular War* (London: Murray, 1899)
Von Vechelde, C. F., *Aus dem Tagebuche des Generals Fr. L. von Wachholtz* (Braunschweig: Vieweg und Sohn, 1843)
Wardell, J. (ed.), *With the Thirty-Second* (Dublin: Hodges, Figgis & Co., 1904)
Warre, W., *Letters from the Peninsula* (London: Murray, 1909)
Wellington, Duke of, 2nd (ed.), *Supplementary Despatches, Correspondence and Memoranda of Field Marshal Arthur Duke of Wellington* (London: Murray, 1858-72)

Index

Abadía, *Mariscal de Campo* Francisco Javier 34, 36
Adige, river 79, 81
Aitchison, Ensign John 170, 189
Albuera, Battle of 34, 166, 168
Alessandria 85, 87–88
Alexander I, Czar 91–100, 102–103, 106, 108–109, 114, 144
Almeida 21, 23, 31–32, 161, 163–164, 166
Alvinczi, *Feldzeugmeister* Joseph 72, 79–81, 85
Amiens, Peace of 126, 132
Andalucía 33, 41
Arcole, Battle of 72, 80
Astorga 15–47
Asturias, the 17–18, 42
Austerlitz, Battle of 49 71, 91, 93, 95, 97, 99, 101, 103–107, 109
Austria 51, 53, 61, 63, 67, 97–98, 125, 192

Badajoz 23, 34, 36
Bagration, *General-leitenant* Prince Pyotr 97, 102, 105–106, 109
Barossa, Battle of 176, 189
Bavaria 50, 59, 65
Belgium 55, 59, 103
Belgrade 50–51
Bélizal, *Capitaine* André-Marie Gouzillon Vicomte de 120, 124
Belvedere, Conde de 43–46
Benavente 22, 36–38, 40, 44–45
Beresford, *Marechal* William184, 194
Berezina, river 139, 141
Berlin 70, 91, 143–144, 150, 158
Berthier, *Maréchal* Louis-Alexandre 27–28, 85
Bessières, *Maréchal* Jean-Baptiste 34, 170
Bohemia 98, 104
Bologna 79, 81
Bonaparte, Napoleon, see Napoleon I
Bonnet, *Général de division* Jean-Pierre-François 34, 36, 40
Borghetto 81, 83
Boulogne 65–66, 162
Bourrienne, Louis Antoine Fauvelet de 84–86
Brescia 78, 82
British Army, foot regiments of; 28th 188–189; 43rd 183, 194, 202, 204; 45th 187, 190–191, 196–197, 200; 50th 197, 201; 60th 168, 176, 185, 191–194, 196–200, 202–203; 71st 195, 198, 204; 79th 198–199; 95th 166, 183–185, 190–191, 194, 198–199, 201, 204; Foreign Corps; Chasseurs Britanniques 195; Dillon Regiment 128–129, Duke of Brunswick's Light Infantry 168, 176, 185 192–193, 195, 199; King's German Legion 168, 194–195, 198; Loyal Emigrants 111–112, 125; Régiment d'Autichamp 113–114, 116, 125, 127, 132; Régiment de Béthisy 113–114, 116, 124, 127; Régiment de Castries 113–114, 116, 122, 124–127, 132; Régiment de Dresnay 113–114, 117–120, 125–126, 132; Régiment d'Hervilly 113–115, 117–120, 122, 124–126, 132; Régiment de Montmorency-Laval 113–114, 121–122, 127, 132; Régiment de Vioménil 113–114, 116, 121–125, 127
Brittany 112, 117, 125
Broglie, *Maréchal de France* Victor-François, Duc de 115–116, 122, 125, 127, 132
Brunn 91, 98–99, 102, 104
Brunswick, Duke of 51–53, 176
Buçaco, Battle of 161, 166–167
Bunbury, Major Thomas 194, 201
Burgos 21, 36, 41–42, 46, 163
Buxhöwden, Frederick Wilhelm Count von 94, 106–107

Caçadores, Portuguese 167, 176, 194–195, 199–200, 202–205

Cádiz 33, 36
Campbell, Major Neil 183–184
Castañón, *Mariscal de Campo* Frederic 40
Castaños, *Teniente-General* Francisco Javier 33–34, 36, 40–41, 45
Castilla 33, 42–43
Charles, Archduke 52, 54–55, 57, 60, 64, 66, 91
Ciudad Rodrigo 20–21, 23, 31–32, 34, 36, 162
Clausel, *Général de division* Bertrand 21–23, 33, 42–43
Clausewitz, Carl Von 68, 71–72, 75, 92, 158–160, 165
Clerfait, *Feldzeugmeister* François, Comte de 52, 54, 60
Coburg, Prince Josias von 51–57
Condé, Prince de 123–128
Confederation of the Rhine 143, 146–147
Corsica 73, 118, 127–128
Coruña 17–18, 24, 37, 44
Corunna Campaign 189, 196
Craig, Colonel Sir James 59, 61
Craufurd, Lieutenant Colonel Charles 125–127
Czartoryski, Adam 96, 107

Davout, *Maréchal* Louis-Nicolas 104, 140, 186
Delft 130, 136, 149
Den Helder 135, 142
Dietz 142, 145–146
Dillenburg 116, 127, 145
Dillon, Colonel Edward 127–129
Dokhturov, *General-leitenant* Dmitry 93, 105–107
Dolgorukov, *General-major* Prince Peter 93–94, 103
Dorsenne, *Général de division* Jean-Marie 34, 163
Duero, river 36–41
Dumouriez, *Général* Charles François 54–56
Dundas, General David 177–178, 183–184
Dutch Army, regiments of; Legion of Orange 144–145, 149–151, 153; 2nd Nassau Infantry Regiment 148, 151

Elbe, river 99, 125–126
El Bierzo 19–22, 34, 44, 46
Enschede 116, 150
Esla, river 34, 38–40, 42–43, 45

Ferdinand, Archduke, 64–66
Flanders 45, 51, 58, 61, 115
Foncebadón 20, 22, 24, 33–34, 46
Foy, *Général de division* Maximilien 43–46, 170, 185
French Army, regiments of; Régiment Royal-Louis 118–119, 122; 3rd Regiment of Foot Grenadiers of the Imperial Guard 138, 139, 141; 33rd Light Infantry 137, 139, 141; 124th Line 137, 139; 125th Line 137, 139; 126th Line 137, 139, 140
Fuentes de Oñoro, Battle of 34, 170–171, 198

Galicia 17–19, 22–23, 33, 36–37, 39, 92
Gardiner, Richard 128–132
Genoa 73–74, 80, 85–88
Goetsenhoven 53–54
Graham, Lieutenant General Thomas 149, 176

Hamburg 123, 125–126, 141, 145
Hanover 51, 91, 99, 194
Hoegaarden 53–54
Hohenlohe, Prince Frederick 56–57, 59
Holland 91, 103, 130, 135, 142

Italy 64, 66, 71–74, 77, 79–84, 86–88, 97, 99, 103, 127, 158

Jerningham, Charles 127–128, 130
Joubert, *Général de division* Barthélemy 79–81, 85
Junot, *Général de division* Jean-Andoche 21–22, 25–28, 31, 33, 81, 164

Kinsky, *General der Kavallerie* Count Franz Joseph 50, 60
Krasnoi, Battle of 139–140
Kutuzov, *General ot infanterii* Mikhail 91–101, 103–109, 139

La Bañeza 19, 21–22, 26, 34, 36–37, 46
Landrieux, *Adjudant-général* Jean 71, 78
Langeron, *General-leitenant* Louis Alexandre Andrault de 93–95, 101, 105–108
Laval 113–114, 121–122, 127, 132
León 15, 17–19, 22, 33–34, 37, 42–43
Lisbon 31–32, 159, 189
Lugo 18–19, 37, 40
Lymington 124, 193

Lyon 33, 82
Lys, river 60, 114–115

MacDonald, *Maréchal* Etienne 63, 86, 89
Mack, *Feldmarschalleutnant* Johann Christoph Carl 49–69, 98
Madrid 15, 17, 24, 36, 41–44, 163
Mahy, *Teniente-General* Nicolás de 22–23, 25
Mantua 71–72, 74, 79, 82, 86
Manzanal 15, 20, 22, 33–34, 46
Marengo, Battle of 71, 82, 84–88
Marmont, *Maréchal* Auguste Frédéric Louis Viesse de 34, 36–43, 45, 161–163, 199
Masséna, *Maréchal* André 20–21, 23–24, 31–32, 34, 80, 81, 83, 85–86, 160–161, 163–165, 171
Melas, *General der Kavallerie* Michael von 82, 85–87
Milan 71, 74, 77–78, 82–88
Moore, Lieutenant General Sir John 17–18, 21–22, 187, 194, 196
Moravia 91–92, 99–100

Naples 61–63, 78, 86, 91
Napoleon I, Emperor of France 49, 53, 63–64, 66, 79–84, 91–94, 96–97, 99–105, 107–108, 135–139, 142–147, 152–153, 159–160, 162, 165, 167, 171–172
Nassau 116, 145–153
Neerwinden 53, 55
Nelson, Vice Admiral Horatio, Viscount 49, 62, 70–89
Netherlands, the 55, 59, 61, 115–116, 136–138, 142, 144–146, 149–153
Ney, *Maréchal* Michel 18–19, 67, 161–162, 165, 167

Obispo 17, 20, 26, 31, 34, 36, 39
Olmutz 91–92, 94, 98–99, 102
Oporto 18, 165, 194, 201
Órbigo 20, 34, 37, 45–46

Paris 34, 63–64, 78, 87, 89, 99, 102, 115, 151, 164–165
Pico, Angelo 79–81, 83–85, 89
Picton, Lieutenant General Sir Thomas 196–197, 203
Piedmont 73, 79–80, 86
Pitt, William 57, 130
Portugal 17–21, 23, 31, 34, 36, 43, 126, 158–161, 163–165, 170–172, 175, 184, 186, 188, 190–191, 193–194, 201
Potsdam 91, 99
Pratzen Heights 104–106, 108
Prussia 53, 91, 99, 146
Pyrenees 160, 189, 192
Pyrmont 116, 121, 123, 127

Quiberon 125, 127, 132

Raussnitz 102, 104
Reitivia 20, 23–26, 33, 36
Rémond *Général de brigade* Victor-Urbain 37–39, 42, 44–45
Rhine, river 115, 121, 143, 145–147
Rhineland 97, 116, 142
Rivoli 20, 79–81, 83, 85, 89, 97
Rome 62–63, 78, 129
Rottenburg, Lieutenant Colonel Baron Francis de 178–179, 183–184, 191
Russia 93, 96, 136, 138, 140–142, 144–145, 153, 169, 172

Salamanca 21, 32, 36, 41–44, 161–162, 199, 202
Savary, *Général de division* Anne-Jean-Marie-René 99–100, 102–103
Schèrer, *Général de division* Barthélemy 73, 83
Schwarzenberg, Prince Karl zu 67, 94
Silesia 99, 143
Soult, *Maréchal* Jean de Dieu 18–19, 41, 43, 104, 160, 162, 165, 168, 192
Spain 15, 17–19, 21, 33–34, 36, 129, 135, 145, 147–148, 153, 158–161, 163–165, 168, 170–172, 176, 186, 188, 190, 194, 204
Stutterheim, *Feldmarschallleutnant* Joseph von 84, 92, 102, 104
Suvorov, *Generalissimo* Alexander 95–97
Switzerland 74, 81–83, 103, 121

Thugut, Johann Amadeus von 55, 59, 61, 64
Tirlemont 53–54
Tordesillas 36–37, 42, 44
Toro 41, 45
Toulon 57, 61, 117–118
Tourcoing, Battle of 58, 60–61, 64
Turin 72, 78, 80, 86, 89

Ulm, Battle of 49, 65–67, 91–92, 94, 99
Utrecht 116, 121, 150

Valladolid 15, 40, 42–44
Venice 74, 78–80, 89
Vienna 56, 61–62, 64–65, 72, 78, 89, 92, 95, 97–98, 100, 104, 106, 153
Vittoria 189, 196, 202
Vizana 45–47
Volkonskii, Prince Peter 106–107

Wagram, Battle of 143, 193
Waterloo, Battle of 151–153, 166, 204
Wellington, Field Marshal Sir Arthur Wellesley, Duke of 18, 20–21, 32, 34, 36–44, 148–149, 159–160, 165, 169–170, 175–177, 184–187, 190–192, 194–196, 198–200, 202–204
Werneck, *Feldmarschalleutnant* Franz von 65–66
West Indies 127, 176, 184–185
Weyrother, *Generalmajor* Franz von 81, 97–98, 101, 104, 106–108
Windham, William 114, 119, 123–124, 128–131
Wischau 102, 104
Wittenberg 141, 144
Woodford, Emperor John Alexander 114, 116, 121, 124, 127–128, 130–132
Wurmser, *Feldmarschall* Dagobert Sigmund Graf von 81–82

Yermolov, Alexei 102, 109
York, Field Marshal HRH Prince Frederick, Duke of 56–61, 116, 178, 185

Zach, *Generalmajor* Anton 87–89
Zamora 36–38, 40–41
Zeeland 135, 138
Zwolle 116, 150

From Reason to Revolution series – Warfare 1721-1815

http://www.helion.co.uk/series/from-reason-to-revolution-1721-1815.php

The 'From Reason to Revolution' series covers the period of military history 1721–1815, an era in which fortress-based strategy and linear battles gave way to the nation-in-arms and the beginnings of total war.

This era saw the evolution and growth of light troops of all arms, and of increasingly flexible command systems to cope with the growing armies fielded by nations able to mobilise far greater proportions of their manpower than ever before. Many of these developments were fired by the great political upheavals of the era, with revolutions in America and France bringing about social change which in turn fed back into the military sphere as whole nations readied themselves for war. Only in the closing years of the period, as the reactionary powers began to regain the upper hand, did a military synthesis of the best of the old and the new become possible.

The series will examine the military and naval history of the period in a greater degree of detail than has hitherto been attempted, and has a very wide brief, with the intention of covering all aspects from the battles, campaigns, logistics, and tactics, to the personalities, armies, uniforms, and equipment.

Submissions

The publishers would be pleased to receive submissions for this series. Please contact series editor Andrew Bamford via email (andrewbamford@helion.co.uk), or in writing to Helion & Company Limited, Unit 8 Amherst Business Centre, Budbrooke Road, Warwick, CV34 5WE

Titles

No 1 *Lobositz to Leuthen: Horace St Paul and the Campaigns of the Austrian Army in the Seven Years War 1756-57* (Neil Cogswell)

No 2 *Glories to Useless Heroism: The Seven Years War in North America from the French journals of Comte Maurés de Malartic, 1755-1760* (William Raffle (ed.))

No 3 *Reminiscences 1808-1815 Under Wellington: The Peninsular and Waterloo Memoirs of William Hay* (Andrew Bamford (ed.))

No 4 *Far Distant Ships: The Royal Navy and the Blockade of Brest 1793-1815* (Quintin Barry)

No 5 *Godoy's Army: Spanish Regiments and Uniforms from the Estado Militar of 1800* (Charles Esdaile and Alan Perry)

No 6 *On Gladsmuir Shall the Battle Be! The Battle of Prestonpans 1745* (Arran Johnston)

No 7 *The French Army of the Orient 1798-1801: Napoleon's Beloved 'Egyptians'* (Yves Martin)

No 8 *The Autobiography, or Narrative of a Soldier: The Peninsular War Memoirs of William Brown of the 45th Foot* (Steve Brown (ed.))

No 9 *Recollections from the Ranks: Three Russian Soldiers' Autobiographies from the Napoleonic Wars* (Darrin Boland)

No 10 *By Fire and Bayonet: Grey's West Indies Campaign of 1794* (Steve Brown)

No 11 *Olmütz to Torgau: Horace St Paul and the Campaigns of the Austrian Army in the Seven Years War 1758-60* (Neil Cogswell)

No 12 *Murat's Army: The Army of the Kingdom of Naples 1806-1815* (Digby Smith)

No 13 *The Veteran or 40 Years' Service in the British Army: The Scurrilous Recollections of Paymaster John Harley 47th Foot – 1798-1838* (Gareth Glover (ed.))

No 14 *Narrative of the Eventful Life of Thomas Jackson: Militiaman and Coldstream Sergeant, 1803-15* (Eamonn O'Keeffe (ed.))

No.15 *For Orange and the States: The Army of the Dutch Republic 1713-1772 Part I: Infantry* (Marc Geerdinck-Schaftenaar)

No 16 *Men Who Are Determined to be Free: The American Assault on Stony Point, 15 July 1779* (David C. Bonk)

No 17 *Next to Wellington: General Sir George Murray: The Story of a Scottish Soldier and Statesman, Wellington's Quartermaster General* (John Harding-Edgar)

No 18 *Between Scylla and Charybdis: The Army of Elector Friedrich August of Saxony 1733-1763 Part I: Staff and Cavalry* (Marco Pagan)

No 19 *The Secret Expedition: The Anglo-Russian Invasion of Holland 1799* (Geert van Uythoven)

No 20 *'We Are Accustomed to do our Duty': German Auxiliaries with the British Army 1793-95* (Paul Demet)

No 21 *With the Guards in Flanders: The Diary of Captain Roger Morris 1793-95* (Peter Harington (ed.))

No 22 *The British Army in Egypt 1801: An Underrated Army Comes of Age* (Carole Divall)

No 23 *Better is the Proud Plaid: The Clothing, Weapons, and Accoutrements of the Jacobites in the '45* (Jenn Scott)

No 24 *The Lilies and the Thistle: French Troops in the Jacobite '45* (Andrew Bamford)

No 25 *A Light Infantryman With Wellington: The Letters of Captain George Ulrich Barlow 52nd and 69th Foot 1808-15* (Gareth Glover (ed.))

No 26 *Swiss Regiments in the Service of France 1798-1815: Uniforms, Organisation, Campaigns* (Stephen Ede-Borrett)

No 27 *For Orange and the States! The Army of the Dutch Republic 1713-1772: Part II: Cavalry and Specialist Troops* (Marc Geerdinck-Schaftenaar)

No 28 *Fashioning Regulation, Regulating Fashion: Uniforms and Dress of the British Army 1800-1815 Volume I* (Ben Townsend)

No 29 *Riflemen: The History of the 5th Battalion 60th (Royal American) Regiment, 1797-1818* (Robert Griffith)

No 30 *The Key to Lisbon: The Third French Invasion of Portugal, 1810-11* (Kenton White)

No 31 *Command and Leadership: Proceedings of the 2018 Helion & Company 'From Reason to Revolution' Conference* (Andrew Bamford (ed.))

No 32 *Waterloo After the Glory: Hospital Sketches and Reports on the Wounded After the Battle* (Michael Crumplin and Gareth Glover)

No 33 *Fluxes, Fevers, and Fighting Men: War and Disease in Ancien Regime Europe 1648-1789* (Pádraig Lenihan)

No 34 *'They Were Good Soldiers': African-Americans Serving in the Continental Army, 1775-1783* (John U. Rees)

No 35 *A Redcoat in America: The Diaries of Lieutenant William Bamford, 1757-1765 and 1776* (John B. Hattendorf (ed.))

No 36 *Between Scylla and Charybdis: The Army of Friedrich August II of Saxony, 1733-1763: Part II: Infantry and Artillery* (Marco Pagan)

No 37 *Québec Under Siege: French Eye-Witness Accounts from the Campaign of 1759* (Charles A. Mayhood (ed.))

No 38 *King George's Hangman: Henry Hawley and the Battle of Falkirk 1746* (Jonathan D. Oates)

No 39 *Zweybrücken in Command: The Reichsarmee in the Campaign of 1758* (Neil Cogswell)

No 40 *So Bloody a Day: The 16th Light Dragoons in the Waterloo Campaign* (David J. Blackmore)

No 41 *Northern Tars in Southern Waters: The Russian Fleet in the Mediterranean 1806-1810* (Vladimir Bogdanovich Bronevskiy / Darrin Boland)

No 42 *Royal Navy Officers of the Seven Years War: A Biographical Dictionary of Commissioned Officers 1748-1763* (Cy Harrison)

No 43 *All at Sea: Naval Support for the British Army During the American Revolutionary War* (John Dillon)

No 44 *Glory is Fleeting: New Scholarship on the Napoleonic Wars* (Andrew Bamford (ed.))

No 45 *Fashioning Regulation, Regulating Fashion: Uniforms and Dress of the British Army 1800-1815 Vol. II* (Ben Townsend)

No 46 *Revenge in the Name of Honour: The Royal Navy's Quest for Vengeance in the Single Ship Actions of the War of 1812* (Nicholas James Kaizer)

No 47 *They Fought With Extraordinary Bravery: The III German (Saxon) Army Corps in the Southern Netherlands 1814* (Geert van Uythoven)

No 48 *The Danish Army of the Napoleonic Wars 1801-1814, Organisation, Uniforms & Equipment: Volume 1: High Command, Line and Light Infantry* (David Wilson)

No 49 *Neither Up Nor Down: The British Army and the Flanders Campaign 1793-1895* (Phillip Ball)

No 50 *Guerra Fantástica: The Portuguese Army and the Seven Years War* (António Barrento)

No 51 *From Across the Sea: North Americans in Nelson's Navy* (Sean M. Heuvel and John A. Rodgaard)

No 52 *Rebellious Scots to Crush: The Military Response to the Jacobite '45* (Andrew Bamford (ed.))

No 53 *The Army of George II 1727-1760: The Soldiers who Forged an Empire* (Peter Brown)

No 54 *Wellington at Bay: The Battle of Villamuriel, 25 October 1812* (Garry David Wills)

No 55 *Life in the Red Coat: The British Soldier 1721-1815* (Andrew Bamford (ed.))

No 56 *Wellington's Favourite Engineer. John Burgoyne: Operations, Engineering, and the Making of a Field Marshal* (Mark S. Thompson)

No 57 *Scharnhorst: The Formative Years, 1755-1801* (Charles Edward White)

No 58 *At the Point of the Bayonet: The Peninsular War Battles of Arroyomolinos and Almaraz 1811-1812* (Robert Griffith)

No 59 *Sieges of the '45: Siege Warfare during the Jacobite Rebellion of 1745-1746* (Jonathan D. Oates)

No 60 *Austrian Cavalry of the Revolutionary and Napoleonic Wars, 1792–1815* (Enrico Acerbi, András K. Molnár)

No 61 *The Danish Army of the Napoleonic Wars 1801-1814, Organisation, Uniforms & Equipment: Volume 2: Cavalry and Artillery* (David Wilson)

No 62 *Napoleon's Stolen Army: How the Royal Navy Rescued a Spanish Army in the Baltic* (John Marsden)

No 63 *Crisis at the Chesapeake: The Royal Navy and the Struggle for America 1775-1783* (Quintin Barry)

No 64 *Bullocks, Grain, and Good Madeira: The Maratha and Jat Campaigns 1803-1806 and the emergence of an Indian Army* (Joshua Provan)

No 65 *Sir James McGrigor: The Adventurous Life of Wellington's Chief Medical Officer* (Tom Scotland)

No 66 *Fashioning Regulation, Regulating Fashion: Uniforms and Dress of the British Army 1800-1815 Volume I* (Ben Townsend) (paperback edition)

No 67 *Fashioning Regulation, Regulating Fashion: Uniforms and Dress of the British Army 1800-1815 Volume II* (Ben Townsend) (paperback edition)

No 68 *The Secret Expedition: The Anglo-Russian Invasion of Holland 1799* (Geert van Uythoven) (paperback edition)

No 69 *The Sea is My Element: The Eventful Life of Admiral Sir Pulteney Malcolm 1768-1838* (Paul Martinovich)

No 70 *The Sword and the Spirit: Proceedings of the first 'War & Peace in the Age of Napoleon' Conference* (Zack White (ed.))

No 71 *Lobositz to Leuthen: Horace St Paul and the Campaigns of the Austrian Army in the Seven Years War 1756-57* (Neil Cogswell) (paperback edition)

No 72 *For God and King. A History of the Damas Legion 1793-1798: A Case Study of the Military Emigration during the French Revolution* (Hughes de Bazouges and Alistair Nichols)

No 73 *'Their Infantry and Guns Will Astonish You': The Army of Hindustan and European Mercenaries in Maratha service 1780-1803* (Andy Copestake)

No 74 *Like A Brazen Wall: The Battle of Minden, 1759, and its Place in the Seven Years War* (Ewan Carmichael)

No 75 *Wellington and the Lines of Torres Vedras: The Defence of Lisbon during the Peninsular War* (Mark Thompson)

No 76 *French Light Infantry 1784-1815: From the Chasseurs of Louis XVI to Napoleon's Grande Armée* (Terry Crowdy)

No 77 *Riflemen: The History of the 5th Battalion 60th (Royal American) Regiment, 1797-1818* (Robert Griffith) (paperback edition)

No 78 *Hastenbeck 1757: The French Army and the Opening Campaign of the Seven Years War* (Olivier Lapray)

No 79 *Napoleonic French Military Uniforms: As Depicted by Horace and Carle Vernet and Eugène Lami* (Guy Dempsey (trans. and ed.))

No 80 *These Distinguished Corps: British Grenadier and Light Infantry Battalions in the American Revolution* (Don N. Hagist)

No 81 *Rebellion, Invasion, and Occupation: The British Army in Ireland, 1793 -1815* (Wayne Stack)

No 82 *You Have to Die in Piedmont! The Battle of Assietta, 19 July 1747. The War of the Austrian Succession in the Alps* (Giovanni Cerino Badone)

No 83 *A Very Fine Regiment: the 47th Foot in the American War of Independence, 1773–1783* (Paul Knight)

No 84 *By Fire and Bayonet: Grey's West Indies Campaign of 1794* (Steve Brown) (paperback edition)

No 85 *No Want of Courage: The British Army in Flanders, 1793-1795* (R.N.W. Thomas)

No 86 *Far Distant Ships: The Royal Navy and the Blockade of Brest 1793-1815* (Quintin Barry) (paperback edition)

No 87 *Armies and Enemies of Napoleon 1789-1815: Proceedings of the 2021 Helion and Company 'From Reason to Revolution' Conference* (Robert Griffith) (ed.))